D1283005

THE INTERNATIONAL FARM CRISIS

The International Farm Crisis

Edited by

David Goodman
Senior Lecturer in Economics
University College, London

and

Michael Redclift
Reader in Rural Sociology
Wye College

St. Martin's Press   New York

First published in the United States of America in 1989

Printed in Hong Kong

ISBN 0–312–02682–X

Library of Congress Cataloging-in-Publication Data
The International Farm Crisis/edited by David Goodman and Michael
  Redclift.
  p. cm.
Includes index.
ISBN 0–312–02682–X
1. Agriculture—Economic aspects. 2. Agriculture and state.
I. Goodman, David, 1938–   . II. Redclift, M. R.
HD1415.I59 1989
338.1—dc19   88–28314
                                                                  CIP

Contents

v

List of Figures

List of Tables

Acknowledgements

This book originated in a Research Workshop held at CEAS, Wye College, on 13 and 14 December 1986. We are grateful to the Nuffield Foundation for supporting that seminar and, under its Small Grants Scheme, for meeting some of the costs of preparing the papers for publication. Without the close collaboration of the contributors, which marked both the original workshop and subsequent discussions, this volume would not have appeared. Jessie Anwell helped with the translation of the paper by Delorme and Coulomb. The other translations from French and Spanish were undertaken by the editors. Thanks are also due to Anne Weekes and Pratiba Kochhar for their help with typing. The index was compiled by Nadia Blackburn.

Notes on the Contributors

Frederick H. Buttel is Professor of Rural Sociology at Cornell University.

Pierre Coulomb is a member of the Department of Economics and Rural Sociology in the National Institute of Agricultural Research (INRA), Paris.

Graham Cox lectures in Sociology at the University of Bath.

Hélène Delorme works in the Centre for International Studies and Research, National Foundation of Political Science (FNSP) in Paris.

Miren Etxezarreta teaches in the Department of Applied Economics, Autonomous University, Barcelona.

David Goodman is Senior Lecturer in the Department of Economics, University College, London.

Geoffrey Lawrence teaches Rural Sociology at the Riverina-Murray Institute of Higher Education, New South Wales, Australia.

Vincent Leclercq is a researcher in the National Institute of Agricultural Research (INRA) working in the International Economics Group in Montpellier.

Philip Lowe is Lecturer in Countryside Planning at University College London.

Max J. Pfeffer is a member of the Department of Human Ecology, Rutgers University.

Clive Potter teaches Economics and Environmental Studies at Wye College, University of London.

Michael Redclift is Reader in Rural Sociology at Wye College, University of London.

Steven E. Sanderson teaches Political Science at the University of Florida.

Laurence Tubiana is the Research Director of the International Economics Group, National Institute of Agricultural Research (INRA) based in the Mediterranean Agricultural Institute, Montpellier.

Lourdes Viladomiu teaches in the Department of Applied Economics, Autonomous University, Barcelona.

Michael Winter is Director of the Centre for Rural Studies at the Royal Agricultural College, Cirencester.

1 Introduction: The International Farm Crisis

David Goodman and Michael Redclift

Writing in 1927, Sir Alfred Mond set out the terms on which agriculture could make a recovery from prolonged depression:

> Knowledge is power, and knowledge is just as much power in the pursuit of agriculture as in the pursuit of any other human (activity) . . . in other countries scientific research, the breeding of the best kind of plants to use on the land, improvements in stock, research in a hundred directions, has been the best business investment governments have made . . . Governments cannot go on treating agriculture as a kind of stepchild. You must build on the fundamental basis of tenure by the means of credit, better methods and marketing and when you have combined these you will see in this country more prosperous and flourishing agriculture, and as it is more flourishing industries will benefit, because farmers and the soil are the basis of prosperity of all countries (Mond, 1927: pp. 293, 303)

Mond was writing at a time when the farm crisis gripping Europe and North America, was one of falling prices, repossession of farms and unemployment. But his words proved prophetic, and the alliance between industry, government and farmers which he sought was the basis of sustained recovery some two decades later. The man who, as Chairman and founder of ICI, was to lead industry into this alliance, not simply in the United Kingdom but throughout the world, could not have predicted that sixty years after he wrote, the 'farm problem' would be just as severe, but in some ways almost unrecognisable by comparison with that of the 1920s and 1930s. For the 'triple alliance' between farming, industry and government, was to produce a new, structural crisis which we are only now beginning to fully understand. The international farm crisis of the late 1980s is a crisis founded on success at bringing science and technology to bear on the uncertainties of agriculture, and developing policies to provide a more secure

1

social and political context in which farmers can operate. The 'break-down of the old system' (op. cit., p. 292) which Mond played a significant part in advancing, was to lead to the apparently intractable problems of agriculture in the industrialised countries today.

This book examines the causes and dynamics of the international farm crisis of the 1980s and its effects in restructuring the rural economies and societies of Western Europe, the United States, and selected 'third' countries, namely Australia, Brazil and Mexico. As agriculture and the rural environment have claimed the headlines the international farm crisis has entered mainstream political debate. Readers and television viewers have become accustomed to a litany of familiar news items: successive EEC budgetary crises and reform proposals for the Common Agricultural Policy (CAP); the threat of a US–EEC trade war; bankrupt Mid-West farmers in the United States; milk quotas and the plight of British hill farmers; the burning of imported lamb carcasses by irate French farmers; tractorcade protests in Canberra, and GATT negotiations for a new system of international agricultural trade. The comparisons with developing countries are particularly galling: the affluence of the advanced industrial countries, expressed in food 'mountains' and wine 'lakes', and famine and hunger in Africa provide striking contrasts. In addition, there is a rising awareness of the causal nexus that links the protectionist agricultural policies of the industrialised (OECD) countries with the Third World food crisis, an awareness that forces us to redefine the politics of overproduction in global terms. In Europe, 'set-aside' schemes, custodial 'environmental service' payments, and agro-forestry programmes are increasingly presented as possible ways to remove excess productive capacity and diversify farm incomes, but they are solutions to 'our' problem, rather than that of developing countries.

These proposals to reduce farm surpluses, reveal the dramatic change in the agenda of international agricultural policy. In little over a decade, the centre of debate has moved away from the fears of global food scarcity voiced in 1973–74 towards trade war and the threatened collapse of the agricultural trading system. This shift has occurred despite continued widespread malnutrition in the Third World, the disarray of national food policies, and the renewed spectre of famine in much of Africa. In the North at least, the leading issues of the 1980s concern overproduction, demands for structural reform of agriculture, the rising importance of environmental politics, as well as the GATT agricultural trade negotiations. Following the collapse in the 1970s of the international food order erected under US hegemony, the future structure of world agricultural markets and their regulation is now at stake.

These issues have arisen in the context of the increasingly acrimonious and costly dispute for export markets as the United States attempts to extend its domination of the world food system and restrict its loss of market share to competitors, particularly the European Economic Community. The intensity of this competition reflects the acute internal imbalances which characterise the farm crisis in the United States and Europe, creating strong political pressures to increase the disposal of surpluses in overseas markets. Heavily subsidised export programmes essentially shift the burden of domestic adjustment on to 'third countries', weakening national food security in importing countries and restricting markets for traditional agricultural exporters.

The repercussions of the 'farm crisis' in developing countries demonstrate how spurious and misleading it is to suggest that the farm crisis is limited to the North. Food systems in the post-war period have become increasingly internationalised as a result of the closer integration of national markets, common technologies, more uniform patterns of food consumption, and the overarching strategies of international agribusiness. This integration and interdependence of food systems is a direct result of the post-war internationalisation of production and accumulation in the world economy. It would be misconceived to see the 'international farm crisis' merely as a conjunctural or cyclical abberation, when it is a logical consequence of the restructuring of the global food economy.

The shifting focus of international concern, from world food shortages in the early 1970s to overproduction in the 1980s, illustrates the instability of agricultural production, prices and farm incomes. Historical experience since the formation of world commodity markets in the late nineteenth century suggests that such instability is the rule rather than the exception. Indeed, many writers argue that instability is an intrinsic characteristic of agriculture, given the natural or biological base of the production process and the atomised, competitive structures of commodity supply. Nevertheless, world agricultural markets enjoyed a remarkable period of stability in the 1950s and 1960s. One of the leading questions posed by the current crisis is whether these conditions can be restored. Is it possible to establish mechanisms of international regulation and adjustment that can eradicate the sources of instability in world markets and bring renewed prosperity to farm households and rural communities? The present Uruguay Round of GATT trade negotiations acquires special significance in this context.

The papers in this volume examine the farm crisis in different 'national agricultures' in the context of the interdependent world food system and explore possible avenues out of the crisis. The present crisis is the *international* expression of structural tendencies determined by modern agricultural policies, whose contradictions at the domestic level have long been acknowledged. These contradictions are embedded in the protectionist, and fundamentally expansionist, policies adopted to overcome the earlier agricultural crisis of the inter-war period. These policies initiated a new cycle of agroindustrial accumulation to propagate the mechanical and genetic-chemical technologies developed in the 1920s and 1930s. Farm price support and other investment incentives generated intense technological competition, reinforcing long-term secular trends in the developed industrial countries, such as rural migration, declining farm numbers, and increasing concentration and specialisation within agriculture. The potentially destabilizing effects of the formidable post-war expansion of agricultural productive capacity on farm prices and incomes were regulated by drawing off production surpluses into government stockpiles, food aid and other concessionary outlets, and commercial exports.

This system worked effectively so long as excess productive capacity was concentrated in the United States but the internationalisation of modern intensive technologies and the associated protective structures of regulation carried the seeds of future instability of world agricultural markets. With increasing competition to export surplus output, these markets have indeed become more volatile and this instability has been transmitted back to domestic markets, resulting in the precipitous rise in the financial costs of farm programmes during the 1980s. These cumulative long-term tendencies are now accompanied by such conjunctural features of crisis as falling land values, farm bankruptcies, foreclosures and financial 'stress', and the accelerated exodus of farm families. As these conjunctural effects intensify, there is a renewed chorus of demands for farm policy reform, ranging from the corporatist claims of farm organisations to proposals for the wholesale restructuring of world agricultural trade. The crisis of the 1980s thus marks the end of the post-war cycle of agroindustrial accumulation and the structures of regulation which sustained its internationalisation throughout the OECD countries and, via the Green Revolution, to selected sectors of Third World agriculture.

The current farm crisis is fundamentally a structural crisis arising as the direct consequence of the global dissemination of an agroindustrial model and the inability of governments to subordinate their own national interests to a wider, historical compromise. What is occurring cannot be reduced to a system aberration for conjunctural problems in the international farm economy are the direct effect of the system's inability to address its own contradictions. We need to recognise that agriculture and agricultural crises fit into a long wave perspective of tendencies in capitalist accumulation. Beginning with the New Deal in the United States, and later prompted by the Marshall Plan for European recovery, a framework was established for the regeneration of agriculture as well as industry, which depended for its success on both the stimulus of the market and the political backing of the state. Farmers entered the post-war world in a state of grace, believing that by pressing their individual demands on governments they were expressing national, rather than sectional, objectives. Governments in the United States and Western Europe, willingly accepted the role of handmaiden to the new Prometheus, providing the policy context essential to the technological revolution in agricultural production. Once the framework had been established it was assumed that the model's success could be measured in productionist terms – economic restructuring had a different connotation in the halcyon days of farm recovery. What were not foreseen were the consequences of increased technological competition in 'domestic' agriculture on world markets, and particularly as multilateral organisation of these markets under United States' leadership gave way in the 1970s to bilateralism and cut-throat competition.

These are the consequences with which we are concerned in this volume, which attempts to bring apparently fragmented events and issues into a coherent perspective, emphasising that the farm crisis is an interdependent, world-wide phenomenon arising from the development of the modern global food system. Although the effects of this crisis are acute in the Third World, its dimensions extend beyond the Procrustean bed of North-South relations. The international farm crisis has its origins in the collapse of the long post-war boom of industrial capitalism and the erosion of United States' hegemony in world agricultural trade.

The breakdown of the Bretton Woods system in 1971, exchange rate realignment, the 1974 oil shock, and the increasing international mobility of capital, ushered in a period of significantly greater instability in the world economy. The full impact of these changes on the agriculture of the industrialised (OECD) countries was delayed by higher world market prices in the mid-1970s, and the associated political decisions to bear the rising cost of farm support and overproduction. However, the 1980s world recession and the fiscal crises in the United States and European Economic Community have thrown these contradictions into sharp relief, with damaging consequences for 'third' countries dependent on agricultural exports. The intensity of world price fluctuations has increased significantly, and this instability has been exacerbated in the 1980s by the vigorous, heavily subsidised efforts of the EEC and the United States to expand their exports. These recent tendencies have further distorted agrarian structures in the Third World but the farm crisis there, which is not the central concern of this volume, is one of food scarcity rather than overproduction, fiscal constraints, and farm indebtedness.

The main components of the international farm crisis can be identified as follows:

(a) the development in the United States of a model of technological innovation and market intervention for agriculture and its international dissemination;

(b) the breakdown of the post-war system of regulation of world agricultural trade managed by the United States;

(c) the crisis of political representation and legitimation between farmers' organisations and the state; and

(d) the failure to anticipate or contain the environmental problems associated with the new agricultural technology/policy model.

THE DEVELOPMENT OF AN AGRICULTURAL TECHNOLOGY/POLICY MODEL

An understanding of the present international farm crisis must begin with the sustained productivity growth achieved by the capital- and energy-intensive agroindustrial model developed in the United States after 1930. The technological base for this model of agroindustrial accumulation was created by the convergence of mechanical and agrichemical technologies on the flow of genetic innovations, which began with hybridisation in the 1930s (Goodman, Sorj and Wilkinson, 1987). This emphasis on plant genetics as the main focus of technical progress gave rise to complementary, integrated technological 'packages' in major crop sectors. In the 1960s these technologies provided the main vehicle for the transformation of selected sectors of Third World agricultures, the so-called 'Green Revolution', and the further internationalisation of the United States' agroindustrial model.

In a regulated climate of price supports and production incentives, technological innovation and diffusion in the advanced industrial economies were maintained by the efforts of public agricultural research systems, extension services and the accumulation strategies of agroindustrial capitals. With farm income support tied directly to production volume, and profitability thus dependent on unit cost levels, producers were forced to walk a 'technological treadmill' in order to escape the cost-price squeeze, or risk leaving agriculture altogether. Technological competition and increasingly intensive production methods have brought high and sustained productivity gains since the 1930s, but this process has been accompanied by a massive exodus of the farm population and a pervasive trend towards the concentration of agricultural production and farm assets. Nevertheless, it would be naive to reduce the farm crisis to the failings of the capital-intensive, high input model which now dominates the agriculture of the OECD countries. If we discount its adverse environmental impacts and other costs not captured by the market, this model undoubtedly retains potential for continued productivity growth and the further centralisation of productive capacity. The roots of the present crisis are rather to be found in the contradictions of domestic structures of regulation and the collapse of the international food order, which has accompanied the decline of United States' hegemony in the world economy since the early 1970s.

At the time when genetic innovations were reversing the long-term decline of US crop yields and provoking technological convergence, US New Deal programmes of protection, price stabilisation, farm income support and investment incentives, and their complements in other industrial countries, were stimulating agricultural recovery from the depressed inter-war years. This evolving structure of market regulation established the institutional foundations for the sustained growth of output and productivity, which in the post-war period has resulted in increasing overproduction and rising fiscal burdens. This institutional apparatus of regulated markets and intense technological competition, which was consolidated and extended in the 1940s and 1950s, confirmed the grain-feed-livestock complex as the cornerstone of the US food system and patterns of food consumption.

Advances in animal genetics, nutrition and health, together with the downward pressure on feed prices exerted by continuously rising yields and output, have reduced the prices of meat and dairy products in real terms, increasing their importance in the diet of advanced industrial societies.

The model of agricultural regulation and technological competition, which emerged from the New Deal period and war-time emergency controls, thus played an important role in the post-war consolidation of the 'Fordist' regime of accumulation (Friedmann, 1987; Kenney, Curry and Stockwell, 1987). 'Fordism' in US agriculture is typified by the corn-soybean-livestock equation as the source of cheap food for the industrial working class and the burgeoning suburban white-collar labour force. This model similarly sustained the expansion of the off-farm sectors of the food and fibre system as technological competition provided markets for agroindustrial inputs and low cost supplies for downstream food processing industries. The cheap food policy centred on basic food and feed grains and livestock products is the rural complement to the mass production of industrial 'Fordism'. This functional relationship is neatly captured by Roosevelt's oft-quoted promise to put 'a car in every garage and a chicken in every pot'. In the post-war period, the strategies of multinational agroindustrial capitals and US foreign policy interests have resulted in what Rama (1985) calls 'the international homogenisation of wage goods'.

The growth of intensive, grain-fed livestock production systems and animal protein-based consumption are absolutely crucial to the workings of the agroindustrial model. This symbiosis provides the vital outlets for the huge productive potential in food and feed grains. These patterns are at the root of global imbalances in food consumption. Thus it is estimated that in the early 1980s Western nations fed 400 million tons of grain to livestock, an amount equal to total Third World consumption. Moreover, scarce agricultural resources in the Third World are diverted from staple food crops to produce animal feed for international markets, as in the case of Brazilian soybeans and cassava from Thailand. The structural changes in world demand associated with the diffusion of intensive livestock systems and the 'Fordist' diet have transformed international agricultural trade and the position of Third World primary commodity producers in the global division of labour. The impact of these changing production patterns in countries such as Mexico also reveals how rising domestic consumption of meat and dairy products by the wealthier urban classes has provoked land use changes which have undermined national food security.

THE BREAKDOWN OF INTERNATIONAL REGULATION: DISORDER IN WORLD MARKETS

Marshall Aid and other US programmes of post-war reconstruction stimulated the adoption of this agroindustrial model in Western Europe. As these countries in turn pursued cheap food policies and technological modernisation, national structures of negotiation and legitimation emerged based on the corporatist alliance of the State, farm unions, commodity associations and agroindustrial interests. (Whether these structures will retain this central role in any transition to a post-productionist agriculture is a leading issue in the current farm crisis.) The dissemination of the US model of production/consumption to Western Europe and other OECD countries, combined with the technological leadership and unchallenged supremacy of the US in world markets, effectively established an international food order under American hegemony. The long period of capitalist expansion in the 1950s and 1960s was one of unprecedented stability in world commodity markets. This stability was founded on US production control mechanisms, notably acreage set-aside schemes and storage programmes, and the market-creating role of concessionary export sales and food aid, especially under Public Law 480 enacted in 1954. As in the domestic sphere, the international food order maintained low prices of basic food and feed grains and other staple foodstuffs, reinforcing the wider framework of international economic regulation instituted by the Bretton Woods agreement and managed by the United States by virtue of its dominant position in the world financial system and world trade.

However, the consolidation of the US agroindustrial model in Western Europe and other developed countries carried a growing threat to US dominance and the regulation of world commodity markets. With the powerful production incentives introduced under the Common Agricultural Policy, the growth of agricultural output in the EEC increasingly has outstripped the slowly rising, and inelastic, aggregate demand for food. Following the example set by the United States, the EEC since the 1970s has placed increasing reliance on export expansion to resolve the contradictions of its domestic policies and reduce mounting structural surpluses. The ensuing heavily subsidised competition for world export markets between the two agricultural 'super powers' has had serious adverse effects on the developing and 'third' countries, as we see below. From an historical perspective, the diffusion of the US production/consumption model to other OECD countries gave the *coup de grace* to 'imperial preference' which traditionally had dominated North-South trade, and with it the understanding that countries possessed 'comparative advantages' in the export of agricultural commodities.

Until the 1980s, the export strategies pursued by the US and the EEC were mutually sustainable due to world food shortages in the early 1970s and continued debt-financed purchases by Third World countries and increasing sales to capital-surplus oil producers. US exports then fell back from the record 1981 level of $44 billion under the impact of the strong appreciation of the dollar and world recession. However, the rise of the EEC as a major food exporter, in addition to the market-orientated changes in domestic US agricultural policies after 1972, had already contributed to the greater volatility of world commodity markets. This intensifying competition undermined the international food order and the conditions of relative price stability which had prevailed in the 1950s and the 1960s. The US regulatory role and multilateral commodity agreements have been superseded by bilateral arrangements and other forms of trade as the EEC and the United States have adopted increasingly aggressive trade policies.

The Position of 'Third' Countries

The slower growth of agricultural trade in the 1980s, as the result of world economic recession and the international debt crisis, has accentuated the intensity of EEC – US competition to the point of virtual trade war. At the same time, major international debtors, such as Argentina, Brazil and Mexico, have been forced to redouble their export efforts in these conditions of deteriorating markets and unfair competition, in order to meet the costs of servicing their mounting external debts. The consequent diversion of land from staple food to cash crop production has aggravated internal food shortages and the incidence of malnutrition amongst the rural and urban poor. The transmission to 'third' countries via world export markets of the distortions caused by the domestic agricultural policies of the EEC and the US is shown with great clarity in the case of Australia, Mexico and Brazil.

Recent trade developments in the Mediterranean Basin illustrate this interdependence of world markets and the impact of US and EEC policies on 'third' countries. This region has been chosen by the United States as 'the arena' in which to confront the increasing export competition from the EEC, and reassert its domination of the international food system. The US strategy is to weaken the EEC by attacking its preferential agreements with Mediterranean countries, undermining these traditional export markets for EEC surpluses and thereby accentuating internal divisions between member states. However, the force of this confrontation has also been felt strongly by specialised 'third' country agricultural exporters. Thus Egypt is Australia's largest wheat market, Saudi Arabia is the leading customer for Canadian barley and Argentina, Brazil and Thailand are also important exporters to this region. Heavily subsidised EEC and US exports of cereals to these markets consequently present a direct threat to the export earnings and farm incomes of these 'third' countries. Such countries are thus drawn inexorably into the farm crisis of the advanced industrial economies. Nevertheless they lack the resources to subsidise exports heavily or wage a trade war. Their vulnerability arises from the way in which they are integrated in world markets, itself testimony to the *disadvantage* of 'comparative advantage' in a period of recession, when increased export competition for agricultural goods opens the door to further rationalisation of production, forcing the more marginal farmers to abandon production altogether. About half the wheat farmers in New South Wales faced the prospect of loan default during 1987. Land values in Australia's prime sheep-wheat zone decreased by 40 per cent in the period 1985–87.

The Impact on Developing Countries

In developing countries, low and stable world prices of basic food grains in the 1950s and 1960s and the availability of concessionary supplies encouraged increasing reliance on imports to meet the demands of rapidly growing urban populations. Policymakers were concerned that allegedly inflexible traditional agricultural structures would create supply rigidities, leading to rising food prices and higher real wages which would threaten accelerated industrialisation programmes. Closer integration in the postwar international food order has had a debilitating impact on traditional agriculture, as peasant producers have struggled to compete with heavily subsidised imports and adapt to the rapid shift in urban consumption patterns towards wheat products, dairy products and meat. Concomitant charges in land use away from traditional staple food grains toward animal feed and forage crops have further undermined domestic food production and accentuated Third World import dependence.

The disarticulation of peasant agriculture has been intensified by technological modernisation programmes and regulatory policies modelled on the US prototype: selective fiscal and credit incentives, public research and extension services, agroindustrial promotion and price support measures. Some small producers have adapted to the demands of modernisation and increased commodity production through greater cash-crop specialisation, but the majority are condemned to an uncertain future of rural poverty and irregular wage employment. Agricultural modernisation and the internationalisation of domestic food consumption patterns have transformed many developing countries into net importers of farm products, reversing the balance of world agricultural trade flows which characterised the inter-war period. This reversal is even more evident if we exclude Argentina, Brazil and Thailand as special cases of integration in the new international division of labour in agricultural trade. By the early 1980s, two-thirds of agricultural exports were from OECD countries, while developing countries accounted for about half the world's agricultural imports.

THE CRISIS OF POLITICAL REPRESENTATION AND LEGITIMATION

The farm crisis has exposed current production regimes to a crisis of legitimacy. Both the State and farm organisations now accept that it is essential to reduce overproduction and contain public expenditures. Agricultural policy reform is assuming higher priority on the political agenda, both domestically and internationally, and initial positions have now been established for the present Uruguay Round of GATT negotiations. Although the urgency of restructuring is widely acknowledged, there is little common ground between the proposals for the reform of world agricultural trade policy made by the European Community and those of the United States and the 14-strong Cairns Club of 'third countries'. The EC position, reinforced by the February 1988 Brussels summit agreement on CAP budget guidelines, recommends a gradualist approach to the task of dismantling farm subsidies. By contrast the US and the Cairns Club countries propose a rapid phased transition toward free trade by eliminating export subsidies, import restrictions and all forms of farm support not linked to production by the year 2000. The complexities and social costs of implementing the sweeping restructuring implied by the so-called 'zero–2000' proposal would be very considerable in both developed and 'third' countries with large farm populations.

The issue of legitimation reveals a vital dimension of the current farm crisis, and it is certainly central to its management and resolution, even if it were possible to put aside international geopolitical rivalries. The farm crisis has all the characteristic features of a structural economic crisis, with farm bankruptcies, falling farm incomes, low returns on capital, and the decline of rural communities whose prosperity is closely linked to the fortunes of the farm industry. In the United States, for example, increasing exports and relatively favourable world market prices in the 1970s combined with farm support programmes to insulate agriculture from growing world economic instability. These factors, reinforced by low real interest rates before 1979, together with investment incentives, stimulated high levels of debt-financed investment in agricultural assets. Highly-leveraged producers are the main casualties of the US farm crisis which has largely been a debt crisis, and therefore uneven in its effects. These producers were caught in a classic debt trap by the sharp upward adjustment of real interest rates in 1979–80, collapsing land values and, since 1984–85, declining farm prices, which have aggravated cash flow problems.

EEC farmers have faced broadly similar conditions, although the sudden imposition of milk quotas in 1984 posed exceptional adjustment problems, which may well illustrate the difficulties of restructuring that lie ahead. Farmers' claims to official support and protection have not remained unchallenged and the restructuring process calls into question the ability of farmers' groups to represent all their members. Farmers' organisations in North America and Western Europe have sought to identify their members' interests with that of liberal, democratic, capitalist society. They have identified private property ownership in land as the cornerstone of democracy and an effective bulwark against both private and state monopoly. In a period when increased food production was a strategic necessity, and agricultural jobs could be shed more or less painlessly, this was not difficult. The rhetoric of farmers' organisations, and governments, often echoed a nationalist, anti-urban bias that drew popular support. Food surpluses, accelerating public subsidies and widespread urban unemployment have altered the picture. Today farmers' organisations are met by increasing public suspicion. Their claim to official legitimacy is likely to be increasingly challenged, both by members who sense their isolation, and governments increasingly aware of the political liability that farmers represent.

By the mid-1980s the emergence of Neo-Liberal economic policies in most Western economies, whether under social democratic or conservative governments, drew increased attention to the subsidies which farmers receive from the state. The model of economic development based on open economies and comparative advantage, which appeared to work within a context of agreed multilateral procedures to regulate markets, had effectively been abandoned. In its absence, individual governments sought ways of avoiding writing a 'blank cheque' for agriculture, at the expense of the consumer and taxpayer. Within the confines of the EEC, it became more acceptable to challenge the system under which food was produced and food prices 'supported', although new member states, especially, sought to retain commodities which were already in surplus, notably such 'Mediterranean' products as wine, cooking oil and citrus fruits. Nevertheless, without an effective 'structural policy' to further the rationalisation of farm structures by the voluntary withdrawal of 'marginal' producers from production, governments have continued to support agriculture for social and political reasons, especially in regions economically dependent on agriculture. Governments that were committed to remove government support from other sectors of the economy have been ambivalent about removing public support from agriculture, knowing that the alternative (some form of enhanced structural policy) might be even less politically acceptable.

Alternative policies to the Common Agricultural Policy could only work through greater differentiation between agricultural producers. In a period of contraction, the issue of who represents farmers has to be addressed, but can it be left to the farmers' organisations themselves? Some organisations have sought to restrict debate about alternative policies for agriculture in the hope that they would, by these means, continue to attract the political support of government. Other groups have tried to enlarge the debate, calling for action on behalf of 'worker-peasants' or disadvantaged commodity groups. Much of the rhetoric and much of the lobbying is sectional and regionalist, rather than national, in orientation. The most insistent questions demand that extremely difficult political decisions be made: how should limited markets be shared? Which farmers should be allowed to remain in agriculture, those who are most profitable, or those who are most 'valued' for their social characteristics or environmental practices? The discussion is taking on another dimension. It is not simply a question of whether farmers' groups represent their members. The issue now is both wider and simpler: the future of agriculture involves choices for society as a whole. The debate can not be left to the farmers alone.

THE NEW AGRICULTURAL TECHNOLOGY MODEL AND THE ENVIRONMENT

The effects of modern agriculture on the rural environment have been recognised for some time (Shoard, 1980; Green, 1981). Nevertheless most attempts to incorporate a concern with the environment into the analysis of agriculture's crisis have been confined to the developed countries. It needs to be understood that the environmental consequences of the agricultural technology/policy model developed in the United States are not confined to the industrialised countries, where the imprint of this model is clearest (Redclift, 1987). In the developing countries, major shifts in land-use and the adoption of modern technology have been associated with the changing international division of labour, and the processes of agricultural specialisation and concentration which have marked recent decades. As we have seen, crops such as soya, sorghum and cassava are grown for export to feed animals in Europe. At the same time, the expansion of international agribusiness in developing countries has had a marked effect on the labour process there, increasing seasonal and casual labour. In addition, agribusiness has contributed in many cases to increased pressure on natural resources, as simple commodity producers are forced to cultivate land more intensively, or make excessive demands on available supplies of water, fuelwood and forest resources.

The principal environmental problems in developed countries are linked to the intensification of agricultural production, which has had both direct and indirect effects. Among the direct effects we should note the loss of important habitats, such as wetlands, and the widespread pollution of water resources. The specialisation of crop production, and the accompanying mechanisation, have increased soil compaction and reduced soil quality. The intensification of crop production, made possible by chemical fertilisers and pesticides, has also contributed to other features of resources degradation, such as resistance in natural pests and, indirectly, it has also contributed to the increase of toxic residues in food. High levels of contamination from sprays and antibiotic residues in food are often impossible for the consumer to detect. The existing legislation to protect food quality from agricultural pollution is, according to the EEC (1986, 17), rarely complied with in practice. The intensification of animal production has, in turn, led to other severe environmental problems. The disposal of animal slurry is now a major environmental problem for West European farmers, as millions of tons of animal manure enter the water system. The cost of returning groundwater supplies to acceptable levels requires action both to reduce the amount of nitrates entering the soil and water systems, and to reduce animal waste disposal in river courses. In most EEC countries intensive animal units are now so large that necessary measures to combat pollution cannot be undertaken without shaping future farm structures in important ways.

The impact of international competition in agricultural products and the relentless effects of the 'technological treadmill' have thus served to underline the precariousness of renewable natural resources in developed and developing countries alike. Only the manifestations of the environmental crisis have differed. Where commercial agriculture is most advanced, as in the United States, the environmental degradation most closely linked with agricultural change on the farm is often 'invisible' even to much of the rural population. Similarly, the 'countryside' of the United Kingdom and some other West European nations, can increasingly be seen as an ideological construct as well as an objective 'reality', a vision made inevitable by increasing urbanisation and the accompanying need for recreation, amenity and landscape in industrial society.

The environmental effects of the farm crisis cannot be reduced to an increased interest in conservation at the margin, when the governments of most industrialised countries continue to support high-input, capital-intensive farming. In those European countries, such as France, where a small-farming ideology persists, the maintenance of farmers on the land is associated with environmental protection. Environmental policy is thus linked to structural policy for farming. Even in these countries, however, the public legitimation of family farming has developed hand-in-hand with widespread use of chemical sprays, 'controlled' production of livestock and the erosion of natural habitats. It needs to be recognised that the very resonance of 'family farming' in ideological terms has made it more difficult for governments to urge effective action on farmers, reversing the trend towards further specialisation and environmental degradation.

Although agricultural intensification is sometimes seen as the 'problem', from an environmental point of view, the measures taken to protect the environment are usually 'reactive', seeking to reduce the damage in specific areas of countryside, notably those with particularly rich ecosystems. Protecting habitats is clearly only part of any 'solution' since the damage to the environment is associated with the inputs into the system, not simply the effects of production. In most EEC countries, preserving farm structures, and with them farm livelihoods, is considered an essential plank in any attempt to reduce the effects of agricultural intensification. At the same time withdrawing land from agricultural production ('set-aside') for environmental or budgetary reasons, does not guarantee that the environment will be returned to greater scientific or aesthetic quality. Farming contraction may alter the appearance of the countryside without enabling farmers to practice agriculture in a more sustainable way. It may mean little more than abandoning the land. The point is that both structural and environmental policy are heavily dependent, for their success, on the relationship between the state and farmers. At the same time, as we have seen, the developing food system is changing this relationship.

The international farm crisis began with the application of industry and science to farming. As Sir Alfred Mond observed, systematically pursuing a new technology and policy model would inevitably herald a new agricultural revolution. In this book we assess the effects of that revolution.

The papers in this collection explore the dimensions of the 'farm crisis' within an international context emphasising both the specific nature of the crisis at the national level and the structural interrelationships which give the crisis an international character. The first two papers, by Tubiana and Buttel, examine the origins and current manifestations of the crisis by exploring the agricultural technology and policy model developed first in the United States, and the effects of its dissemination on other developed countries. Tubiana views the international contradictions of the model from a global perspective, while Buttel is principally concerned with the domestic causes, and consequences of the 'US farm crisis'.

Tubiana shows how the organisational mechanisms governing world markets in basic agricultural products were undermined at the beginning of the 1970s following the introduction of more market-orientated agricultural policies in the United States. Price instability, the breakdown of multilateral agreements, and trade wars characterise the recent period. At the same time, this organisational crisis is also a crisis of diffusion of the prevailing model of production and consumption.

After a long period of stable and low prices in which US food aid (via Public Law 480) was a strong stabilising factor, these markets have become fiercely competitive. The United States is no longer willing to play its role as 'the policeman' of the world market, and new exporting countries in Europe and the Third World have emerged to challenge the hierarchical structure of the international agrofood system. With the diffusion of common technological and consumption norms, Tubiana argues, the consensus on the regulation of world trade and the international division of labour has broken down, most notably in relations between the United States and the EEC.

It is therefore necessary to analyse the crisis of world agricultural trade in the framework of the threat to American hegemony. Tubiana's paper raises some critical issues, in a particularly cogent form: has the dominant post-1945 production-consumption model encountered structural limits to its further integration and internationalisation? What are the consequences of the growth of bilateralism? Since the importance of the current technological/policy model promises to be reinforced by new developments in biotechnology and genetic engineering, will the contradictions of international 'deregulation' of markets exacerbate agricultural instability? What new forms of national and international regulation will emerge from the present crisis and restructuring?

Buttel's paper explores both the different manifestations of the US farm crisis, and the explanations that have been advanced for its occurrence. The paper argues that the most salient dimensions of the farm crisis are associated with farm indebtedness, itself a response to the 'technological treadmill' that has held American farmers in its grip since the 1950s. Other papers in the collection, notably those by Graham Cox and colleagues (United Kingdom), Steven Sanderson (Mexico) and Geoff Lawrence (Australia) pay similar attention to the problems that have accompanied indebtedness and the financial problems besetting vulnerable groups of farmers.

Buttel examines a range of explanations which have been offered for the US farm crisis. He argues that although some aspects of policymaking in the United States elucidate elements of the problem, these 'policy-based' explanations are inadequate in themselves. Instead he argues, like Tubiana, that secular trends in the world economy, together with the inherent contradictions of accumulation in developed country agriculture, are the principal causes of the farm crisis. Unlike Tubiana, he sees policy shifts within the United States as a response to domestic problems, rather than as necessary preliminaries to the 'export' of the agricultural technology/policy model. The clear implication of both papers is that the international farm crisis can only be intensified by the continuance of bilateral policies, and the further elaboration of the 'Fordist' model at the international level.

The following five papers each examine the impact of international markets and policy shifts on several of the countries of the European Economic Community (EEC). Coulomb and Delorme look at the farm crisis in France, both as a policy crisis and a crisis of political legitimation. Cox, Lowe and Winter examine the British case, concentrating their attention on the maintenance of a 'corporatist' framework, within a context of economic restructuring. Potter focuses on the difficulty, in the United Kingdom, of continuing farm support when the political and economic advantages of agricultural contraction are compounded by environmental policy objectives. The contrast with France is obvious: does increasing farm livelihoods provide a way of realising environmental objectives or create problems for improved conservation? In their paper, Etxezarreta and Viladomiu examine a country which has only recently become a member of the EEC, Spain. They argue that Spain's membership, which is looked upon in some quarters as an answer to the farm crisis, is in fact likely to complicate the position of Spanish agriculture. Spain has become increasingly integrated within international agricultural markets, at the consumption as well as the production 'end', but this has served to weaken the agricultural sector's autonomy. Etxezarreta and Viladomiu draw attention to the large number of family farmers who remain in agriculture without making an adequate livelihood from it, a situation found in most EEC countries, although in a less stark form. This 'marginalisation' of family producers, combined with the rationalisation of large-scale capitalist agriculture, linked to foreign inputs and markets, resembles the situation in developing countries. Pfeffer's paper examines the situation of farmers in the agriculturally disadvantaged regions of West Germany, and reveals that farm price support programmes, however costly, aggravate farm income inequalities without addressing structural deprivation. The papers on Western Europe each demonstrate the cost of continued state support within a climate of economic restructuring, the principal 'protection' for the agricultural sector being provided by the mechanism of the EEC, notably the Common Agricultural Policy.

The next group of papers takes up the issue of the 'farm crisis' from the perspective of 'third countries', variously opposed to the kind of regional protectionism demonstrated by the CAP. Lawrence, in his paper, addresses the peculiarities and characteristics of the Australian farm crisis, examining the political lobbies and pressure groups which have sought to defend farmers' interests. In a trenchant, carefully documented paper, he demonstrates that the very qualities which have contributed to the past success of the Australian model make it extremely vulnerable to international changes. The 'openness' of Australia to foreign capital, together with 'New Right' opposition to interventionist policies, have exposed the agricultural sector to the development of monopoly capitalism without much protection for family producers from the cold winds of international competition.

The contrast with Mexico, similarly 'dependent' economically, but with closer links to the United States, is instructive. In Mexico, 'agrarian' policy (rather than 'agricultural' policy) has traditionally sought to guarantee a minimum livelihood for peasant farmers. This social and political accommodation to the interests of the poor rural majority has been undermined, especially since Mexico's debt crisis surfaced in 1982. The central thesis of Sanderson's paper is that the United States and Mexico are so inextricably linked that policies to correct rural poverty and increase agricultural productivity in Mexico are placed in jeopardy by US adjustments to the international farm crisis. The effects of economic restructuring have been particularly painful for Mexico, which has come to depend even more heavily on its agricultural exports, as oil prices weaken and the peso loses value against the US dollar and other currencies. Sanderson suggests that the very success of US farm policies, to increase exports and streamline production, poses problems for Mexican attempts to secure social objectives such as cheaper food and better nutrition for the rural and urban poor.

The paper by Leclercq considers the situation of another 'third' country, Brazil, focusing on its rise to become the world's second largest soybean exporter. Leclercq examines the effects of this integration into world soybean markets on agrarian structures and the adjustment process provoked by the debt crisis and international recession. Economic stabilisation and fiscal retrenchment have exposed the limited capacity of the state in Brazil, as in other 'third countries', to protect farmers from the increasing instability of world commodity prices and to maintain their position in world markets against the heavily subsidised competition of the US and the EEC. Leclercq focuses on one commodity, soya, which links developing and developed economies, but his paper also addresses some of the problems raised by Sanderson and Lawrence in their contributions to this volume.

Bibliography

Buttel, F. (1982), Environmental quality in agriculture: some observations on political economic constraints on sustainable resource management, *Cornell Rural Sociology*, Bulletin No 128.
Buttel, F. and Gertler, M. (1982), Agricultural structure, agricultural policy and environmental quality: some observations on the context of agricultural research in North America. *Agriculture and Environment*, 7 (101–119).
EEC (1986), *Report on behalf of the Committee on the Environment, Public Health and Consumer Protection*. European Parliament Working Document A–2–207/85.
EEC Commission (1986), *A Future for Community Agriculture: Commission Guidelines*. (Brussels: EEC).
Friedmann, H. (1987), 'Everyone's food comes from abroad: class specific diets and the international specialization of agricultural production'. Paper presented at the Rural Sociology Society meetings. (Madison, Wisconsin).
Goodman, D., Sorj, B. and Wilkinson, J. (1987), *From Farming to Biotechnology* (Oxford: Basil Blackwell).
Green, B. H. (1981), *Countryside Conservation*. (London: Allen & Unwin).
Kenney, M., Curry, J. and Stockwell, T. (1987), 'Contextualising agriculture within postwar US society: Fordism as an integrative theory'. Paper presented to the Rural Sociology Society meetings. (Madison, Wisconsin).
Mond, Sir Alfred (1927), *Industry and Politics*. (London: Macmillan).
OECD (Organisation for Economic Co-operation and Development) (1985), *Environmental Data*. (Paris: OECD).
Rama, R. (1985), 'Some effects of the internationalization of agriculture on the Mexican agricultural crisis'. In S. Sanderson (ed.) *The Americas in the New International Division of Labor*. (New York: Holmes & Meier).

Redclift, M. R. (1987), *Sustainable Development: exploring the contradictions*. (London: Methuen).
Shoard, M. (1980), *The Theft of the Countryside*. (London: Temple Smith).
Vogtmann, H. (1985), 'Environmental and socio-economic aspect of different farming practices' in *The Other Economic Summit* (London: unpublished MS).

2 World Trade in Agricultural Products: from Global Regulation to Market Fragmentation

Laurence Tubiana

From the mid-1960s, the development of agricultural trade between the North and South led to a decisive collapse of the traditional colonial models of the division of labour. The increasing complexity of trade patterns has destroyed the old systems of 'imperial preference': what F. Braudel termed 'les Economies-monde', have been incorporated into the world economy. The traditional role of the South – low-cost provision of agricultural raw materials to the industrialized nations – is no longer of decisive importance to trade flows and to the world economic system. Indeed, we have witnessed a significant reversal in these flows. Today the countries of the South are increasingly the major customers for the surplus agricultural products, both processed and unprocessed, exported by the advanced economies. According to a recent study by the OECD, the developed nations now account for more than 65 per cent of world agricultural exports.

The sustained increase in agricultural trade during the last two decades (1960s and 1970s) is essentially due to the growth in the exports of the developed nations, while the share of the developing nations has been in constant decline.[1] This tendency would be even more clear cut if certain surplus-producing areas in the Southern hemisphere, notably Argentina, Uruguay, Brazil and Paraguay, but also certain Asian countries, including Thailand, were excluded. Conversely, on the import side, the share of the OECD countries in agricultural trade has declined steadily, while that of the LDCs has increased significantly: in 1980 the developing countries represented 26 per cent of the world demand for agricultural products (as against 16 per cent in 1967); 51 per cent of the world demand for cereals; 54 per cent for dairy products (20 per cent in 1967); 46 per cent of world sugar imports (19 per cent in 1967); and 25 per cent of the world

23

demand for meat (5 per cent in 1967). Even in the market for feed grains and oilseeds, where the developed nations have traditionally been both the principal producers and consumers, demand from the South has increased. In 1985 the demand from the developing nations for feed grains represented 29 per cent of total world imports (4 per cent in 1967), and that for oilseeds 25 per cent (9 per cent in 1967).

These trends in North-South trade relations were underpinned first by the organisational structure of trade in primary products and manufactures introduced in the post-war period, and later consolidated following the Korean War, the process being completed in the 1960s. The rapid expansion of agriculture in the developed nations, which has undergone a technical and economic transformation without precedent in the history of modern agriculture, gave further momentum to this dynamic.

The beginning of the 1970s saw these long-term tendencies reinforced: the final breakdown of colonial relations; the technical and economic pre-eminence of the agriculture of the advanced industrial countries (especially of North America) and the reversal of trade flows. At the same time, however, those factors which seemed to assure the continuation of this pre-eminence, namely, the stability of dollar-linked currencies along with the stability of prices in expanding world commodity markets due to United States' agricultural policy, were put in question. In 1973/4 prices on the world cereal and soya markets soared and gave rise to fears of famine on a global scale, food shortages in the developing nations, and the risk of a breakdown in supplies for European livestock producers. This crisis provoked wide-ranging debates on the world food system and posed a number of leading questions. Did the crisis provide striking confirmation of North American hegemony over world food markets? Was the crisis conjunctural, arising from the technical modernisation of Third World agriculture, the extension of commodity relations and insertion into the world trading system? Or, on the contrary, did the crisis reflect deep-seated problems and obstacles?

If we look at the development of North-South agricultural trade since the early 1970s we can discern several very contradictory trends. On the one hand, there has been a profound transformation in food consumption patterns in the towns and cities of the South, and food deficits have become more acute. The unification of the world economy and the worldwide diffusion of the North American model of production/consumption have continued, impelled by internationalised agro-industrial capital. On the other hand, today there are strong signs of an upheaval in the organisational structures of world agricultural trade, and of the beginning of a period of uncertainty as to the economic rules of the game and future development.

This area of discussion is both too vast and too complex for us to provide a comprehensive interpretation here. Accordingly, we shall limit ourselves to several hypotheses and suggest further directions for thought. In particular, we will examine the contradictory process, which is at once unifying and dividing the world economy, whereby agricultural products are produced in the North and sold to the South.[2]

Two periods, we feel, must be distinguished. The first period saw the perfection and diffusion of the 'North American model of production/consumption' as the dominant national international model of regulation.[3] In this period, the tendencies towards unification of the world economy and the interpenetration of national agro-food systems were strong, as they were in other sectors of economic activity. The second period, which dates from the crisis in the international commodity markets (1972–4) is characterized by the increasing fragmentation of the world economy. This occurred, however, without any decline in the volume of trade, contrary to developments in other sectors of world trade.

In this second period, there are many indications that the model of production/consumption and the methods of national and international regulation proposed by the United States in the aftermath of the Second World War (for agriculture and the food system as for other sectors of activity), have entered a period of crisis.

THE DIFFUSION OF THE PRODUCTION/CONSUMPTION MODEL AND THE ORGANISATION OF WORLD TRADE.

American Supremacy – Domination and Hegemony?

The 1960s and 1970s witnessed the technical and economic supremacy of North American agriculture. The United States progressively won a growing share of world markets, and in 1970 it accounted for nearly 35 per cent of wheat exports, 50 per cent of maize exports, 90 per cent of soybean exports, and 30 per cent of cattle-cake. For the American agricultural economy the conquest of foreign markets was vital, since, from the end of the Korean war, surpluses had continued to accumulate. Exports supported domestic prices and agricultural income, as well as allowing the continuing expansion of production.

The development of stable and growing trade with other developed nations (first with Europe and then Japan and other Eastern countries), relied specifically on the diffusion of the model of agricultural production and food consumption established in the United States. The diffusion of this model was the vector for the establishment of American hegemony over agricultural markets, and the pre-eminence of its norms of production, consumption and trade.

Immediately after the Second World War, the United States 'proposed' to the developed nations – and notably to Europe – a model for the restructuring of agriculture and livestock farming as part of the effort towards economic reconstruction. One by one different nations adopted capital-intensive and labour-saving agricultural systems, though at different speeds and with diverse forms (Coulomb and Delorme, 1981). But the essentials never changed: the capitalisation of farms (mechanisation) and a massive reduction in the agricultural workforce; specialisation according to locality and within the production process (arable crops, breeding, livestock fattening); a technical revolution through the use of industrial inputs (fertilisers, pesticides) and of genetically improved seeds; and the intensification of livestock production (poultry, pigs and cattle) on the basis of industrially-processed feed (cereals, soybean).

The expansion of US wheat, maize, and soya exports accompanied this modernisation. After bitter negotiations with the EEC during the 'Kennedy Round' of 1964–67, a compromise was reached which established an agreed division of labour, with Europe protecting its production of cereals but increasing its deficit in oilseeds (Chabert, 1976; Berlan, 1976). American soya complemented European cereals in the feed of European livestock, as high European wheat and corn prices encouraged the consumption of soya bought at low world market prices. Patterns of consumption quickly changed: within twenty years, in most developed countries, the consumption of beef doubled, while that of poultry increased threefold.

Marshall Aid encouraged the extension of this model of production/consumption in those developed nations devastated by the war. In their turn, the 1960s and 1970s saw the birth of aid programmes for the Third World. These programmes established the financial channels necessary for the adoption of the model, which had been re-baptised as 'the Green Revolution'. Its diffusion had led, ten years later, to the transformation of certain sectors of agricultural production, to the partial restructuring of livestock-raising, and to the modification of consumption patterns, especially in urban areas: wheat, bread, or rice tended to replace traditionally cultivated cereals (maize in Central America or in Egypt, millet or sorghum in West Africa), and the consumption of meat and dairy products increased.

Numerous studies, notably those of the United Nations Research Institute for Social Development, have analysed these programmes and their repercussions on Third World agriculture. For many writers,this link between domestic sectors of the US economy and world markets, supported by the solid alliance of the American state, farmers, industrialists, and consumers, was evidence of an increasing monopolisation of the international food system. The United States, the world's leading economic power, played a determining role in the organisation of the international division of labour, and here, as in other sectors, trade was 'managed' to its own advantage (George, 1976). In support of this thesis one need only underline the vast amount of public funds used to encourage the international expansion of US agriculture and agro-industry. The increase in American exports to weak or insolvent economies is the most striking example of this immense support.

From 1954, programmes to subsidise exports were introduced in the name of food aid (Public Law 480). Wheat, wheat-flour, corn, and soya oil were then provided as aid or virtually so (40 years' credit at 1.3 per cent interest), to insolvent countries. Consumption habits were changed even before local farmers were in a position to respond to the new demands, and often before they were given the means to do so. Important markets were thus opened up. These in turn supported the growth of agro-industrial markets stimulated by the agricultural modernisation programmes formulated to 'respond' to these new consumption demands.

Within this model of the international division of labour, the Americans kept for themselves the export of basic feed and food products, in which they considered their comparative advantage to be the greatest, along with their position as technological leader. This left nations with a greater available workforce to concentrate on livestock activities, thus creating a steady outlet for the American agro-industrial complex. Numerous institutions were created to defend this position: the United States Feed Grain Council, the American Soybean Association, the US Agency for International Development, and the US Wheat Association. These organisations made considerable efforts in developing countries to encourage the consumption of wheat and animal proteins.

At the same time, one could advance the hypothesis that the American influence on agricultural trade is at once more restricted and more important than might be suggested by analyses framed in terms of US 'domination'. In fact, this influence, in certain respects, is limited, since the agreements and compromises reached with the EEC and certain developing nations are numerous, the diffusion of the model is very unequal, and world demand does not permit all American surpluses to be absorbed. Its domination of the markets has not been complete, and it has had to accommodate a certain amount of 'sharing', notably with other members of the 'exporters' club', of temperate zone agriculture – Canada, Australia, France, and Argentina (Berlan, 1975).

But the 'American' influence goes far beyond the task of regulating markets and commercial relations. This 'domination' is an effective hegemony since it relies on the strength of the State and the power of the principal actors (notably multinational US agro-industrial companies), and is legitimated by the efficiency of its technical, scientific, economic, social, and political systems.

The Organisational Model of Trade

These same technical and economic norms allowed a new codification of trade and international relations. This 'organisational model' encompassed a price system, the international regulation of economic relations, and the creation of financial institutions. These were entrusted with the task of encouraging growth compatible with the imperatives of the development and organisation of the world food trade.

The Liberalisation of Agricultural Trade

The United States has waged a constant battle in favour of the liberalisation of agricultural trade and the abolition of preferential relations within the framework of specialist trade organisations such as the General Agreement on Trade and Tariffs (GATT). This position has been widely adopted by the developing countries, notably through UNCTAD, which since the beginning of the 1960s has attacked the restrictions imposed by developed nations on LDC exports. This free trade stance is not just a facade: even though the

United States uses a whole arsenal of measures to protect its own agriculture, its primary interest in the international arena is the expansion of trade.

This anti-protectionist position is shared by almost all the international development organisations. The latter, and primarily the most important of them – the World Bank (IBRD) – although in principle not directly concerned with the organisation of trade, never cease to intervene in such matters. The IBRD has always vigorously defended the principle of trade liberalisation (in the North as well as the South), and supported agricultural specialisation according to 'comparative advantage' in order to encourage growth and development. In many cases, this principle of liberalisation (itself a corollary of the United Nations system and of the post-war boom), and growth in an open economy seem to govern the activities of these 'agencies'.

The Maintenance of Stable World Prices

From 1956–72 the prices of agricultural products exported by the developed nations were exceptionally stable.[4] These low and stable prices encouraged the growth of new demand and inhibited the competition from tropical products, which were substitutes for those supplied by the developed nations (Marloie, 1974). This stability in world prices, which seems to have disappeared in recent times, has been widely discussed. For many observers, this phase of stability was exceptional because agricultural markets by their very nature are unstable. Proponents of this view believe that price instability characterised these markets in the period 1914–49, and is again evident today.

It seems to us, however, that the 'abnormality' of price stability in the period 1956–72 was not a deviation, but a product of a trading system closely attuned to the regulatory influence of the hegemonic economy. The stability of prices was the pre-condition of the diffusion of the US model of production/consumption. The adoption of new production techniques, the localisation of activities (intensive livestock production relying on imported feed-grains and soya), and the transformation of consumption habits all depended on the expectations of economic agents, who could rely on plentiful supplies and on predictable terms.

This stability was also the fruit of the internal management of American agriculture. The stability of farm incomes was maintained either by high guaranteed prices (compared with the world price), or by compensatory payments (especially after 1964). Similarly, supply adjustments were made via control of the level and capacity of production, changes in stocks, and through exports (subsidies, food aid, and so on). The stability of world prices thus was achieved largely by the financing and management of the surplus production of American farmers.

The Development of Multilateral Agreements.

The international regulation of economic relations in agricultural production was dictated by the need for stable world prices in order to expand trade and diffuse the model of development. The example of the International Wheat Agreement is most indicative. The first convention, signed in 1949, was modified by an uninterrupted series of further conventions until 1969. Until 1967, this agreement revolved around the price range which had to be respected in at least 50 per cent of transactions, both by the exporters and importers who were signatories to the agreement. From this date, the agreement was extended to all transactions, even those concluded with non-member countries.

At the 'Kennedy Round' negotiations, which were meant to result in the signing of a broader agreement, the US failed to obtain the dismantling of European protection on cereals but did reach agreement with the Europeans on a readjustment of prices and the institution of a multilateral food programme.

For some analysts, the agreement on wheat never really worked; the International Wheat Council set up by the 1949 convention hardly ever intervened to force buyers and sellers to respect their commitments. Agreement on prices was, more often than not, reached directly between exporters. Supporters of this view take as an example the 'break-up' of the agreement from 1969 onwards, under the impact first of declining prices and then price increases, and the insuperable difficulty of getting an agreement signed that would go to the root of the problems affecting the market. Today, the renewed agreement is limited to guaranteeing the continued existence of the International Council and the accord on food aid. However, between 1959 and 1967 wheat prices stayed within the price limits determined by the international agreement, despite important and irregular purchases by the USSR and India. This stability would seem to arise more from the consensus between the principal exporters (Canada and the US) than from the agreement itself. Until 1970, the

US and Canada accounted for more than 70 per cent of the trade in wheat and held more than 80 per cent of the stocks. They were able, therefore, to control the level of competition and the price. The Agreement did not work only in so far as it failed to express this *de facto* situation.

For the United States, it was important to have this explicit agreement on price levels and market shares with the international community. In the same way, the US fought to ensure that the other cereal-exporters joined in the food aid agreement of 1971, in order to avoid an increase in competition in commercial markets (Eiseneman, 1982).

THE CRISIS

In the early 1970s this system of organising trade was thrown into crisis. The most obvious symptoms were: the beginning of a period of great instability in world market prices; increasing difficulties with the operation of multilateral accords and, concomitantly, the triggering of increased competition in export markets. Co-operation between members of the 'exporters club' gave way to a 'trade war', to the proliferation of bilateral accords and agreements on compensation. Today, this crisis of organisation has led to a slowing down of world agricultural trade (though at different rates, depending on the country in question). Several phenomena combined to accentuate the situation, including the maintenance throughout the 1970s of high economic growth rates in developing countries, accompanied by a slowing down in the growth of their agricultural production.[5] Since 1975 we have seen both a boom in food imports by the South and a fall in their agricultural exports.

The Instability of Prices

Since 1972–3 and the sharp rise in world prices, agricultural markets have entered into a marked phase of instability (Figure 1) Periods of surpluses and shortages have succeeded one another. Thus since 1973 we have seen a period of lower demand (1974–76), followed by a new period of tight demand (1979–80), and then finally shortages have again reappeared on world cereal markets (in 1981, 1982, and 1983). This instability also affects prices: since 1970 price fluctuations have been from three to five times as great, depending on the product, as

Figure 2.1 *World Price Trends of Major Agricultural Commodities* (Average annual prices in cents US $)

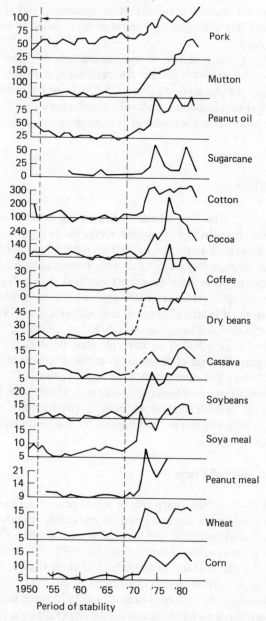

Source M. Marloie, *L'internationalisation de l'agriculture française*, (Paris, Editions Ouvrieres, 1984, page 14). Calculated from selected price series of the FAO.

those in the period 1950–70. In the early 1980s this instability was accompanied by a slight fall in prices. Indeed, the mechanisms used in earlier periods to adjust supply and demand on a global scale have largely lost their effectiveness; and the most important of these are the forms of regulation of the world market.

The Breakdown of Multilateral Agreements

As we have already observed, the 'Kennedy Round' negotiations had demonstrated a growing consensus in favour of multilateral trade liberalisation. This consensus was shattered by the crisis in the commodity markets. The rise in protectionism and the uncertainties of badly regulated markets rendered most of these multilateral agreements obsolete.

Thus after 1969 the wheat agreement became unworkable in the trade war which broke out between exporting countries following the contraction of demand. Successive meetings in 1971, 1974, 1979 and again in 1981 of the International Wheat Council, the World Food Council, FAO, and UNCTAD failed to reach agreement between exporting and importing countries. The negotiating parties could not agree on price levels, the system of stockpiling (national and international), nor the organisation of markets. The same obstacles emerged in the negotiations of international agreements for coffee (finally re-established in 1980) and sugar.

While multilateral procedures lost much of their importance, the number of bilateral agreements, on the other hand, grew rapidly. The OECD recently estimated that 40 per cent of the trade in cereals takes place on a bilateral basis. Credit agreements negotiated contract by contract, and the expansion of mixed financing involving public and private sources, [6] especially in the later 1970s, made it increasingly difficult to establish the 'world price' of certain products. The Soviet purchases of wheat and corn from Argentina after the US embargo were made at well below world price levels. Similarly, the 'market prices' at which the United States sold wheat or corn to Latin American and North African countries were combined with so many different terms of credit (maturity, interest rate, and so on), that contracts without such favourable terms had to be made at below the world price. Multilateral agreements failed to halt the expansion of these bilateral accords and export credits. Indeed, when international agreement to limit these credits was finally reached in 1976 and 1978 it did not include agricultural products (RAMSES, 1982).

In North-South relations, barter agreements, now called 'compensatory agreements', have emerged in response to the twofold instability of prices and currencies. Representing an estimated 20 per cent
of world trade, these agreements have been expanding since the early
1970s, in much the same way as they grew in the crisis of the 1930s
(Outters-Jaeger, 1979).

These new forms of trade are linked to the financial crisis of the
Third World in the 1980s. But they are also the consequence of the
trade wars between exporting countries to win markets in the South.
In this struggle to redeploy exports, certain regions have become
highly coveted. Thus North Africa and the Middle East, for example,
have been the arena of fierce battles between the European Community, the United States, Australia, and Canada because the oil-
producing countries and 'middle-income' countries were the only
export markets still growing in the early 1980s.[7]

This 'trade war' between the advanced industrial countries over
world agricultural markets goes hand in hand with the crisis of
multilateral institutions, such as the World Bank and the IMF (Leclercq and Tubiana, 1983). Their repeated demands for increased
resources have foundered on the United States' refusal to increase its
capital contribution to these agencies.

In the late 1970s, the weakening influence of GATT was met by an
increase in bilateral consultative agreements, the creation of informal
groups, and attempts to settle litigation on a case-by-case basis, as
emphasised in the 1982 RAMES-IFRI report. We have witnessed 'a
kind of exhaustion or ageing of the system in use. After the tri-
umphant progress of free trade in the 1950s and 1960s, and its
consolidation and apogee with the "Tokyo Round", in the 1970s,
perhaps the time of its decline has arrived' (RAMSES, 1982, 80). As
far as agricultural trade is concerned, this decline of free trade has
confirmed the breakdown of the consensus on the 'international
division of labour', most notably in United States–EEC relations.
This statement is borne out by the hostility provoked by the 'Uruguay
Round' of GATT.

These changes in the methods of trade have occurred against the
background of food crisis in the Third World. Long-term factors
(population growth, urbanisation) have combined with the slowing
down of agricultural growth to provoke a rapid increase in LDC
agricultural imports, which today are scarcely offset by their global
agricultural exports (George, 1983).

Comments on the Interpretation of the Crisis

The new face of world agricultural trade – instability, Third World food deficits, bilateralisation, and trade wars – has prompted a number of different analyses. The initial reaction was to interpret the 1973–74 crisis as the prologue to world-wide shortages of staple commodities. That is, would the waste of resources and the growth in demand for agricultural products which accompanied the generalisation of the American model of production/consumption be offset by the expansion of output?

Many projection studies have examined this question, including work at the Universities of California and Michigan, USDA, OECD, FAO and, finally, at Wageningen on a world agricultural model (the MOIRA model). These studies rejected the thesis of food shortages, demonstrating that potential productive capacity, especially in the developed countries, would be sufficient to meet world needs. Yet the hypothesis is still relevant: for some observers, the present fall in world prices is only a transitory phase that could be followed by higher prices pushing the more dependent countries into a food crisis (George, 1983).

The receding risk of world food shortages in the short-term led most commentators to argue that the American model of production/consumption (and its diffusion) had emerged strengthened from the 'food crisis' of 1973–74 (Revel and Riboud, 1980). Subsequently, this crisis appeared as a conjunctural event, without major significance for the organisation of world trade.

In this way, writers such as Pierre Chalmin (1983) regard unstable agricultural markets as the norm, and the preceding period of stability as exceptional.[8] The 1973–74 crisis had no effect on the interplay of international forces. For Susan George, on the other hand, the crisis demonstrated that the United States exerted excessive power over the world food system. The upsurge of prices bore witness to the capacity of the American state and multinational firms, which dominate trade, to manipulate the markets and impose higher prices.

In similar fashion, analyses of the internationalisation of agro-industrial capital interpret recent trends in terms of the maintenance and deepening of the international division of labour. Thus Kostas Vergopoulos examines the connection between Third World agricultural exports and the development of intensive livestock production in the North: the 'cash crops' previously restricted to tropical products now comprise animal feeds, such as Brazilian soybeans and cassava from Thailand (Vergopoulos, 1983). The expansion of these crops limits the production of staple foodstuffs for the domestic market and further undermines food production and consumption in peripheral countries. The role given to Third World agricultural economies, within the logic of the internationalisation of capital, is to supply animal feed to the North, which is accompanied by a decline in food consumption, the creation of food deficits, and the greater dependence of Third World countries.

For Pierre Salama (1983), the food crisis, beyond the well-known conflict between cash crops and food staples, is linked to the system of capital accumulation and the expansion of commodity production in agriculture. The decline in food consumption arises from the 'marginalising' process of capital accumulation which, by encouraging commercial production for export markets, accelerates the rural exodus and the decline of the subsistence sector.

For many writers, therefore, the process of the internationalisation and unification of world agriculture was not called into question by the crisis which began in the early 1970s. On the contrary, they stress the continued domination of world markets by the United States, manifest in the dynamism of agro-industrial multinationals which are well adapted to the crisis and the climate of instability, in order to demonstrate that the unification of the world economy is continuing apace (Caillet, 1984).

Several factors lend support to these analyses. The United States, cornerstone of the world food system, has again increased its exports especially at the end of the 1970s, and seems to rule alone over world market prices. Patterns of food consumption continue to be transformed, as shown by the increasing imports by LDCs of oilseed cake and animal feed for livestock production. The management of exports, as an integral part of agricultural policy, has long characterised the United States' approach to this sector. More and more developed countries, under the pressure of intensified production and rising surpluses, have adopted aggressive export policies. As Coulomb and Delorme (1981) suggest, with the growing export specialisation of the advanced countries underway since the 1970s, at the same time as agricultural production was expanding throughout the world, does not the world crisis represent a new extension of the model? The diffusion of new production techniques and consumption patterns continues, as a tendency, in each economy, reinforcing the changes in international trade.

Whether we examine national processes of capital accumulation or the supranational aspects of the world food economy (that is, the multinationals), the conclusion is that the crisis has confirmed the model of organisation and agricultural trade established in the post-war period.

MARKET FRAGMENTATION AND DIFFICULTIES OF REGULATION

There are clear indications, however, that the process of internationalisation has run into major contradictions.

Intensified Competition

The earlier discussion of changes in the forms of trade revealed that the trading structures favoured by the United States have encountered major obstacles.

First, as producing countries have gradually adopted the same techniques of production, competition in world markets has intensified, undermining the hierarchical structure of the world food system. Thus conflicts between the major grain exporters, especially the struggle over the Soviet, Chinese, North African and Middle Eastern markets, have destroyed the geo-political organisation of markets and areas of influence.

Second, certain Third World countries and traditional exporters of basic foodstuffs have greatly increased their exports in recent years. Argentina's exports of cereals have expanded from 10 to 25 million tonnes since the early 1970s, and Thailand has increased its exports of corn and cassava. Brazil and Argentina have invaded the soybean market, previously reserved for American exports, and together they now account for almost 30 per cent of the world total. These exporters participate in world trade on the basis of very heterogenous agricultural sectors in terms of production techniques and, more generally, state policies. Less controlled agricultural economies and producers less protected from world market fluctuations thus have been drawn into competition with other producers who benefit from permanent transfers and subsidies, thereby introducing contradictions and factors of instability into organised markets.

Other indications of the profound transformation of the world agricultural economy and trade patterns also deserve emphasis, most importantly the changes in American agricultural policy.

Less Stable US Policy

Since 1974, the American state has experienced greater difficulty in controlling domestic output and prices and in exercising decisive influence over international prices. From 1953, American agricultural policies were largely successful in supporting prices, stabilising farm incomes, and maintaining a rate of output growth consistent with the expansion of manufacturing industry. The legislation governing agricultural policy, and notably the Food and Agriculture Act of 1965, provided the USDA with a very diversified range of measures to control farm production and incomes. The programmes to withdraw land from production have been the main instrument of supply management. Farm incomes have been controlled by a dual intervention system:
(a) direct transfers (compensatory payments) to support farm incomes.
(b) a subsidised system of on-farm storage to regulate market prices.

In 1974, greater priority was given to controlling market prices, and farm income support, which had previously been related to parity prices, was reduced and linked henceforth to costs of production. Following the marked decline in farm incomes, the US government has reinforced its efforts to control prices via stockpiling and, since 1981, by further policies to reduce the area under cultivation, such as the PIK programme. These measures have failed to reverse the declining trend of farm incomes and the control of supply has remained very uneven. Furthermore, since 1978 the capitalisation of agriculture has continued at the cost of rising indebtedness and, since the early 1980s, numerous farm bankruptcies.

The greatest difficulty, both for the State, whose agricultural budgets have declined under the Reagan administration, and for producers, is to dampen world market fluctuations by supply adjustments (output and stocks). This problem is clearly related to the reduction of surplus production capacity that has been underway since the early 1970s.[9] In the case of wheat, for example, it can certainly be argued that the adoption of intensive production systems has made it harder to control output and the acreage under cultivation, especially when farm operators are in difficulty (Chaminot and Jacquet, 1983).

This increasing instability in domestic supply management has been accompanied by changes in export policy. Food aid programmes used since the early 1950s to support world prices have been reduced in both relative and absolute terms, even in years of substantial surplus production. Food aid which amounted to 15 million tonnes of cereals in 1960 is now less than 7 million tonnes. Such shipments represented 64 per cent of American wheat exports in 1960 compared to only 10 per cent today. In the same period, the total volume of exports has more than doubled. Since 1974 American food aid has tended to be concentrated on a small number of countries as well as playing, in times of crisis and financial difficulty, more a political than commercial role.

The development of export credits in the early 1980s, which in part took the place of food aid programmes in facilitating the disposal of US production, has had a very marked effect on the working of the world market. By diversifying the conditions of sale and the types of bilateral trade, these export promotion programmes are unable to reduce price fluctuations. Mixed export credits have reached an important level and in 1982 they could be used for agricultural products up to a limit of US$ 1 billion. This change in the support mechanisms for American export markets can be seen as a simple technical adjustment intended to facilitate continued accumulation in the agricultural sector (Perelman, 1981).

It seems to us that this interpretation significantly underestimates the effect of the financial and budgetary restrictions felt by all countries, North and South. One thing is clear, however: the stabilisation of world prices and farm incomes achieved by massive state transfers to agriculture is a questionable strategy by virtue of both its cost and the current uncertainty about its efficacy.

Structural Adjustment Policies

The problems faced in controlling the American economy must be set within an international framework shaken by a series of profound changes in monetary and financial systems, energy and manufacturing industry. These transformations emphasise how the conditions of economic growth and trade have themselves changed. Third World countries have experienced a similar upheaval in the conditions of their insertion in the world economy. Rising import costs, unstable export earnings, fluctuating interest rates and mounting indebtedness have made 'external imbalances' a major preoccupation.

Policy responses to this new situation have been varied but increasingly, under the pressure of deficits and the need to negotiate
external financing and debt rescheduling, Third World countries have
been forced to apply 'structural adjustment policies'. These essentially comprise a series of stabilisation measures applied to monetary
and credit systems, fiscal management and the labour market, in
order to resolve imbalances resulting from policies considered to be
'unrigorous and expansionist' (Lichtensztein, 1978). In the
mid-1980s, these policies were seen as the only 'way out' of the crisis,
as the instruments of a necessary 'structural transformation'. It must
be noted however, that 'structural' aspects have always been secondary to policies, which are dominated by the short-term management
of budget deficits and external payments problems. Indeed, these
policies basically have sought to resolve the balance of payments
deficits provoked by the rising cost of oil, industrial imports and debt
service. They have thus focused on increasing export surpluses in
order to avoid the cumulative growth of deficits which could imperil
the whole international financial system (Cline and Weintraub 1982).
   Confident in market processes of resource allocation, the international organisations have supported anti-protectionist policies.[10]
This policy orientation can be seen as the continuation of the norms
or rules under which, in different circumstances, the internationalisation of the world economy took place. However, when applied to
agricultural economies weakened by structural disequilibria, such
policies come up against extreme situations in social and political
terms. These force the international institutions to adjust their approach, as in the case of the cost-of-living riots in Tunisia or in
Morocco in January 1984, for example. In addition to these domestic
factors, the crisis in the advanced industrial countries has restricted
outlets for Third World agricultural products and increased competition
and protectionism.
   Consequently, given the uncertain results of adjustment policies,
especially in the agricultural sector, where the re-allocation of resources is necessarily slow, an important debate has arisen on the question of 'food strategies'. With the extension of the 'American model'
and the adoption of 'outward oriented' growth strategies, some
analysts in the wake of the 1974 FAO Conference have insisted on
the integration of national networks, the linking of national food
requirements with local production, and the reintegration of marginal sectors into the national economy.[11] However, these strategies
presuppose the strengthening of national mechanisms of control and

protection which cannot be obtained simply by the 'return' to a system of international regulation based on competition and comparative advantage.

The Fragmentation of Third World Markets

In the 1970s, the trends observed in Third World countries varied widely under the differential impact of economic shocks. The rhythms and forms of growth, the patterns of insertion in world trade, then the unfolding of the crisis, all these aspects diverge, whether we are talking of capital surplus oil-producing countries or those with a high absorptive capacity, or of less advanced developing countries, or even of the newly-industrialising countries. This diversity, at the heart of the Third World, extends also to the contrasting performance of the agricultural sector. Growth rates are negative in sub-Saharan Africa, stable in East Asia, and have slowed down in Latin America.

In the oil-producing countries, which constitute the most dynamic sector of world agriculture, certain factors have emerged which interfere with the normal processes of consumption, production, and trade. The diffusion of oil wealth provoked an increase in urban demand, though this was quite differentiated. Middle-class consumption patterns changed significantly and, with high income-elasticities of demand, markets for cereals, animal feedstuffs, and processed food products increased rapidly. The income from oil production, although unequally distributed, stimulated rural-urban migration, swelling the size of marginal groups. These provided a specific demand for cheap basic foodstuffs (Lerin and Tubiana, 1980; 1983). Faced with several different patterns of consumption, parts of which have to be subsidised, the State has attempted to compartmentalise food markets in order to control the various segments of food demand separately (Egg, Lerin, and Tubiana, 1982).

These policies have absorbed considerable public expenditure in importing foodstuffs to stabilise prices, financing subsidies to local consumption, and stimulating domestic production. However, the segregation of markets, although necessary to cope with income inequalities and varied patterns of demand, is hardly conducive to the diversification and expansion of internal production. The system of relative prices, inflation, rising agricultural wages, and higher consumer goods prices, even for foodstuffs in rural areas, all combine to inhibit the development of agriculture.

This fragmentation of organised markets, which is characterised by different price systems, is reinforced by the development of parallel markets. Thus in the 1970s the State adopted important administrative and financial measures to regulate subsidised markets and offset the effects of world market fluctuations. On the other hand, the private sector in many cases has developed parallel markets, which are fostered by the contradictory relations within the apparatus of State intervention. Indeed, they exist in its shadow thanks to the many profitable opportunities created by this intervention. Thus the parallel markets between Benin, Niger and Nigeria depend on shifts in exchange rates and local requirements. These extremely active and flexible trading systems accentuate the fragmentation of markets and economic activity (Igue, 1983). Such systems are at odds with the model of world market integration, creating economic circuits which function according to their own logic rather than the logic operating to deepen the international division of labour.

CONCLUSION

The imbalances and anomalies of Third World agricultural economies define the limits of the organisational model of world trade established since 1945. The diffusion in the Third World of American production techniques and consumption patterns today has run into too many obstacles and contradictions to be able to continue as the driving force behind the expansion of production and trade. Food dependence and the decoupling of production and consumption trends have resulted in a dual crisis. That is, the crisis of the models of economic development based on open economies and comparative advantage, and the breakdown of the multilateral procedures used to unify the world market. The crisis is one of American hegemony, and therefore of the movement toward integration and internationalisation.

One point worth noting is that just at the time when American domination over world agricultural markets is most perceptible the discussion of alternatives is at its strongest. In the Third World, plans for national food strategies are based on the hypothesis that the revival of domestic agricultural growth depends upon the integration of small peasant producers and marginal consumers into the market. These plans stress the need for the selective protection of agricultural production and, more generally, for measures to shield domestic systems from unstable world markets which are too competitive for producers who do not have the benefit of massive State transfers. The formation of protected regional markets and the search for technical and economic alternatives to the prevailing model, both in production and consumption, define the terms of the current debate on agricultural development.

In the present context of economic warfare, this debate expresses the failure of the dominant economy to put forward a model of production and trade to 'get out' of the crisis. However, even if the economic crisis, which can be seen as a crisis of the regulation and diffusion of the dominant model, paves the way for alternative strategies, short-term macroeconomic constraints make their viability uncertain.

Notes

1. The share of the developing countries has remained stable as far as tropical commodities, notably beverages, and sugar are concerned. A marked increase in the market share of developing countries has occurred only in the case of oilseeds due to Latin American soybean exports, first by Brazil, later by Argentina.

2. This discussion draws on various studies undertaken by the Department of Rural Economics and Sociology of the National Agricultural Research Institute (INRA) and, of course, the research now in progress in the International Economics Workshop in Montpellier.

3. Regulation here is understood as defined by M. Aglietta, R. Boyer or J. Mistral; that is, 'the conjuncture of mechanisms and adjustment principles associated with a given structure of the wage relation, competition, State intervention and the international economic order'. *Revue des Annales*, Le Temps présent: la Crise (I), p.488. In the United States, the process of regulation in agriculture is characterised by the strong role of the State in adjusting productive capacity to demand, managing financial transfers, and promoting exports. At the international level, regulation involves efforts to organise and codify economic relations (that is, multinational agreements) and to maintain price stability. See also M. Aglietta, *Régulation et crise du capitalisme* (Paris: Calmann-Lévy, 1980).

4. In the case of wheat, the variance between the average annual US export prices was 0.06 in the years 1963–72 and 0.20 between 1972 and 1983.

5. These rates were very unequal between countries, and depended on the massive financial transfers to OPEC countries and, given the crisis of the advanced industrial economies, the recycling of these funds to a select number of supposedly creditworthy developing countries.

6. That is, loans which combine public funds, often in the form of grants, and publicly guaranteed private credits.

7. Consider, for example, US shipments of wheat and dairy products to Egypt and Morocco.

8. P. Chalmin has suggested that continued price instability on world markets will lead to the predominance of forward market mechanisms.
9. This thesis is defended by J.P. Penn, who suggests that agriculture will return to an 'equilibrium' position; that is, the virtual disappearance of excess factor supply (land, labour, and capital). See J. P. Penn, 'Economic Developments in US Agriculture in the 1970s' in D. G. Johnson (ed.), *Food and Agricultural Policy for the 1980s* (Washington, D.C.: American Enterprise Institute, 1980).
10. The appointment of William Clausen as Chairman of the World Bank occurred in this new context of financial crisis. A reading of the *World Development Report* in this period emphasises the change in perspectives. Thus the analysis of growth and poverty is superseded in 1983 by reflections on economic adjustment and management. The financing of structural adjustment and the conditioning of lending agreements on the execution of economic adjustment programmes approved by the International Monetary Fund moved to centre stage.
11. Some writers have suggested that the extension of the American model to the Third World is impossible. Apart from a handful of countries which may, with time, become integrated in the 'club' of developed economies, this model thus creates a 'dualism' not only in production but also in consumption.

Bibliography

Berlan, J.P. et al. (1975), 'Blé et soja: pénuries sur commande', La Recherche, no. 56, mai.

Berlan, J.P. et al. (1976), 'Approvisionnement en protéines de l'élevage français et complexes oleoproteagineux des Etats-Unis et du Sénégal'. Paris. GEREI-INRA.

Caillet, F.(1984), 'Où va l'investissement direct international (USA/monde). Le cas du secteur alimentaire'. CFCE/D.P.A.

Chabert, J.P. (1976), 'Le complexe francais du blé, INGRA-GEREI.

Chalmin, P. (1983), 'Crises et conflits surles marchés, des matières premières (Paris: CNAM).

Chaminot, A. and F. Jacquet (1983), 'Un avenir prometteur pour le "grenier à blé du monde"' Le Monde diplomatique, no. 352, juillet.

Cline. W.R. and S. Weintraub (1982), Economic Stabilization in Developing Countries, Washington, D.C., The Brookings Institution

Coulomb, P. and Delorme, H. (1981) 'Points de repères: La crise internationale', Etudes internationales, vol.12(1), mars.

Egg, J., Lerin, F. and L. Tubiana (1982), 'Choc pétrolier et crise agricole: notes sur la situation de l'agriculture dans deux pays exportateurs de pétrole sans excédents de capitaux. (Mexique-Nigeria)', Economie Rurale, no. 147–8.

Eiseneman, M. (1982), 'L'Organisation internationale du commerce des produits de base'. Faculte de Droit, Bruxelles.

George, S. (1976), How the Other Half Dies (London: Penguin).

George, S. (1983), 'Vers un nouvel ordre alimentaire mondial'. Communication au colloque Vers quel nouvel ordre mondial? (Paris).

Igue, J. (1983). 'L'officiel. le Parallele et le clandestin (commerces et intégration en Afrique de l'Ouest)', Politique Africaine, no.9, mars.
Leclercq, V. and L. Tubiana 1983, 'Les enjeux du conflit agricole entre la CEE et les USA', *Le Monde Diplomatique*, juillet.
Lerin, F. and L. Tubiana (1980), 'Intentions et contraintes de la politique agricole mexicaine, 1976–80', *Problèmes d'Amérique Latine*, no. 57, juillet.
Lerin, F. and L. Tubiana (1983), Intentions et contraintes de la politique mexicaine, II 1980–83, Problèmes d'Amérique Latine, no. 70, décembre.
Lichtensztein, S. (1978), 'Sobre el enfoque y el papel de las politicas de estabilisacion en América Latina', *Economía de América Latina*, no. 1, September.
Marloie, M. (1974), 'Le marché des tourteaux oléagineux, une nouvelle division internationale du travail'. INRA–ESR (1981), *L'instabilité des marchés agricoles* (Paris: OECD).
Outters-Jaeger, I. (1979), 'L'incidence du troc sur l'économie des pays en voie de développement'. (Paris: OECD Development Centre).
Perelman, M. (1981), 'La politique agricole et l'accumulation du capital, le cas des USA', *Etudes Internationales*, vol. 12(1), mars.
RAMSES (1982), *Rapport annuel de l'IFRI* (Paris: Economica).
Revel, A. and C. Riboud (1980), *Les Etats-Unis et la stratégie alimentaire mondiale* (Paris: Calmann-Lévy).
Salama, P. (1983). 'Endettement et disette urbaine', *Critique de l'economie politique*, no.24.
Vergopoulos, K. (1983), La transnationalisation agro-alimentaire de la périphérie. Communication au colloque *L'avenir du sous-développement* (Paris: CIP).

3 The US Farm Crisis and the Restructuring of American Agriculture: Domestic and International Dimensions[1]

Frederick H. Buttel

INTRODUCTION

The US farm crisis – or 'farm financial stress', as it is often referred to euphemistically in America – is actually an ensemble of many crises of national and international political economy. Its most immediate and salient components, as experienced directly by farmers, are heavy debt loads (and hence onerous debt service obligations), rapid declines in the value of farm land and other agricultural assets, low prices for many of the most important US farm commodities (especially soybeans, wheat, and corn), and a somewhat heightened pace of voluntary and involuntary liquidation of assets since 1981. More structurally, the US farm crisis is closely rooted in extraordinarily high real interest rates that have prevailed due to Reagan Administration fiscal and monetary policy, which have had a dramatic effect on the capital-intensive – and hence interest-rate-sensitive – agricultural sector. The farm crisis also reflects the contradictions of continued increases in US (and world) productive capacity in the basic grains and oilseeds due to technological change. The capacity to produce has relentlessly increased even as the means for purchasing and valorising this expanded production have stagnated. The US farm crisis is also a policy crisis – a protracted struggle among many contending forces that makes it virtually impossible to arrive at a political solution to problems of the agricultural economy without (and, in some respects, despite) massive state intervention and subsidy programmes. Finally, it can be seen that the US farm crisis is a reflection of a more fundamental crisis in the world economy: a long phase of global contraction which began in 1974 and

46

which continues to plague most continents in the world. This long phase of economic contraction has led to declines in prices of virtually all raw materials commodities and has exacerbated the debt problems not only of American farmers, but also of Third World countries whose appetite for borrowing vast sums of low or negative interest rate dollars in the 1970s only slightly exceeded that of US farmers.

Not since the Great Depression has there been such widespread attention to farm problems among virtually all the advanced countries in the world. There has been no shortage of policy proposals among US farm groups, agricultural economists and policy analysts, food and commodity trading interests, public interest groups, and political parties for addressing the current crisis. But there does not yet appear to be any viable political programme for dealing with the farm crisis which has much chance of being enacted by the US government. All prevailing proposals would exact major costs on one or more of the traditional farm policy constituencies (farmers, commodity groups, grain-trading and other agribusiness firms, proponents of food stamp programmes for the poor, and so on). Indeed, given the range of interests that have historically been accommodated within US farm policy legislation, implementation of any of the current proposals would presuppose the virtual dismantling of the farm policy structure that has led to the Food Security Act of 1985, which reflects a marginal adjustment of the farm policies of the past several decades.

The purpose of this paper, however, will not be largely that of advancing particular policy proposals for resolution of the US farm crisis, though I will make some concluding comments in which it is argued that the centrepiece of a policy strategy for rationalising US agriculture will need to be a partial nationalisation of agricultural land along with state intervention in land markets. The major goal of the paper will instead be to make some preliminary notes toward an analysis of how the farm crisis will contribute to a restructuring of US agriculture and the possible features of such a structure. As will become apparent later, this analysis must remain highly preliminary because of the lack of a data base on changes in the nature and pace of entry into, exit from, and differentiation within American agriculture over the past two or three decades.

I begin by describing some of the most salient dimensions of the farm crisis – in particular, rising debt loads, crop surpluses and declining commodity prices, the decapitalization of agriculture in the form of declining land and other asset values, an accelerated rate of voluntary and involuntary liquidation of agricultural assets, and the increased pace of exodus of commercial-scale farmers from the land. The following section explores a range of explanations of the origins of the farm crisis. I argue that the two most prevalent conventional explanations – that the farm crisis was largely due to an aberrational economic and policy environment of the 1970s and/or that the farm crisis was engendered by abrupt policy shifts during the 1980s – have an element of truth, but they are, by themselves, incomplete explanations. I suggest that two other forces – long swings of expansion and contraction in the world economy and some inherent contradictions of accumulation in industrial-country agriculture – constitute a fundamental backdrop to the farm crisis. These latter two factors, which have been largely ignored in current analyses of the farm crisis and its impacts, have major implications for how one assesses proposals for farm policy reform and makes inferences about the restructuring of agriculture over the coming decades.

HISTORICAL PERSPECTIVES ON THE US FARM CRISIS

The current farm crisis is often compared with that of the Great Depression, especially in terms of its severity. There are, however, a number of important respects in which the two crises differ (see, for example, Kloppenburg and Buttel, 1987). Nonetheless, the Great Depression era is of tremendous importance in understanding the roots of the contemporary farm crisis.

The agricultural depression of the 1930s was preceded by more than a decade of agricultural recession which was decisively deepened following the rapid world economic downturn that was precipitated by the stock market crash of 1929. Foreclosure rates accelerated rapidly, and as a result tenancy increased greatly, peaking at 42 per cent of US farm operators in 1935 (Hottel and Harrington, 1979). These severe economic dislocations led to a resurgence of agrarian radicalism in the early 1930s, which is generally credited with having contributed to President Roosevelt's resolve in pursuing the establishment of federal commodity programmes (Breimyer, 1983; Rasmussen, 1983). These programmes essentially remain in effect to this day.

In 1935 there were nearly 7 million farms, most of which were relatively small and non-specialized by contemporary standards. In due course, however, federal commodity programmes, in conjunction with wartime and post-war general economic prosperity, were to contribute to a dramatic change in the socioeconomic and political structure of American agriculture. By placing a floor under farm prices, federal commodity programmes along with federal credit programmes blunted the most severe edges of the Depression and reduced the risk of agricultural production. Foreclosure and tenancy rates began to decline, and, given the scientific and technical developments of the late 1930s onward (especially new mechanical technology, hybrid corn, and chemical means of plant protection and nutrient provision), farm productivity and production capacity registered continual increases. With the security afforded by commodity programmes and the benefits to be gained from modern mechanical and biochemical technologies, farms became steadily larger and more specialised. Commodity programmes thus played a major role in underwriting post-war capital accumulation and technological change in agriculture in a potentially unstable milieu of excess capacity and volatile world market prices.

The trajectory of agricultural capital accumulation set forth in the aftermath of commodity and credit legislation of the 1930s was not socially equal. In large part this was because state intervention underwrote massive technological changes that disadvantaged smaller operators in several respects. Mechanical technologies led to widespread labour displacement, principally among small, tenant farm household members who were in a disadvantageous position to gain access to or benefit from such technology. Biochemical technologies put an increasing premium on farmers' access to credit. A share of the benefits of technological change and commodity programmes became capitalised in farm asset values (especially land), making it increasingly difficult for small farm households to expand their holdings to be able to benefit from new technologies and farm programmes (Cochrane, 1979). By the late 1960s farm numbers had declined to roughly 2.7 million, and to roughly 2.2 million by 1982 (OTA, 1986).

State intervention in agriculture along with technological change and a generally favourable post-war economic environment also led to a dramatic change in agricultural politics. Whereas agricultural politics prior to the Great Depression involved minimal intervention (and focused principally on disposition of the public domain, facilitating agricultural co-operatives, and expansion of exports), post-Depression farm policy came to focus largely on commodity programmes (especially support levels, mandatory vs voluntary participation, production controls, and so on). Commodity programme legislation contributed to the formation of large commodity associations whose major role came to be that of advancing the cause of producers of specific commodities in farm bills and related legislation. As farm programmes and technological change led to increased concentration, larger farms, and greater specialisation, the role of commodity groups as the focal point of farmer representation in the political process was progressively strengthened at the expense of general farm organisations, such as the American Farm Bureau Federation and the National Farmers Union. At the same time, the historic social base of agrarian radicalism – small and medium-sized, full-time family farmers – rapidly diminished in absolute and especially relative terms during the post-war period. Depression-era commodity programmes thus temporarily 'saved' the family farm but laid the groundwork for the rapid decline in family farming in the decades that followed.

Because of the abundance of farm land in the US and the country's low population density, American agriculture had faced chronic overcapacity and recurrent overproduction problems for many decades prior to the Great Depression. A number of largely unsuccessful attempts had been made to sell more surplus US farm commodities in world markets so as to alleviate farm surplus and income problems (Friedmann, 1982). These strategies were to bear little fruit until the passage of PL 480, the Agricultural Trade Development and Assistance Act of 1954, through which disposal of surplus commodities became tied to American foreign policy objectives of promoting international trade with and capitalist development in Third World countries and of containing the spread of communism. World trade in grains and the US share of the world grain trade accelerated sharply from the mid-1950s to the mid-1960s. By the mid-1960s, over 35 per cent of world wheat commerce was accounted for by US aid under PL 480. This foreign-aid/foreign-policy-dominated post-war grain trade regime was instrumental in reducing surplus problems and, moreover, was crucial in facilitating the maintenance of domestic price support and quasi-protectionist farm commodity policy.

It is widely agreed that the decade of the 1970s witnessed major departures from post-war trends in American agriculture and that several 'aberrations' of this decade sowed the seeds of the farm crisis that became manifest in the 1980s. The early 1970s can now be seen in retrospect as the final years of the post-Second World War global economic boom and as the harbinger of massive global dislocations that would soon follow. The buoyant world economy of the 1960s and early 1970s was characterised by tightened raw materials markets, especially in grains. World grain prices began to increase slowly in the late 1960s and then rapidly in the early 1970s, providing President Nixon with an unprecedented political-economic opportunity: to greatly reduce federal outlays for PL 480 programmes and commodity programmes while simultaneously benefiting farmers and solving balance of payments problems by liberalising agricultural policy and increasing US farm exports. Early 1970s legislation eliminated mutual defence uses of US food aid funds while *détente* expanded trade to the socialist countries, especially the Soviet Union. Later in the decade *détente* would become subordinated to US domestic policy – especially foreign exchange considerations – as the basis of state policy agricultural exports (Friedmann, 1982). With the collapse of the 1950s and 1960s aid-based world food regime, largely as a result of US policy changes, the world food economy became far more market-orientated. Vast growth in foreign demand for grains and oilseeds enabled the US government to reduce budget outlays for commodity programmes and to increase export revenues at the same time that US productive capacity increased substantially.

The domestic environment of US agriculture was also characterised by significant discontinuities that would ultimately usher in a 1980s farm crisis of massive proportions. Largely induced by rising export sales and relatively favorable prices, grain and oilseed production became somewhat more profitable even as productivity and output increased. Also, given the inflation originally engendered by the financing of the Vietnam War and subsequent federal budget deficits and by the two major 1970s oil price shocks, real interest rates (especially for subsidised farm loans) in the 1970s were very low and, at times, were negative, which provided a further incentive to invest in agricultural assets. Further, federal tax provisions, such as favourable tax treatment of capital gains and subsidies to capital investment, deepened the incentive to invest in farm land, buildings, and equipment. The result was a near doubling of farmer debt in real terms during the decade, tremendous pressure on land markets, and startling inflation in farm asset values. In retrospect, we can see that surging export sales served to maintain commodity prices at the same time that farmers were dramatically increasing their debt levels, purchasing expensive farmland, and increasing their capacity to produce the basic grains and oilseeds. Available data show that the rising debt load was incurred by a minority of farmers who had expanded aggressively, largely for speculative reasons in order to take advantage of farm asset appreciation (Shepard, 1985).

Several other changes during the 1970s would ultimately prove to be influential in shaping the completion of the 1980s farm crisis. First, the 1970s represented a major turning point in the pattern of structural change in agriculture. In contrast to previous decades, from the early 1970s on there was relative stability in farm numbers, with stable farm numbers largely being accounted for by increases in the number of relatively small, part-time, 'subcommercial' farms. Second, while there was a continuing trend toward concentration of farm assets and sales during the decade, this was in substantial measure a reflection of the declining position of medium-sized, full-time family farms (OTA, 1986), rather than a decline in the number of small farms, as had been the case in the years after the Second World War. The result was a trend toward a more dualistic farm structure in which both small (subcommercial) and large (that is, 'larger-than-family' enterprises relying primarily on wage labour) farms increased in numbers (and large farms increased their share of sales) at the same time that there was a 'disappearing middle' of medium-sized family operations (Buttel, 1983; OTA, 1986). As we will see below, the farm crisis has had relatively little effect on small farms because of their generally low debts and access to off-farm income. Medium-sized and large (larger-than-family or corporate-industrial) farms have borne the brunt of the debt problem.

A further dimension of the farm crisis that has its roots in the 1970s was a series of changes in Third World economies. Concurrent with the massive increase in farm debt was a comparable escalation of Third World debt. This was to culminate in a general Third World debt crisis shortly before there emerged awareness of the severity of the US farm problem. Heavily-indebted Third World countries, as a condition of access to their further loan and debt restructuring programmes, were subjected to increasingly stringent demands by international lending institutions that have led many such countries (most notably, long-standing agro exporters, Argentina and Brazil, as well as more recent Asian agroexporters such as Thailand and India) to become increasingly formidable competitors with US farmers for world commodity markets. Debtor countries were required to devalue their currencies, reduce budget deficits, decrease their imports, and increase their exports as conditions for receiving further loans and credits from the World Bank and International Monetary

Fund. It was also during the late 1960s and 1970s that many third world countries began rapidly to deploy 'green-revolution' technology which increased their productive capacity, and in some cases reduced the need for imported food and enabled them to become net exporters.

It should be stressed, however, that heavily indebted Third World countries that have experienced major green revolutions have by no means been uniformly successful in challenging US dominance in food and feed grain export markets. Several Latin American nations, most notably Mexico (Sanderson, 1986), have actually experienced deterioration of their level of food self-sufficiency during the 1980s. Mexico is now a larger food importer and is more closely tied to US markets for agricultural exports than it was in the 1960s.

DIMENSIONS OF THE US FARM CRISIS

The major quantitative parameters of the continuing US farm crisis have for some time been well established from federal statistical sources. It is widely recognised that the following factors have been integral in the dislocations experienced in American agriculture during the early and mid-1980s.

Debt

Shepard (1985) has reported time-series data showing that, in constant 1984 dollars, the debt of the US farm sector increased nearly twofold from 1972–82, from roughly $110 billion to $215 billion. Aggregate farm debt declined slightly after 1983, apparently as a result of foreclosures and debt restructuring. Nonetheless, in the early 1980s, US agriculture, with a total capital stock valued at roughly $1 trillion, had a debt position that was highly leveraged by comparison with one and two decades earlier. Interest expenses paid by farmers in the early 1980s averaged about $23 billion annually, which exceeded or represented at least 50 per cent of income from farm assets, depending upon the year (due to fluctuations from 1980 to 1985 in net income from assets).

It should be noted, however, that the farm sector's overall debt-asset ratio of roughly 20 per cent in the early 1980s was not particularly high by the standards of other industries. Farmers were far more 'leveraged' in relation to net income from assets than in relation to total net worth. Also, many industrial farmers in the Sunbelt states for several years had debt-asset ratios in the 30 to 40 per cent range without experiencing financial trouble. As will be emphasised later, the persistent key problem of the US non-industrial farm sector has been its low rate of return to assets, which can be attributed to factors such as the special characteristics of land as agriculture's principal input, the nature of agricultural commodities in the sphere of circulation, and other factors. Accordingly, with low margins characterising direct farm production, farm operations are highly sensitive to even modest adverse changes in debt loads and interest rates.

Changes in Fiscal and Monetary Policy and in Real Interest Rates

The 1970s were largely characterised by high inflation and very low – and, at times, negative – real interest rates which were generally in the 1 to 2 per cent range. These very low real interest rates, in a milieu of rising farm asset values and generous tax subsidies to capital investment, were, of course, the major factors leading to the rapid rise of farm indebtedness that has been noted several times earlier. Global inflation, the general slump or slowdown in the world economy, and dollar gluts associated with the surplus of 'petrodollars' caused these low real interest rates and made real estate an attractive haven for lenders and investors alike. This situation, however, was to change abruptly beginning in 1979 when the Carter Administration took steps to control inflation through restrictive monetary policy. This policy was intensified by the Reagan Administration in the early 1980s. In addition, Reagan Administration policies of major tax cuts (especially for corporations and high-income individuals), the expansion of military spending, and heavy government borrowing to finance the rising federal budget deficit led to real interest rates in the 6 to 8.5 per cent range, which are extraordinarily high by historical standards. Many farmers who had incurred large debts in the late 1970s at nominal interest rates approaching 20 per cent were faced with the prospect of repaying these loans with unexpectedly dear 1980s dollars. Abrupt shifts in fiscal and monetary policy have led to especially severe consequences for a capital-intensive, interest-rate-sensitive, and heavily debt-leveraged industry such as agriculture.

Declining Land Values and the Decapitalisation of US Agriculture

The 1970s economic environment that we have just portrayed resulted in phenomenal appreciation of farm asset values. From

1973–81, the average per acre value of US farm real estate increased by 98 per cent in real terms. Real estate values increased roughly threefold or more in real terms in several Midwestern states (Minnesota, Iowa, Illinois, and Indiana) where the farm crisis has been most severe. In the early 1980s, however, the land bubble burst, resulting in a 19 per cent decrease in the per acre value of US farm real estate from 1981–85, with further 7–9 per cent annual decreases expected in 1985–86 and in 1986–87. Decreases in real estate values have been most severe in the Midwestern states where land price inflation was most pronounced in the 1970s; declines in excess of 39 per cent were recorded in Iowa, Illinois, Nebraska, Indiana, Ohio, and Minnesota during 1981–85.

While it has been conventional to treat the recent decapitalisation of American agriculture in terms of devalorisation of both land and other means of production (for instance, machinery, building), I wish to give principal emphasis to land. This is not only because land is agriculture's key input and a distinctive one in that it cannot be manufactured, as will be discussed at greater length below, but also because the devalorisation of land and of non-land assets likely has different causes and implications. Declining land values have been due primarily to adverse changes in the balance sheet of the farm sector, while the decline in non-land asset values is likely to have been caused by the devalorisation of land. Also, in relation to the behaviour of agriculturalists, land has special importance in terms of retaining land in the family and easing the entry of new generations into farming, whereas non-land assets are far less important in this regard. Thus, the devalorisation of land can be expected to have different consequences for farmer behaviour than will the devalorisation of non-land assets.

There have been two principal impacts of declining farm land values. The first has been a fundamental shift in the economics of agricultural investment. In the 1970s capital gains income generally was well in excess of operating returns, so that investment strategy became heavily focused on leveraging low real interest rate loans and purchasing farm land in order to take advantage of asset appreciation. With the collapse of the farm land market, investment and operating strategy has shifted to cash flow and operating returns considerations. Second, declining farm land values have resulted in rising debt-to-asset ratios, causing a growing proportion of farmers to have debt-to-asset ratios in excess of 40 per cent even as the aggregate debt load of American agriculture has declined somewhat and

farm cash flow has improved over the past two years (USDA, 1986a).
In 1985, 21 per cent of farms, which accounted for 66 per cent of
aggregate debt, had debt-asset ratios over 40 per cent (compared to
19 per cent of farms and 62 per cent of debt in 1984; ibid). About 20
per cent of commercial farms (those with gross sales of $40 000 or
more) had a debt-to-asset ratio of 40 per cent or more and had a
negative cash flow. Even though there have been continued declines
in farm asset values and further deterioration in the aggregate debt-
to-asset ratio in US agriculture over the past two years, ongoing
restructuring of debt and farm organisation has resulted in a slight
decline in the prevalence of severe 'financial stress'. The proportion
of farms with the most serious financial problems – those with
debt-to-asset ratios of 40 per cent or more and with negative cash
flows – declined from 12.5 to 11 per cent from 1984 to 1 January 1986
(USDA, 1986a); these most severely stressed farms accounted for 45
per cent of farm operator debt in 1984 compared to 37 per cent as of 1
January 1986.

Declines in Export Sales and Commodity Prices

It is widely acknowledged that the export dependence of US agriculture increased sharply during the 1970s. From 1969–70 to 1980–81,
US exports of wheat and feed grains increased from roughly 35
million tons to 111 million tons. Since 1980–81, US exports have
declined each year, to an estimated 75 to 80 million tons in 1985–86,
and from 55 to 40 per cent of world wheat and feed grain markets.
Declining export sales are often seen as the result of declining
commodity prices. Indeed, current prices (at this writing in early
1987) of the major export commodities (wheat, corn, and soybeans)
are somewhat lower than in 1980–81, the peak year of export sales.
Nonetheless, it should be recognised that declining US export sales
have not led to a major secular decline in the prices received by US
farmers for these basic food and feed grains. Prices for all three
commodities in 1983–84 were, in fact, roughly comparable to those in
1980–81. The principal declines in commodity prices received by US
farmers did not begin until mid–1984, when soybean and wheat prices
began to decline precipitously, followed by corn in mid-1985. These
more recent commodity price declines, nonetheless, closely parallel
changes in farm asset values, which averaged −12 per cent per acre in
1984–85 and an estimated −9 per cent change from 1985–86. On
balance, declining commodity prices played a minor role in triggering

the US farm crisis, which has largely been a debt crisis. The most recent USDA (1986a) data, in fact, suggest that net farm income has remained remarkably stable during the course of the farm crisis, even during 1985 when prices for the major food and feed grains declined. This was largely because of the $18–20 billion annual expenditures on farm commodity programmes that prevailed in the 1980s. Nonetheless, it is quite plausible that grain and oilseed prices received by US farmers will continue to decline as target prices and loan rates are decreased to match world market price levels and to realise the Reagan Administration goal of a more market-oriented American agriculture which can compete in an unsubsidised fashion on world markets. Continued erosion of commodity prices could severely exacerbate the farm crisis in the next few years by thrusting a sharply higher proportion of commercial farmers into a negative cash flow situation.

The decline in export sales had a number of causes: the overvalued US dollar; the debt crisis and stagnation of many Third World countries, which, under IMF conditionality provisions, have led to declines in their food imports; trade wars among and export subsidies by the major exporting countries; periodic US grain export embargoes, which have caused some countries to see the US as an unreliable supplier; the emergence of new export competitors in the Third World due to the green revolution, contraction of their domestic markets, and the imperative to earn foreign exchange to service their staggering debts; and the high relative production costs of US grains and oilseeds.

It should be recognised, however, that world imports of wheat and feed grains, while fluctuating significantly from year to year, have remained relatively stable since 1979–80, at about 200 million tons annually. World imports during 1985–86 were roughly 20 million tons below that level, mainly due to a large Soviet grain crop. Thus, since the late 1970s, world trade in wheat and feed grains has peaked while the US share has declined precipitously. One of the consequences of declining US export sales has been huge carry-over stocks of American wheat and feed grain commodities. These stocks rose from roughly 30 million metric tons in 1975 to 80 million tons in 1980, and to 140 million tons in 1983. These carry-over stocks were sharply reduced in 1983–84 due to the (very costly) PIK programme and poor weather in the 1983 growing season to about 70 million metric tons. But with sluggish export demand and large harvests since 1984, US carry-over stocks had by 1986 ballooned to roughly 150 million metric tons, representing 75 to 80 per cent of total annual world import demand. These large carry-over stocks portend a difficult set of political choices over the next year: to allocate $10 billion or more to another PIK programme (which would pay farmers with grain for idling a significant portion of their land) and/or $30 billion to price supports and deficiency payments (with set-aside provisions), or to permit wheat and feed grain prices to plummet.

The Uneven Incidence of 'Farm Financial Stress'

The rapid increase in aggregate farm debt during the 1970s and early 1980s did not occur evenly among US farms. Debt-asset ratios are greatest among large farmers, among younger farmers, among grain and general livestock producers, and in the Midwest, Northern Great Plains, and the Lake states. About 40 per cent of US farms, in fact, had no debt as of 1 January 1986; these farmers were generally relatively old operators of small farms.

Figure 3.1, taken from USDA (1986a:19), provides the most recent data on the relationship between farm size and debt-asset

Figure 3.1   Percentage of farms in each sales class by debt/asset ratio, 1 January 1986

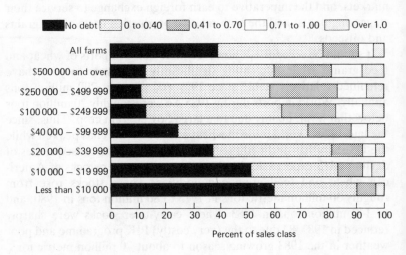

SOURCE: USDA (1986a:19).

ratio. These data indicate that there is a strong linear association between farm sales class and debt-asset ratio, with the exception that very large farms with annual sales of $500 000 or more had somewhat lower-debt asset ratios and a higher incidence of zero debt than did farms in the $250 000–499 999 sales class. This is likely because of the fact that a major portion of very large farms in the US are actually large cattle feedlots with relatively little land, the operators of which tended to be less involved in speculative purchases of farmland during the late 1970s.

Exit Rates

One aspect of the US farm crisis on which there are inadequate statistical data is that of changes in farmer exit rates since the late 1970s. In large part this is because the federal government has historically not permitted researchers to utilise intercensal matches of farm-level data from the census of agriculture in order to develop estimates of rates of entry into and exit from agriculture over time (as can be done with Canadian census of agriculture data; Ehrensaft *et al.*, 1984). Nonetheless, USDA (1986b) has summarised the results of a January 1986 survey conducted by the Midwest Association of State Departments of Agriculture. These eight states (Illinois, Iowa, Kansas, Michigan, Missouri, Nebraska, North Dakota, and Wisconsin) plus Minnesota and South Dakota have borne the brunt of the farm crisis thus far. The results of the survey as reported by USDA suggest that judging by stated intentions of farmers to remain in or leave agriculture in 1986, the farm crisis has not led to an unusually large exodus from farming. Roughly five per cent of the farmer respondents indicated that they planned to leave farming in 1986, while 'in a normal year, 4–5 per cent of operators cease farming for a variety of financial and personal reasons' (USDA, 1986b:21). While this 4–5 per cent estimate of a 'normal' exit rate may be high, it would seem that the pace of foreclosure and voluntary exit has tended to be overestimated in much of the literature on the US farm crisis, perhaps because there is inadequate recognition of the fact that a relatively small percentage of US farms are highly debt-leveraged and have negative cash flows.

Nonetheless, these Midwest data are suggestive in several additional respects. One is that Midwestern farmers generally indicated personal reasons, rather than financial problems, as the major factor leading them to expect to leave farming in 1986. Second, however, financial problems were a more important consideration for leaving agriculture by 'family-size commercial' farmers than for either larger or smaller farmers. Third, it was found that delinquency rates on real estate and non-real estate loans were generally high, with Iowa farmers having the highest rates at 11.9 and 14.5 per cent, respectively. Nonetheless, most farmers who were delinquent on loan repayments intended to remain farming in 1986. Fourth, however, intention to leave farming in 1986 was strongly correlated with farmers' current loan delinquency problems. Finally, the farmer respondents indicated that the lack of off-farm employment opportunities has played a major role in contributing to farm operators remaining in agriculture.

Distribution of Farm Debt by Lender

Table 1 provides the most recent data (USDA, 1986a) on the distribution of farm operator debt by debt-asset ratio and lender. These data show that commercial banks are the single most important holder of debt claims in American agriculture, accounting for 27.4 per cent of total operator debt as of 1 January 1986. Federal land banks and the Farmers Home Administration are the next most important holders (22.2 and 15.1, respectively). Roughly 66 per cent of debt is accounted for by highly-leveraged farmers (that is, with debt-asset ratios greater than 0.40). The Farmers Home Administration has the highest incidence of at-risk loans, with 35.3 per cent of its portfolio loaned out to farmers whose debt-asset ratios exceed 1.0 (and who are thus technically insolvent). Among farmers who are technically insolvent, 33.2 per cent of their loans are held by the Farmers Home Administration, 23.4 per cent by commercial banks, and 14.6 per cent by federal land banks. The farm credit system (which includes the Production Credit Associations, federal land banks, and the Bank for Cooperatives) is widely regarded as being in grave trouble and as being unlikely to survive 1987 without a federal cash infusion.

Federal Commodity Programme Payments

At the beginning of the decade, annual federal outlays for farm commodity programmes were approximately $4 billion. The cost of farm commodity programmes soared during the 1980s and was generally in the $18–20 billion range during 1983–85. In the 1986 fiscal year, however, these outlays increased again, to $25.6 billion, and are projected to be $30 billion or more in Fiscal Year 1987, which will equal or exceed net farm income. There is little doubt that federal commodity programme payments have served to blunt the impact of the farm crisis, principally by placing a floor under commodity prices or by providing deficiency payment income to participants in commodity programmes. As will be noted below, however, continued escalation of commodity programme expenses in a milieu of fiscal crisis and Gramm-Rudman deficit reduction legislation is creating immense pressure for a restructuring of farm programmes. This may well result in an unprecedented major rewriting of the farm bill, the Food Security Act of 1985. (Farm bills have heretofore been written in the first year of a Presidential administration and have remained in effect during the entire four-year term.)

EXPLANATIONS OF THE US FARM CRISIS

The foregoing account of the anatomy of the US farm crisis suggests that the crisis had its origins in the aberrational character of American agriculture in the 1970s and a combination of adverse changes in the 1980s (abrupt shifts in US fiscal and monetary policy and the Third World debt crisis). Indeed, these are the principal explanations of the debt crisis that have appeared in the current literature (see, for example, Harl, 1986; Boehlje *et al.*, 1985). That each of these two factors has played a major role in inducing and deepening the farm crisis is clear. I would argue, however, that previous analyses of the farm crisis have given inadequate attention to two other factors – the tendency toward long cycles of expansion and contraction in the world economy, and inherent contradictions in industrial-country agriculture – that can be seen to make 'farm crises' a normal ingredient in the process of accumulation in advanced capitalism.

Agriculture and Long Waves of Expansion and Contraction in the World Economy

The world economy has since 1974 been in a sustained contractionary phase characterised by high unemployment, stagnant and declining real incomes, high real interest rates, and sagging levels of investment.

TABLE 3.1 Distribution of debt owed by farm operators by debt/asset ratio and lender, 1 January 1986[1]

Lender	Debt/asset ratio					1 Jan. 1986, all farms	1 Jan. 1985, all farms[2]
	0 to 0.10	0.11 to 0.40	0.41 to 0.70	0.71 to 1.0	Over 1.0		
	Percent						
Commercial banks:							
Percentage of —							
Row	5.1	33.6	33.8	13.8	13.7	100.0	NA
Column	35.6	30.9	28.2	21.8	23.4	27.4	NA
United States	1.4	9.2	9.3	3.8	3.8	27.4	28.2
Federal land banks:							
Percentage of —							
Row	2.5	30.0	35.5	21.4	10.6	100.0	NA
Column	14.3	22.3	24.0	27.3	14.6	22.2	NA
United States	.6	6.6	7.9	4.7	2.4	22.2	25.0
Farmers home Administration:							
Percentage of —							
Row	1.1	14.3	28.6	20.7	35.3	100.0	NA
Column	4.3	7.2	13.1	18.0	33.2	15.1	NA
United States	.2	2.2	4.3	3.1	5.3	15.1	13.5
Production Credit Association:							
Percentage of —							
Row	6.3	35.7	33.5	12.7	11.8	100.0	NA
Column	12.6	9.3	7.9	5.7	5.7	7.8	NA
United States	.5	2.8	2.6	1.0	.9	7.8	9.9

Commodity Credit Corporation:							
Percentage of —							
Row	3.9	28.3	36.2	17.8	13.9	100.0	NA
Column	7.2	6.9	8.0	7.5	6.3	7.3	NA
United States	.3	2.1	2.6	1.3	1.0	7.3	1.4
Other individuals:							
Percentage of —							
Row	4.3	35.6	31.3	16.6	12.2	100.0	NA
Column	12.3	13.3	10.6	10.6	8.5	11.1	NA
United States	.5	4.0	3.5	1.8	1.4	11.1[3]	14.3
Others:							
Percentage of —							
Row	4.7	35.2	33.3	15.3	11.5	100.0	NA
Column	7.6	7.4	6.4	5.5	4.5	6.3	NA
United States	.3	2.2	2.1	1.0	.7	6.3	5.9
Merchants and dealers:							
Percentage of —							
Row	10.5	30.8	24.0	17.0	17.7	100.0	NA
Column	4.4	1.7	1.2	1.6	1.8	1.6	NA
United States	.2	.5	.4	.3	.3	1.6	1.9
Other farmers:							
Percentage of —							
Row	5.1	22.1	18.2	28.9	25.7	100.0	NA
Column	1.6	.9	.7	2.1	2.0	1.3	NA
United States	.1	.3	.2	.4	.3	1.3	NA
All farms:							
United States	3.9	29.8	32.9	17.4	16.1	100.0	100.0

NA = Not applicable. [1] Numbers may not add due to rounding. [2] Source: *Financial Characteristics of U.S. Farms, January 1985.* AIB-495. USDA, Econ. Res. Serv., July 1985. [3] Comparable to other individuals plus other farmers in the 1986 survey.

SOURCE: USDA (1986a:23).

There are, to be sure, some regions and countries that have experienced fewer dislocations and some that have prospered substantially, but the world economy as a whole has become mired in a more-than-decade-long phase in which the pace of accumulation has been sharply lower than that of the 1950s and 1960s. Over the past few years the stagnant world economy and the fear of deep recession have led to a renaissance of theories of long waves of expansion and contraction, of which N. Kondratieff and J. Schumpeter have been the most well-known classical theorists.

A review of such theories – there are, in fact, several which take quite different positions – is beyond the scope of this paper. Suffice it to say, however, that the courtship of many academicians with these theories has been short because of the tendency of many of the classic statements by Kondratieff, Schumpeter, and more recent perspectives by E. Mandel and others to have strong deterministic elements. In particular, objections have been raised that prominent versions of long waves theory are technological determinist accounts of the onset of expansionary and contractionary phases.

My approach to long waves is a cautious one, in which I assume neither that such phases can be accounted for by technological change and technological 'saturation' nor that there is any theoretical or empirical reason to suppose that waves tend toward temporal regularity (that is, 25-year-long expansion cycles followed by 25-year contraction cycles). I lean toward an account, such as that by Gordon *et al.* (1982), that long cycles correspond with the establishment and disintegration of 'social structures of accumulation'. By a social structure of accumulation, Gordon *et al.* (1982:9–10)

mean the specific institutional environment within which the capitalist accumulation process is organized. Such accumulation occurs within concrete historical structures: in firms buying inputs in one set of markets, producing goods and services, and selling these outputs in other markets. These structures are surrounded by others that impinge upon the capitalist accumulation process: the monetary and credit system, the pattern of state involvement in the economy, the character of class conflict, and so forth. . . . Our focus on long swings derives in part from a hypothesis that each long swing in capitalist economies is associated with a distinct social structure of accumulation . . . These social structures of accumulation define successive *stages* of capitalist development. . . . [L]ong swings and social structures of accumulation are interdependent and mutually determining in capitalist economies. A long period of prosperity is generated by a set of institutions that provides a stable and favorable context for capitalists. . . . The boom begins to fade when the profitable opportunities inherent within the existing social structure of accumulation begin to dry up. . . . Long swings are in large part a product of the success or failure of the social structure of accumulation in facilitating capitalist accumulation (emphasis in original).

The relevance of a long wave perspective for present purposes is several-fold. First, as noted earlier, the current world economic downturn has been a protracted one. It is thus similar to the Great Depression in its longevity, though less severe than the preceding long phase of contraction (presumably, at least in part, because of the prevalence of countercyclical economic policies of major developed-country governments). Second, the current long cycle of contraction has, like those of the 1880s and 1930s, led to especially severe impacts on agriculture. This is likely the case because of the character of agricultural commodities in the sphere of circulation (that is, their tendencies toward low price elasticities of demand). Third, the current conjuncture can be seen as one of negotiation and struggle over the parameters of a new social structure of accumulation (Gordon *et al.*, 1982) and the role of agriculture in that structure. As will be noted below, it is likely that there will be some major changes in the position of farmers and agriculture in a new social structure of accumulation and world food regime (see also Friedmann, 1982).

Heretofore there has been very little attention to the relationship between long waves of expansion and contraction and agriculture in advanced industrial countries. To my knowledge the only such inquiry has been that of Ehrensaft (1980), who has examined the correspondence between phases of capital accumulation and technological change in US agriculture, and long cycles of economic growth and decline over the past 150 years. Ehrensaft has noted that before the First World War, the American agricultural and industrial sectors exhibited relatively comparable movements of prices and profits over the course of long waves. As long as agriculture continued to be the predominant industry, crises in purchasing power of farmers became translated quite directly into economic distress in the industrial sector. Ehrensaft argued that while the direct and indirect impact of contemporary agriculture on aggregate economic activity is greater than the small fraction of farmers in the labour force would indicate, it is nonetheless sufficiently low that there has for 70 years been a tendency for relative farm and industrial prices to no longer move in tandem. For example, as noted earlier, the agricultural recession of the 1920s preceded the Great Depression in the economy as a whole. Relative farm prices also declined during the 1950s and 1960s, which were an era of vibrant industrial capital accumulation. Further, while the world economy as a whole moved into a protracted phase of stagflation in 1974, Ehrensaft has noted that industrial-country agriculture, particularly that of the US, continued its expansionary phase through the end of the decade. Ehrensaft nonetheless predicted that US agriculture would move into a contractionary phase in the near future. His explanation of the continued 1970s accumulation in agriculture at the same time that non-farm industry was in a general contractionary phase centred around the aberrational character of 1970s agricultural export markets, the deceleration of technological change in agriculture, and the ability of farmers to behave collectively as an oligopoly by organising politically to maintain farm price support levels. (Farmers, because of their numbers and the hyper-competitive conditions thereby engendered, cannot readily act collectively as an oligopoly in purely market terms, and are forced to resort to political means – establishment and maintenance of farm subsidy programmes – to accomplish this end.)

Ehrensaft's framework, while creative and pathbreaking, gives more attention to technological forces as the prime movers of shifts from long phases of contraction and expansion in agriculture and non-farm industry than may be warranted. Also, Ehrensaft gives little attention to social structures of accumulation, which, as argued earlier, should be seen as central to long cycles. Further, Ehrensaft's framework generally focuses on domestic-societal forces (except for suggesting that long cycles tend to occur globally because the impulses for accumulation and stagnation become internationalised through the synchronising impacts of world trade). Thus, Ehrensaft, while acknowledging the role of world trade in recent phases of expansion and contraction in North American agriculture, does so only exogenously and ignores international trade and monetary 'regimes,' the geopolitics of agricultural commodity markets, and the more fundamental internationalisation of the global political economy (for instance, in the form of off-shore banking, the multinationalisation of agro-industry). But Ehrensaft has provided some of the basic building blocks for understanding agriculture in a long-waves conceptualisation of the world economy. His framework can be usefully extended by incorporating more systematically phenomena relating to the geo-politics and economics of agro-industry and international trade.

Reconstituting Ehrensaft's long-waves perspective is beyond the scope of this paper, but we can identify some further implications of Ehrensaft's (1980) preliminary notes toward a long-waves conceptualisation of agricultural transformation and farm crisis as follows. First, two of the major factors widely seen as being mere aberrations of the 1970s – inflation (and low real interest rates) and stimulation of agricultural export demand – can be seen as being strongly rooted in the long world-economic contractionary phase that began in 1974. Inflation (or stagflation) was the first symptom of the world economic downturn (which has been transformed into very high real interest rates and low inflation due to a very abrupt shift in US fiscal and monetary policy after 1979). Also, stimulation of agricultural export demand in the 1970s can be seen, in part, as the result of a temporary stimulation of Third World economies engendered by capital mobility (that is, First World firms moving to Third World countries in order to deal with stagnation of profits by seeking out cheap sources of labour; Frobel, 1980). Each of these two 'long-wave-related' forces has been transformed in the 1980s – from stagflation and low real interest rates to stagnation with high real interest rates, as noted above, and from Third World growth to crisis as a result of accumulating debt loads, changes in US fiscal and monetary policy, and rising real interest rates.

US agriculture has thus moved into a contractionary phase in tandem with the world economy as a whole. Following Ehrensaft (1980), contractionary phases in agriculture are significant in several respects. First, during contractionary phases less efficient farmers tend to be forced out of business, resulting in a higher proportion of technologically-innovative farmers. Second, assets become devalued, creating the basis for further rapid accumulation when other conditions (low interest rates and expansion of demand) become propitious. Third, contractionary phases in agriculture heighten the scramble for new production technologies, the mass investment in which undergirds a new phase of expansion.

As noted earlier, the tap-root of a new expansionary phase in the world economy should be seen in terms of a new social structure or regime of accumulation – 'the specific institutional environment within which the capitalist accumulation process is organized' (Gordon *et al.*, 1982:9), which includes industrial structures, the monetary and credit system, patterns of state intervention, the nature of class relations and class conflict, and so forth. The specific contours of a new social structure of accumulation and of the timing of the agriculture and non-agricultural upswing phases are as yet quite unclear. (Bergesen [1982] has, nonetheless, made a provocative and persuasive argument that such a structure will revolve around state [and state-directed] 'high-technology' corporate structures which receive massive state financial and diplomatic assistance under the ideological rubric of the 'need' to enhance international competitiveness.)

One of the crucial issues in the configuration of new social structures of accumulation concerns the likelihood of expansion of world trade in cereals and oilseeds and the overall configuration of the international division of labour in food production. In retrospect we can now see that over the past three decades there has evolved an international division of labour in food production in which the advanced Western countries became increasingly specialised in the capital-intensive production of grain and oilseed crops while labour-intensive horticultural crops and land-extensive commodities such as cattle were increasingly produced in the Third World (de Janvry, 1980; Sanderson, 1985). This configuration was based on widening differentials between First World land and labour costs, rapid Third World accumulation (and hence the ability to purchase grains with hard currency), and rapid technological change in food and feedgrain crops. These conditions have changed dramatically over the past ten years. The deepening of the First World farm crisis (outside of the EEC) is resulting in the narrowing of First and Third World land prices: the Third World debt crisis is reducing the ability of middle-income Third World countries to purchase imported grains and oilseeds; and future technological change is likely to be more rapid in horticultural crops and livestock than in the cereal grains and major oilseeds (Barker, 1986). One might go so far as to speculate that the result could be a major transition in the world division of labour in food production in which livestock and horticultural crop production increasingly return to the First World while cereal grain and oilseed production becomes increasingly relegated to the Third World. Given the tendency of horticultural crop and cattle production to utilise a substantial amount of hired labour (while modern cereal and oilseed production can be highly mechanised), a major shift in the commodity mix of American agriculture along the speculative lines suggested above might well lead to a significant change in the social relations of production toward a greater prevalence of wage labour and capitalist agriculture (but see Friedmann, 1980, 1986; and Goodman and Redclift, 1985 for recent debate on the theoretical and empirical significance of the employment of wage labour by large family-proprietor farms).

Contradictions of Accumulation in Industrial-Country Agriculture

In the midst of a long farm crisis for which there is no end in sight there has been a tendency for there to appear recollections of imagined 'golden ages' of agriculture when the agricultural economy was stable and agriculture profitable. But as Johnson (1985) has noted, there are inherent tendencies toward overinvestment, over-production, low returns, periodic capital losses, cash flow problems, and bankruptcies for highly-leveraged farmers. Except for eight of the past 70 years, 'farmers have produced so much output that the consequences have been either (1) undue adverse pressure on prices in the absence of government price support and storage programmes, or (2) the accumulation of surpluses in agricultural storage programmes' (Johnson, 1985, p. 60). Thus, one can see that in an absence of repressive labour systems, monopoly in land ownership, and mechanisms for preventing declines in commodity prices, agriculture as a production sector tends to be subject to a set of forces that cause low returns and crises to be normal, and vibrant periods of accumulation and high returns to be uncommon.

Elsewhere (Buttel, 1983) I have provided a set of interrelated reasons why agriculture tends to be conspicuously less concentrated and centralised than other productive sectors such as the bulk of non-farm industry, which are integrally related to the observations made by Johnson. First, the nature of the production process, which involves discontinuous production in accordance with the seasonal nature of most agricultural activities, leads to the non-identity of production time and labour time (Mann and Dickinson, 1978) that causes returns to be low. Second, given that land is the major input in agricultural production, that the quantity of land is essentially fixed, and the fact that land tends to be consumption as well as productive property, there are significant barriers to the centralisation of agricultural property and to the consolidation of large farm units. Third, most agricultural commodities have relatively low price and income elasticities of demand, which results in sharp declines in commodity prices when production is in excess of demand. Fourth, independent producers, unlike capitalist farmers, need not achieve the average rate of profit to remain in business over the long term; the lack of such a structural imperative for achieving the average rate of profit enables family farmers to squeeze consumption and remain in business even if returns are very low (Friedmann, 1980). Fifth, agricultural research and technological innovation, which have become widely institutionalised in all developed countries, provide a continuing source of productivity improvements which tend to exacerbate overproduction problems and to reinforce the tendency toward low returns. Sixth, the range of food activities conducted by farmers tends to decline with the advance of agro-industry, as activities that permit scale economies and are privately profitable are differentiated away from agriculturalists to non-farm industry and the less profitable activities are relegated to household producers. The result of these six factors historically has been a tendency for agriculture to be relatively unprofitable and unattractive to large-scale capital for direct investment, and for agriculture to remain largely relegated to small production units (that is, family-scale enterprises).

It is thus the nature of agriculture as a production sector that has accounted for an anomaly noted by Ehrensaft (1980) in his examination of agriculture in the context of long waves: the simultaneous occurrence of agricultural expansion and low returns during the 1950s and 1960s. Technological change in American agriculture during this period proceeded so rapidly that an otherwise sustained pattern of capital accumulation in the economy as a whole was insufficient to provide for adequate demand. It was only the aberrational expansion of foreign demand for grains and oilseeds in the 1970s that enabled a high level of capital accumulation in agriculture during that decade. But even so, accumulation primarily occurred in the form of asset appreciation (rather than operating returns from assets; Shepard, 1985), which, in conjunction with low real interest rates, high inflation, and generous tax subsidies to capital investment, led to the high debt loads that remain the central feature of the current farm crisis.

It should be emphasised as well, following Johnson (1985), that there is a strong tendency in agricultural production systems characterised by decentralised ownership structures for the overall use of land to be unresponsive to changes in product prices and returns. When prices are favourable, the fixed supply of land causes 'above-normal' returns to be capitalized in asset values. But when product prices are unfavourable, the unwillingness of landowners to sell land at substantial losses causes most land to remain in production even if it results in cash flow losses. In other words, the value of agricultural assets tends to be highly correlated with the values of the products these assets are used to produce. 'Farm crises' are thus exacerbated because it is not in the interest of an individual farmer to reduce production – hence, most land remains under production even as product prices turn downward.

The current farm crisis is different than that which preceded it in the 1930s. The current crisis is characterised by massive farm debt and overcapacity, while the 1930s crisis was largely one of plummeting product prices caused by a deep world-economic depression in industry, which resulted in widespread foreclosure and tenancy. Nonetheless, it should be noted that we can see a fascinating pattern in which there have been alternating crises of tenancy and debt during the down phases of the past four long waves in the US and world economies. The downswings of 1820–1845 and of the First World War to the Second World War were crises of plummeting agricultural product prices which led to rises in tenancy rates. The downswings of 1873 to the late 1890s and of the current era were both debt-related crises induced by massive farm debts incurred by expanding farmers during preceding periods of rapid overall accumulation. Mooney (1985), in fact, has fashioned an argument that there is a strong tendency in industrial-country agriculture toward alternating crises of tenancy and debt, each of which involves a legitimacy dynamic that tends to result in a political solution – but which sows the seeds of the next crisis. He has noted that the 1930s agricultural crisis was characterised by a rapid increase in tenancy, the legitimacy problems of which led to the establishment of federal programmes to alleviate tenancy. Chief among these programmes were federal credit subsidies designed to make it easier for farmers to borrow capital to be used to purchase land and to climb from tenant to landowner status. Ultimately, in Mooney's view, these farm credit policies sowed the seeds of overinvestment and farm crisis which were manifest in the early 1980s. Mooney argues that the prevalent public policy response to the farm crisis has been arrangements that facilitate land rental-based debt restructuring, which may ultimately create the basis of an agricultural legitimacy crisis of the demise of owner-operatorship.

It should be stressed, however, that while the farm sector can sustain a rate of profit below that of the prevailing industrial average, it can do so only if relatively 'unexposed' to capitalist credit markets via debt (and hence to the discipline of achieving the average rate of profit in the economy to service debts). Historically, American family farmers have tended to be conservative *vis-à-vis* borrowing, as early-1970s data on farm debt levels reported above demonstrate well. American farmers departed from this pattern in the 1970s, partly as a result of the tax and asset appreciation incentives discussed earlier and partly because the social structure of US agriculture had become dominated by 'larger-than-family' farms operated by persons who increasingly resembled portfolio managers in other branches of the economy. As the bubble burst in the early 1980s, many of these heavily indebted, erstwhile portfolio-manager farmers found themselves unable to play by the new rules in a decapitalising agriculture. Many have since left farming.

In sum, then, while US agriculture has experienced a longstanding trend toward differentiation and concentration, there have been continuing barriers to widespread centralisation of farm assets and the consolidation of a large-scale capitalist agriculture. The chief barrier is that agriculture tends to remain unprofitable for direct investment by large-scale non-farm capital. But while there are powerful forces restraining pronounced centralisation of farm assets into a full-blown capitalist agriculture, there has been a cyclical dynamism that corresponds to inherent tendencies toward overproduction, low returns, and repeated crises of accumulation and legitimation. Thus, the current farm crisis, while it does have its distinctive aspects, should nonetheless be viewed as reflecting continuity with longstanding trajectories of American agricultural development.

THE FARM CRISIS AND THE RESTRUCTURING OF AMERICAN AND GLOBAL AGRICULTURE

The prevailing imagery about the ultimate impacts of the farm crisis on the structure of US agriculture has been that lingering high debt loads combined with low product prices will result in a continuing exodus of highly-leveraged family farmers from agriculture along with financial restructuring among those highly-leveraged operators who are able to remain in farming. The result of this process is seen to be a massive reduction in the number of farmers. I would argue that both of these notions oversimplify the nature of the ongoing and future restructuring process.

First, while the aggregate debt load in agriculture is very high and a cause of significant 'stress', roughly 40 per cent of US farms have no debt and another 35-plus per cent have modest debt loads (less than 40 per cent of assets). Thus, debt, by itself, is unlikely to be the major factor in farm structural change.

Second, while large farms tend to have the highest debt loads, large farms are also more likely to have the most favorable cash balances and levels of cash margin after payment of interest and principal. According to USDA (1986a), farm size is strongly and inversely correlated with the incidence of a negative cash balance for the calendar year 1985. But because sub-commercial farms tend to have high levels of off-farm income (averaging over $28 000 for farms with sales of less than $20 000 in 1985), most sub-commercial farms are in little danger of going out of business. The most vulnerable farms would appear to be small family-size operations with gross sales between $20 000 and $99 999 and with low levels of off-farm income.

Third, OTA (1986) suggests that there has been a major change in the extent to which scale economies in US agriculture favour larger operations. OTA reports data showing that the average cost curve continues to decline over a much longer range of scale for most major agricultural commodities than has generally been acknowledged to exist. The consequence is that large farmers can continue to generate positive cash balances even if highly leveraged, provided that commodity prices do not decline to significantly lower levels than at present (which has thus far been the case because of federal commodity programmes).

Fourth, we do not yet have a full dynamic picture of the anatomy of burgeoning farm debt in order to understand the degree to which high levels of debt are 'normal' or 'abnormal' for various types of farms. For example, it is likely that more detailed time-series data will reveal that a high proportion of heavily debt-leveraged 'larger-than-family' farms are actually cattle feedlots, greenhouse operations, and horticultural farms for which there have been high levels of indebtedness for some time and for which the farm crisis has not been a severe setback. It may thus be the case that while moderate-sized family farmers are not as highly debt-leveraged as many of their large counterparts, this additional debt incurred in the 1970s may be more problematic for these medium-sized family farms than for larger operations.

Fifth, we do not yet have adequate information about behavioural aspects of exit from (as well as entry into) agriculture during this period of crisis. To what extent do operators of different types of farms avoid liquidation of assets and exit from agriculture for 'non-economic reasons' (that is, because of attachment to the land or commitment to farming) or for 'economic reasons' (that is, to avoid major capital losses because of declining land values)? Are plummeting land prices, on balance, a barrier to exit (as opposed to the conventional wisdom that they are a factor encouraging more rapid exit)? Data on these issues remain scarce. What modest data do exist (for example, Bultena *et al.*, 1985) suggest that farmers who left agriculture during the early years of the farm crisis are predominantly medium-sized family operators rather than larger operators who are the most debt leveraged.

Sixth, we also lack adequate data on the processes of transfer of ownership of farm land as a result of the farm crisis. There do not exist good data on the degree to which the farm crisis has led to distinctive new trends in the 'freeing up' of land due to involuntary liquidation of assets and on the characteristics of the new owners of this land. Is this process leading to less concentration in agriculture or more, and to a minor or major change in land tenure relations (that is, increased tenancy)? Again, currently available date are inadequate to address these questions.

At present there is little basis to give a definitive account of the likely distributional impact of 'farm financial stress' except to say that it may well accelerate the trend toward a dualistic farm structure. Indeed, it may well be that the ultimate distributional impact of the farm crisis will be in its having paved the way for a more rapid phase of consolidation than has been typical in previous agricultural upswings (see Ehrensaft, 1980). By resulting in a pronounced devaluation of farm assets and causing a substantial amount of land to be held by lending institutions and other creditors, a period of higher and more stable agricultural prices may set the stage for a major consolidation into large-scale units while, at the same time, there is persistence of small farm operations which are not heavily dependent on farm income. This new phase of consolidation may be especially pronounced if, as the OTA (1986) data suggest, there are substantial and growing scale economies in agricultural production.

Likewise, it is very difficult to predict the future of foreign export markets and how trends in export levels will affect the product prices received by American farmers. It is increasingly conventional wisdom that American farmers will not enjoy late-1970s export conditions again – or at least any time soon. This pessimism is probably justified as long as there remains a lingering Third World debt crisis. Moreover, given the tendency of US cereals and oilseeds to be more costly to produce than those sold by the US' newest and some of its most formidable competitors (especially Argentina and Brazil; OTA, 1986), a secular increase in world trade in grain and oilseeds may not result in any significant expansion of the US export trade volume.

Equally problematic to predict is the future shape of US farm policy. If we assume that US export sales will never rebound to late-1970s levels and that there will not be a return to an aid-based international food regime, American farm policy-makers face a difficult choice: either to move toward protectionism in order to restrain production and bolster farm prices, or to permit the further internationalisation of the world food economy and to subject American farmers to increasingly stiffer foreign competition and to a continued long-term decline in farm asset values. The former strategy seems most likely if the farm crisis and overall US economic stagnation wear on, resulting in one or more Democratic Party administrations after 1988. This strategy, however, is constrained by the federal fiscal crisis, the ideological predilections of farmers and commodity groups, and by the likelihood that farm product price increases will lead to food and general inflation. The latter strategy becomes more likely if the fiscal crisis of the US government deepens and there is at least one more conservative Republican administration.

Whichever policy path is taken, the result is likely to be continued concentration and centralisation in agriculture, albeit by different routes and with the constraints on and contradictions of capital accumulation in agriculture discussed above. The protectionist or autarchic path would valorise speculative 1970s investments in farm assets and provide the collateral from which to leverage loans for investment in a new round of technological change. Given the likelihood that these new technologies will tend to be most suitable for larger operators (particularly with regard to the management skills required for their effective utilisation; OTA, 1986), the result would presumably be a 'technological treadmill' and 'cannibalism' pattern like that of the 1950s and 1960s in the US (Cochrane, 1979).[2]

If, on the other hand, the policy road that is taken is in the direction of further internationalisation and 'liberalisation' of the world food order, the route toward further concentration and centralisation would be far different, especially if it proves to be the case that new biotechnologies over the next decade increase productivity in livestock and horticultural crops more rapidly than in the cereal grains and oilseed crops. It would likely take the form of Schumpeterian 'creative destruction' of productive assets (especially those used to produce cereals and oilseeds). One component would be continued low cereal grain and oilseed prices and an absence of commodity programme floors under these prices, and thus continued declines in farm asset values. The other component may well be a decisive shift in the international division of labour in food production that was discussed earlier, as US farmers shift from grain and oilseed crops into higher value-added horticultural and livestock crops (which would be made possible by the fact that biotechnology advances will be more immediate and dramatic in these crops than in cereals and oilseeds; Barker, 1986). Grain and oilseeds would thus be produced largely for livestock feeds and for domestic consumption, rather than for export in increasingly competitive world food markets.

The specific route that will be taken will probably also be shaped, at least in part, by non-agricultural aspects of US state policy and by the outcomes of the Punta Del Este and subsequent rounds of GATT. The Reagan Administration at present would appear to be pursuing the highly contradictory objectives of a more market-oriented world food economy and domestic agricultural policy on one hand, and restrictive monetary policy and huge budget deficits which perpetuate an overvalued dollar on the other. The Administration is seeking a market-oriented agriculture in the US policy arena (chiefly by lowering price support levels, target prices, and loan rates) and at Punta Del Este (by attempting to secure stronger provisions against export subsidies by the US' major competitors). Yet a more market-oriented agriculture would result in further deterioration of US dominance of export markets if the overvalued US dollar prevails, which causes US commodities to be uncompetitive on world markets and keeps real interest rates high (Browne, 1986). It is thus unlikely that the Reagan Administration in its final two years, or subsequent administrations that would pursue comparable policies, will be able to make a decisive turn in elaborating a viable long-term agricultural policy.

In each scenario, however, eventual upswing and accumulation in the agricultural economy would be constrained by the tendency for above-normal profits to be capitalised in farm asset values. The result is that accumulation would increasingly tend to take the form of (unrealised or realised) capital gains, rather than as net operating income from assets. Accordingly, farmers would be able to benefit directly from asset appreciation only if they discontinue direct culti- vation (by either selling or renting their land) or use rising asset values to lever more loans for speculation in farm real estate. Ulti- mately, high land values would reduce operating returns, causing agriculture to return to its historically normal situation of low net return from assets.

CONCLUDING COMMENTS

US agriculture faces unattractive prospects over the short term due to the likelihood that the 'farm crisis' will continue for several more years. The outlook is for continued declines in farm asset values and low and unstable commodity prices even as $30 billion are spent annually on farm commodity programmes. There is no indication that there is any basis for a decisive shift in farm programme politics that can yield relief from the farm crisis. If this is the case, agricul- tural conditions will continue to deteriorate slowly until farm assets have been devalued sufficiently, and enough very highly-leveraged farmers with cash flow problems have been eliminated from farming, so that a new trajectory of agricultural accumulation can proceed. Ultimately, however, such an upswing in the American agricultural economy will hinge on a solution to the Third World debt and global monetary crisis so that there can be growth in incomes and food imports among its trading partners. A general upswing in the larger US and Western economy may not be sufficient to lead to a vibrant agricultural upswing, especially if lower real interest rates eventually make possible more rapid investment in new agricultural technology and set in motion a technological treadmill a la Cochrane (1979).

It is interesting to note that one of the most plausible long-term solutions to the farm crisis – a partial nationalisation of agricultural land – has yet to be mentioned in conventional policy circles. It was pointed out earlier that private land markets tend to play a very significant role in creating alternating cycles of overproduction and low returns, and of the capitalisation of above-normal returns in farm asset values. In a sense it is surprising that in the midst of rapidly shrinking farm land values that there has been no proposal for the federal government to intervene by purchasing the physical property or the 'farming rights' for some (or all) of the farm land that has been thrust on the market due to farm financial distress. In particular,

there are several historical and contemporary precedents for pursuing such a policy, for example, the land purchase programmes of the
US Department of Interior and Resettlement Administration during
the Great Depression, the SAFER land-banking programme in
France, and the Saskatchewan Land Bank. In the US at present, a
quasi-state entity, the Farm Credit System, owns millions of acres of
land (due to foreclosures) that could become the initial base of a
publicly-owned farm land portfolio. Nationalisation of ownership
and/or control of land need not, however, be undertaken largely or
solely by the federal government. There are a number of encouraging
examples of sub-national governments and private non-profit groups
purchasing the 'development rights' to urban and rural lands that
could be the basis for local efforts along this line (Geisler and Popper,
1984).

Nonetheless, the result of such a programme could be, in the short
run, to soften the slide in farm land values and, over the long term, to
give sub-national governments the ability to plan food production
and consumption more in relation to social needs or to provide the
federal government with the leverage to control production at levels
deemed appropriate given 'national objectives'. Also, by giving
preference to particular groups of farm operators in the rental of
land, the federal government would be able to implement a 'structural policy' by putting additional land in the hands of categories of
farmers considered most worthy.

That no such proposal for public ownership and/or control of land
has been made is not surprising since it is out of step with the
conservative tenor of the times (especially *vis-à-vis* the Reagan
Administration) and would probably be resisted on ideological
grounds by farmers as well. Also, a policy of public ownership-
control of agricultural land would be costly during its implementation, which would come at a time when there are multiple competing
pressures on the federal budget. Nonetheless, partial nationalisation
of agricultural land, through a rental policy, would provide a means
for controlling (or expanding) production and resolving the contradictions of agricultural accumulation that is far more effective than
set-aside and other policies that have historically been invoked in the
US. And the capitalised cost of such a programme over a half century
of operation would surely be far less expensive than 50 years of
commodity programmes during which federal outlays might average
$10 billion annually. Perhaps, however, the farm crisis may become
so severe and long-lasting that this nationalisation option may need

to be pursued because of the expense of and political barriers to any alternative policy. The possibility might thus occur that the contradictions of agricultural accumulation could be dealt with more effectively than in the past and that farm crises would no longer be as American as cherry pie.

Finally, it should be noted that it would be misleading to portray the emerging crisis of rural America – particularly the reversal of 1970s trends for non-metropolitan countries to grow faster, in both population and economic activity, and to have lower unemployment rates than metropolitan counties (Henry *et al.*, 1987) – in terms of the farm crisis alone. To be sure, the agricultural crisis has buffeted the rural regions and communities of the Great Plains, sparsely settled areas of the corn belt, and portions of the South. But the crisis of rural America has been more general than the spatial incidence of farm financial stress. This larger crisis has three major origins, each of which is non-farm in nature, and its solutions will accordingly have little to do with the status of the US farm economy.

The origins of the current 'crisis' – the term 'crisis' must be used advisedly because the current situation is by no means universally recognised or acknowledged in such strong terms – can largely be traced to a reversal of three trends that significantly benefited rural regions in the one to two decades prior to the 1980s. These first of the three trends was the elaboration of a major domestic funding apparatus consisting of a wide variety of federal programmes (for example, area development programmes, small business development programmes, the regional commissions, service delivery subsidies, community facility subsidies [for example, for water system and pollution control systems], and planning grants) that together constituted a (largely invisible) 'rural development program' of considerable dimensions. These domestic spending programmes, which were applied across rural and urban America and were thus not often recognised in rural development terms, did nonetheless confer disproportionate benefits on rural places. Second, the 1970s were characterised by a pattern of 'reverse migration.' Non-metropolitan counties grew in population faster than metropolitan counties through net in-migration, which had the effect of stimulating non-metro economic activity. Finally, rural regions benefited from one of the major responses of US firms to the post-1974 downswing – capital mobility to zones of cheap labor. Taken together, these three trends, especially the elaboration of an invisible rural development programme, buoyed the rural economy and represented perhaps the most successful 'strategy' for improvement of rural living standards ever 'implemented' in the western countries.

These three factors that enabled rural America to experience a decisive narrowing of rural-urban disparities in incomes, unemployment rates, and access to services in the late 1960s and 1970s are no longer in effect. The Reagan Administration, which upon taking office indicated its intention to roll back the 'welfare state' has been largely unable to do so with regard to the major 'entitlement programmes' (social security, medicare and medicaid, aid to families with dependent children, and so on). But the Administration has been enormously 'successful' in virtually eliminating major discretionary domestic spending programmes that historically constituted a disguised rural development programme. The growing problems of rural areas have also led to the discontinuation of the 'population turnaround.' Finally, capital mobility to take advantage of cheaper non-metro wage rates has slowed dramatically for a number of reasons (especially declining metro wage scales, the decline of unions, declining federal service subsidies, the greater attraction of cheaper labour in the Third World).

The result of these adverse changes on rural America – both farm and especially non-farm – has been a growing socio-economic crisis that is only now being documented statistically and recognised as such. This larger rural crisis will, over the medium- to long-term, be potentially more severe than the farm crisis. Rural communities in agriculturally dependent regions have been severely affected by the farm financial situation, but these are a distinct minority among the the larger set of non-metropolitan counties. Further relative declines in rural wage rates and increases in unemployment could serve to harm rural places and to reduce the viability of multiple jobholding among farm households, which has over the past two decades come to constitute the backbone of farm numbers in the US. Most importantly, the (non-farm) rural crisis affects far more people – the nearly 56 million residents of non-metropolitan counties, as against the 5.8 million members of farm households – than does the farm financial crisis. Fortunately, the rural crisis may be more easy to address than the farm crisis. A restoration of the major domestic funding programmes, the cuts in which have probably been the single most important cause of the rural crisis, would probably cost less than farm commodity programmes currently do. This restoration of foregone domestic development and service delivery programs would not only be inexpensive relative to farm commodity programmes and MX missiles, but its beneficiaries would include urban as well as rural Americans. Even so, one cannot be sanguine about the resurrection of America's historically successful disguised rural development programme, since the fiscal crises and ideological currents that constrain solutions to the farm crisis will also affect non-farm domestic spending legislation as well.

Notes

1. I would like to thank Michael Redclift, Michael Gertler, and Harriet Friedmann for their helpful comments on an earlier draft of this paper.
2. Smith and Coltrane (1981) have reported data indicating a profound reversal of longstanding trends in the use of hired labour in US agriculture during the 1970s. From 1910 to 1972, hired labour as a percentage of farm employment remained remarkably stable, at about 25 to 26 per cent. This percentage increased sharply, however, from 1972 to 1980, from 26 per cent to 35 per cent.
3. Unlike the 1950s and 1960s when small farms were most likely to be displaced as a result of technological change, however, the victims of a future technological treadmill would likely tend to be medium-sized, full-time family farms (see, for example, OTA, 1986).

Bibliography

Barker, R. (1986), 'Impact of prospective new technologies on crop productivity: implications for domestic and world agriculture.' Paper presented at the Conference on Technology and Agricultural Policy, National Academy of Sciences, December.

Bergesen, A. (1982), 'Economic crisis and merger movements: 1880s Britain and 1980s United States', pp. 27–39 in E. Friedman (ed.), *Ascent and Decline in the World-System* (Beverly Hills, Calif: Sage Publications).

Boehlje, M. D., R. Thamodaran, and A. D. Barkema (1985), *Agricultural Policy and Financial Stress* (Ames, IA: Center for Agricultural and Rural Development, Iowa State University).

Breimyer, H. F., (1983), 'Conceptualization and climate for New Deal farm laws of the 1930s', *American Journal of Agricultural Economics* 65:1153–57.

Browne, W. P. (1986), 'Issues of world food and trade: perspectives and projections', pp. 1–13 in W. P. Browne and D. F. Hadwiger (eds), *World Food Policies: Toward Agricultural Interdependence* (Boulder, Co.: Lynne Rienner).

Bultena, G., P. Lasley and J. Geller (1985), 'The farm crisis: profiles of dislocated and at-risk farm operators in Iowa'. Paper presented at the annual meeting of the Rural Sociological Society, Virginia Polytechnic Institute and State University, Blacksburg, Va., August.

Buttel, F. H. (1983), 'Beyond the family farm', pp. 87–107 in G. F. Summers (ed.), *Technology and Social Change in Rural Areas* (Boulder, Co.: Westview).

Cochrane, W. W. (1979), *The Development of American Agriculture* (Minneapolis: University of Minnesota Press).

de Janvry, A. (1980), 'Agriculture in crisis and crisis in agriculture', *Society*, 17:36–9.

Ehrensaft, P. (1980), 'Long waves in the transformation of North American agriculture: a first statement', *Cornell Journal of Social Relations*, 15:65–83.

Ehrensaft, P., P. LaRamee, R. D. Bollman and F. H. Buttel (1984), 'The microdynamics of farm structural change: the Canadian experience and Canada–U.S.A. comparisons', *American Journal of Agricultural Economics*, 66:823–8.

Friedmann, H. (1980), Household production and the national economy', *Journal of Peasant Studies*, 7:158–84.

Friedmann, H. (1982), 'The political economy of food: the rise and fall of the postwar international food order', *American Journal of Sociology*, 88:248–86.

Friedmann, H. (1986), 'Patriarchy and property: a reply to Goodman and Redclift', *Sociologia Ruralis*, 16:186–93.

Frobel, F. (1980), *Current Development of the World Economy* (Tokyo: United Nations University).

Geisler, C. C. and F. R. Popper (eds) (1984), *Land Reform, American Style*, (Totowa, NJ: Rowman & Allanheld).

Goodman, D. and M. Redclift (1985) 'Capitalism, petty commodity production and the farm enterprise', *Sociologia Ruralis*, 15:231–47.

Gordon, D. M., R. Edwards and M. Reich (1982), *Segmented Work, Divided Workers: The Historical Transformation of Labor in the United States* (New York: Cambridge University Press).

Harl, N. E. (1986), 'Responding to the farm crisis: an evaluation of alternative public policies'. Paper presented at the annual meeting of the American Association for the Advancement of Science, Philadelphia, May.

Henry, M., M. Drabenstott and L. Gibson (1987), 'Rural growth slows down', *Rural Development Perspectives*, 3 (June):25–30.

Hottel, B. and D. H. Harrington (1979), 'Tenure and equity influences on the incomes of farmers', pp. 97–107 in *Structure Issues of American Agriculture*. Agricultural Economic Report 438. Washington, D.C.: Economics, Statistics, and Co-operatives Service, US Department of Agriculture.

Johnson, G. L. (1985), 'Agricultural surpluses—research on agricultural technologies, institutions, people, and capital growth', pp. 57–70 in M. Gibbs and C. Carlson (eds.), *Crop Productivity—Research Imperatives Revisited*. Proceedings of an international conference held at Boyne Highlands Inn, MI, 13–18 October 1985, and Arlie House, Va., 11–13 December 1985.

Kloppenburg, J., Jr. and F. H. Buttel (1987), 'Two blades of grass: the contradictions of agricultural research as state intervention', *Research in Political Sociology*, 3, 1989.

Mann, S. A. and J. M. Dickinson (1978), 'Obstacles to the development of a capitalist agriculture', *Journal of Peasant Studies*, 5:466–81.

Mooney, Patrick H. (1985), 'The transformation of class relations in Wisconsin agriculture, 1945–1982'. Unpublished Ph.D. dissertation, University of Wisconsin-Madison.

Office of Technology Assessment (1986), *Technology, Public Policy, and the Changing Structure of American Agriculture*, Washington, D.C.: Office of Technology Assessment (OTA).

Rasmussen, W. D. (1983), 'New Deal farm programs: what they were and how they survived, *American Journal of Agricultural Economics*, 65:1158–62.

Sanderson, S. E. (1985), 'The 'new' internationalization of agriculture in the Americas', pp. 46–68 in S. E. Sanderson (ed.), *The Americas in the New International Division of Labor* (New York: Holmes & Meier).

Sanderson, S. E. (1986), *The Transformation of Mexican Agriculture* (Princeton: Princeton University Press).

Shepard, L. (1985), 'The farm debt crisis: temporary or chronic?' Paper presented at the annual meeting of the Western Economics Association, Anaheim, Ca., July.

Smith, L. W. and R. Coltrane (1981), *Hired Farm Workers: Background and Trends for the Eighties*. Rural Development Research Report No. 32. Washington D.C.: Economic Research Service, US Department of Agriculture.

US Department of Agriculture (1986a), *Financial Characteristics of U.S. Farms, January 1, 1986*. Agricultural Information Bulletin No. 500. Washington, D.C.: National Economics Division, Economic Research Service, US Department of Agriculture.

US Department of Agriculture (1986b), 'States survey farm financial conditions', *Agricultural Outlook*, (September):21–2.

4 French Agriculture and the Failure of its European Strategy

Pierre Coulomb (INRA) and
Hélène Delorme (FNSP)

Like the policies introduced by the leading industrial nations between the 1930s and the post-war restructuring, the primary aim of French agricultural policy is to prevent the market instability that is inherent in the competitive character of a sector made up of many different producers. Although the conditions of these policies may vary in different States, the underlying principle is the same and rests on the old law of economics that emerges from the observations made by King on the price of wheat in eighteenth-century England: slight overproduction can bring about a marked fall in market prices, just as conversely, a slight shortage can lead to a strong increase in prices. It is necessary and sufficient, therefore, to withdraw excess production from the market by either destroying or stockpiling any surpluses or, a better solution since it can also be profitable, by exporting them in order to reestablish the normal price level. Conversely, stocks should be run down and supplies imported when there is a shortage and market prices have risen excessively. These operations are the essence of the activities of the Commodity Credit Corporation created in 1934 in the United States, of the French FORMA of 1953, and the European FEOGA since 1962.

The 'virtue' of perfect competition is well known; prices are kept at the lowest possible level, permitting the almost instantaneous transfer of productivity gains (at least if one takes economic theory literally). Indeed, perfect competition does not allow capital accumulation since the level of prices prevents the growth of profits. In this respect, agricultural producers are in a far more difficult position than industrial firms: they are caught between the oligopolies that sell them inputs and buy their output, but they are also exposed to natural forces which are sometimes hostile (disasters) and sometimes too favourable (overproduction).

This brief reminder of the economics of agriculture enables us to understand that under the aegis of these modern agricultural policies a common model of production has been created: that of 'productionism' and/or 'intensification'. In a competitive economy, the relative decline in prices which accompanies technical progress requires those producers who are aiming to maintain their incomes to offset this decline by increasing their output. That is, to reinvest, which they can only do if prices are properly supported and/or if investment incentives are available. This competitive behaviour and good policy management are at the root of the tremendous growth of agriculture in the industrial countries, which have now become agricultural powers. This growth has brought the intersectoral integration of agriculture (with upstream and downstream transactions as in industrial sectors) and an abundance of cheap food (food consumption now accounts for only 20 per cent of household expenditure), as well as overproduction. (The industrial countries account for 70 per cent of international agricultural trade.)

The competitive nature of agricultural markets is certainly long-established, if only because it is founded above all on the practical possibilities of realising the value of the land. The need to accumulate stocks against the risk of disastrous harvests is equally long standing. The organisation of the earliest states, from ancient China to Egypt of the Pharaohs, from European feudalism to feudalism in Japan, expresses this need to regulate production. The social forms of this regulation have been varied but basically they have depended on the domination of certain social classes (slaves, serfs, agricultural workers, or peasants), who have borne the risks at the price of their own wretchedness.

Now this brings us to the second characteristic common to modern agricultural policy in advanced industrial countries: these states have learned how to master the two agricultural 'corporatisms' which, from the nineteenth to the twentieth century, appeared to think that they were the natural organisers of agricultural production *vis-à-vis* industry. On the one hand, *rentier* corporatism based on the property rights of the great landowners, led to a significant diversion of resources to the detriment of industrialisation. On the other hand, the protectionist (or Malthusian) corporatism of the big agricultural entrepreneurs, who demanded a sufficiently high level of prices to allow them to secure profits comparable to those obtained by their counterparts in industry (Coulomb, 1978).

In other words, modern agricultural policy is characterised by the revival of the State's authority to regulate prices, and by the refusal to be subordinated to the interests of a rural social stratum seeking to form itself into the ruling class in agriculture. In this sense, these policies are fundamentally anti-corporatist. On the contrary, they aim to ensure continuing competition between producers.

For more than ten years now, the economic crisis has destabilised these two fundamental components of modern agricultural policy. First, it has upset the mechanisms of price and income support, and particularly their regulation through exports. This instability then aggravates the contradictions between different types of producers, as they try to influence policy in their own interest.

Agricultural overproduction in the industrial countries makes it more difficult, and above all more costly, to transfer instability from the domestic market toward the international market. The United States after 1950 had succeeded in dominating world trade by organising it around the 'Fordist' export strategy (the 'corn-soya' model allowed the diffusion of intensive livestock production in importing countries). Today, by virtue of the success of the 'productionist' model, almost all the industrial countries are structural exporters. France, the second leading world exporter in the 1980s, regards its exports as 'green oil'. However, due to the power struggles in the international market the instability which reigns there is instead being transmitted to exporters and no longer provides them with the means to stabilise domestic markets. (Delorme, 1988). Will the various projects such as a 'Marshall Plan' for the developing countries or a return to protectionism (welcomed by producers in the US, West Germany, and so on), be sufficient to get the machinery working again?

The lack of equilibrium on the world market has a devastating effect on the socio-economic conditions underlying the management of competition in agriculture. In the dynamics of productionism, only those producers with high rates of technical innovation are in a position to retain productivity gains for any length of time. These producers quite naturally appear as the model to emulate for others who are trying to join them in the 'march of progress' (Coulomb and Nallet, 1980). But this dynamic presupposes the widening of markets. If these are reduced or blocked (for instance, milk quotas), this dynamic becomes perverse: the 'model peasant' is no longer the hare in the race for technical innovation, but becomes the bearer of a 'new corporatism', who claims the right to produce and reproduce himself.

In this paper, we analyse first the ways in which French agriculture and agricultural policy are adapting to this new context. We then turn to consider how the different currents within agricultural producers' organisations are proposing to re-orientate French agricultural development.

THE CRISIS OF 'L' EUROPE A LA FRANÇAISE'

In the 1960s, France saw in Europe the opportunity to replicate to its advantage the model of agricultural growth developed after the second World War by the United States. With a diversified agriculture and a powerful cereals sector, France sought first to become the dominant producer of animal feed and then, by modernising its livestock industry, to challenge the livestock production of Northern Europe.

However, this strategy met with almost total failure. French agriculture, though already possessing natural advantages (soils, climate) and structural advantages (farm size) has profited much less than its North European competitors from the expansion of the European market. France has failed either to gain the expected benefits from agricultural specialisation or, and above all, to link its cereals sector with the growth of European livestock production. Her partners who have specialised most in livestock production (Holland, Belgium, West Germany) have substituted instead low price imports for cereals in animal feed. Thus, in the late 70s, a significant share of French grain exports was being sold on the world market, where they competed in relative isolation with third countries (above all, the United States) under deeply depressed market conditions.

Agricultural Policy and the Struggle against Inflation

The result is due mainly to monetary factors, and particularly the adoption of an anti-inflationary policy at the end of the 1960s. Scarcely two years after the introduction in 1967 of the common European price system, France devalued the franc in August 1969. In order to respect the system of common prices, this devaluation should have been accompanied by a revaluation of French farm support prices to retain the same accounting value, and hence the same value in relation to the other currencies in the Community. Economic policy-makers, under the direction of Valery Giscard d'Estaing, then Finance Minister, and Jacques Chirac, Secretary of

State for the Budget, rejected such an increase in support prices, arguing that it would have an inflationary impact on the cost of living and the level of the guaranteed minimum wage. Instead, to avoid the disequilibrating effects of the devaluation of the franc on the markets of their EEC partners, they proposed a corrective mechanism: Monetary Compensation Amounts (MCAs), which taxed French exports and subsidised French imports.

These 'negative' MCAs were joined in October 1969 by 'positive' MCAs, this time devised by Germany and Holland to correct the effects of the revaluation of the Deutschmark and the florin. This was the opposite problem: to maintain the system of common European prices, German and Dutch agricultural support prices should have been reduced. This option was refused and their domestic support prices, now too high, were counterbalanced by export subsidies and import taxes. The MCA mechanism was generalised throughout the EEC after 1971, when the devaluation of the dollar and the suspension of gold convertibility brought an end to the Bretton Woods system of fixed parities (Viau, 1984).

The introduction of MCAs rests on a misunderstanding between intervention prices (or administered prices) and prices determined by the market. This had had serious consequences for the expansion of French agriculture. Market intervention can only set limits on the movement of market prices. It follows that the links between intervention prices (whose levels are negotiated in each round of the Brussels 'marathons') and market prices are not automatic: they depend on the degree and level of intervention, which vary from product to product. The intervention price therefore is never really a guaranteed price, even for those products which are most strongly supported, such as grains and dairy products.[1]

In other words, the choice made by France in 1969, which allowed strong currency countries to establish similar MCA mechanisms, was a short-sighted one, which ignored the dynamics of French agricultural growth. In fact, this growth was penalised on two levels: its capacity for capital accumulation and its competitiveness in the intra-European market.

French farmers were first caught in the 'scissors' of declining domestic prices, which were forced down to the lowest possible level, and rising production costs (industrial inputs) which kept pace with inflation. Until 1973, this situation was to some extent disguised by the high prices on world agricultural markets, but it was revealed clearly between 1974 and 1978. In this period of high inflation, often in double figures, the governments of Jacques Chirac and Raymond Barre both refused to 'dismantle' the 'negative' French MCAs, turning French farmers, in François Guillaume's phrase, 'into the undisputed champions of the battle against inflation' (Coulomb and Delorme, 1981). This 'price index politics' had serious repercussions on the profits, and hence investment, of French agro-industry. First of all upstream, by reducing input purchases, but especially downstream, where food processors were caught between producers' demands and the downward pressure on prices exerted, with government encouragement, by the large distributors.

Higher intervention prices would probably not have led in the medium-term to equivalent increases in market prices. First, because market support mechanisms often leave ample room for the play of 'market forces', as in the case of products from Southern France (wine, fruit and vegetables where market controls were only strengthened in 1982–83), and pork and poultry, which are protected only against competition from outside the Common Market. Second, higher intervention prices would have led in the long term to higher productivity levels, resulting eventually in lower relative prices. Finally, the very need to export would have favoured lower prices.

This reasoning explains the reversal of French policy which, from 1979 onwards, has attempted to reduce the 'negative' MCAs in the framework of the European monetary system. However, France has failed to persuade the strong currency countries (Holland, Belgium, West Germany) to give up their positive MCAs. The agreement reached in March, 1984 was only a temporary palliative. The Deutschmark, the strongest EEC currency, was to have become the monetary unit of the CAP, thereby allowing all MCAs to be abolished. However, the German Christian Democrats have refused to accept this policy which, by freezing support prices, threatens to lose them the farm vote.

On the other hand, the relative increase in domestic price levels, made possible by the MCAs, confirms our argument. In the strong currency countries, this has favoured the modernisation of the agro-industrial complex. The same applied to Italy, a weak currency country, because governments have resorted less frequently to negative MCAs at times when the lira has been devalued. MCAs have also encouraged exports from strong currency countries to the intra-European market, while concomitantly protecting their domestic markets from competition from weak currency countries. In the 1970s, Holland has moved ahead of France, despite its standing as the second world exporter, and West Germany has conquered a considerable share of the Italian dairy market. This situation is all the more serious for French agriculture because it has been accompanied by a change in the source of supply of animal feeds for Northern Europe.

The Breakthrough of Cereal Substitutes

Since the earliest days of the CAP, two decisions have weakened the articulation between the growth of French agriculture and that of Europe as a whole. The first is the alliance with West Germany which resulted in the maintenance of high grain prices. The second decision involves the agreement with the United States to allow duty-free imports of oilseeds into the EEC. These two choices were originally considered to be complementary but with hindsight they have proved contradictory.

The first decision was shaped by the agricultural crisis which shook France between 1953 and 1965. This modernisation crisis stimulated the large grain producers to demand higher prices, a demand which was supported for opposite reasons by small farmers, true victims of the mechanisation of production which made their labour superfluous (Coulomb, 1985). This crisis had a double consequence. First, new legislation was introduced in 1960 and 1962 which established the social framework to administer the rural exodus and the growth/modernisation of family farms. Second, the negotiations with West Germany, which defended the position of less competitive producers, culminated in 1967 in an EEC regulation which brought higher prices to the great French grain industry but now also to the wider market in Europe of the Six (Delorme, 1978). This preferential emphasis on grains, characteristic of French policy after 1945, had the dual effect of discriminating against modern livestock production in France and to a very large extent of eliminating French cereals from the European market for animal feed.

The second decision involving US oilseed exports was taken in the framework of trade policy established by the GATT agreement. This agreement incorporated the central aim of US policy to unify the international market (multilateralism). The GATT allows the formation of 'regional' customs unions on condition that they negotiate compensation for the losses inflicted on their trading partners. As signatories of the GATT charter, the founder members of the Common Market were obliged to negotiate with the United States, their main external trading partner. The compromise reached between 1962 and 1967 had two opposing elements. On the one hand, the protection of the grain and livestock sectors under the system of variable levies instituted by the CAP to offset differences between world prices and European prices was accepted. On the other hand, for oilseeds, the compromise maintained the previous system of free trade, with a bias toward soybeans. This product, promoted by the technological, commercial and financial (and military) apparatus of the United States, from the 1950s took the place of colonial oilseeds as the protein supplement in animal feed (Bertrand *et al.*, 1984). This free trade regime later was progressively extended to a number of other products that can substitute grains in animal feed. The two main grain substitutes at present are cassava, whose production was revived with Dutch encouragement in Thailand and Indonesia in the 1970s, and corn gluten, a by-product of the US corn wet-milling industry, which developed towards the end of the same decade.[2]

This compromise has been very beneficial to the North European countries; thanks to it, they have been able to play two aces. The first is their traditional specialisation in livestock production based on imported feed, which developed in the later nineteenth century in the framework of British free trade. The second had already been the basis of the might of the Hanseatic League and Flanders: the efficiency of their ports and the strength of their commercial interests.

By purchasing 80 per cent cereal substitutes, Holland, Belgium and West Germany have been able to lower significantly the prices they pay for animal feed. Between 1975 and 1984, these prices rose at an annual average of 3.5 per cent in Holland, 5 per cent in Belgium, and 2.6 per cent in West Germany, whereas they have increased 8 per cent in the EEC as a whole and 9 per cent in France (European Commission, 1986). Since 1985 animal feed prices have declined but more markedly in the former three countries than in France or the EEC. Pork production, where feed accounts for 80 per cent of total costs and prices are very close to those of a free market, symbolises their success. These three countries, together with Denmark, supply 56.6 per cent of European production, and Dutch and Belgian producers fill gaps in French production. All in all, this redirection or hijacking of the logic of the CAP, at least as envisaged by French interests since 1950, has allowed these four countries to concentrate their exports in the EEC market with its guaranteed and stable prices, and to join the ranks of the top ten world agricultural exporters.

Conversely, when France in the 1980s became the world's second major exporter ahead of its Dutch rival, it did so with a more diversified export structure. Between 1967 and 1973 the EEC absorbed two-thirds of French exports, but this share stagnated at 60 per cent after 1979 and even fell to 51 per cent in 1981. In 1986, the entry of Spain and Portugal into the EEC, although opposed by French agricultural unions, was one of the factors behind the recovery of French exports to the EEC, which absorbed 69 per cent of its total agricultural exports. However, this increased trade with Europe is also due to the decline in exports to world markets, leading to a fall in France's surplus on agricultural trade from 34 billion to 28 billion francs in 1986.

The World Market Crisis

The crisis of the world market is due to the growing discrepancy between the trend of production, which continues to rise, and that of consumption, which is declining. These two trends are caused first of all by the differing economic conditions affecting the developing countries. The majority must contend with heavy external indebtedness and the stabilisation policies imposed by the World Bank and the IMF. Imports are therefore reduced but in different and specific ways. Some countries, such as India, China, Brazil, Indonesia, Argentina and Thailand, have become either specialised or temporary exporters. Most countries, and above all the oil producers, have increased their production in order to reduce their imports. Certain others, notably in Africa, have simply reduced their levels of food consumption. Finally, the Eastern bloc countries who entered world markets in the early 1970s following their adoption of the 'corn-soybeans' model, have tried to stabilise their imports, above all by increasing competition among their various suppliers.

In this heightened competition, the major exporting countries, and particularly the two giants, America and Europe, have attempted since 1980 to exert their influence as great powers to preserve their market share. This 'bilateralisation' of trade, which runs contrary to the GATT charter, accentuates further the instability of the market by restricting its expansion and destroying its unity. With a complex combination of credit conditions, food aid and export subsidies,[3] export prices can vary widely, undermining the role of the Chicago futures market as the basic reference point for world market transactions. Consequently, prices now differ with each agreement and for each customer under conditions that are difficult to comprehend fully as they are often hidden under the cloak of State secrecy.

In this trade war, world market shares are highly prized. This is evident from the rising cost of agricultural support in the United States and the EEC. Expenditure by the CAP to promote exports to third countries doubled between 1981 and 1986, when it reached 8 billion ECU, while the cost of stockpiling surpluses tripled, rising to 4.5 billion ECU. These expenditures now represent half of the budget for farm price and income support (FEOGA – guarantee), whose overall size also doubled in the years 1981–86, increasing from 11.2 billion ECU to 22.1 billion, almost two thirds (63 per cent) of the total EEC budget.

In face of the American trade offensive since 1981, and intensified in 1986, France has been unable to count, as she had hoped, on the whole-hearted support of the EEC. Indeed France, with the UK, is the only major grain exporter. Her trading partners in Northern and Southern Europe may prefer to join the international division of labour that the US is seeking to consolidate, particularly as they fear the consequences of a grain war on the economic and political links between the EEC and the United States.

The 1984 decisions that established 'budgetary discipline'[4] and production controls, above all, milk quotas, make it more difficult to reconstruct a European market for animal feeds. Caught in the vice of milk quotas and the relative fall in milk prices, dairy farmers are trying to maintain their incomes by reducing their outgoings and increasing their access to the cheaper feedstuffs available on the world market. This strategy has forced French grain producers to accept lower prices, particularly since 1984. However, this reduction has only partially restored their position on the European market, while French livestock producers are still at a competitive disadvantage as their North European rivals continue to buy animal feeds more cheaply through the great ports of northern Europe. For French livestock producers, the citadel of grain interests, although admittedly in decline, continues to resist and hinders their growth in the EEC.

Thus the articulation between the grain and livestock sectors, envisaged as the linchpin of France's agricultural strategy, has become disjointed, not only in the context of European agricultural development but also in France itself. When seen through French eyes, the CAP appears irrational: it drags French agriculture into the spiral of surpluses (grains, milk, and so forth) while failing to provide

her with the means to widen market outlets in Europe or internationally. At the same time, France is also caught in a spiral of
deficits (oilseeds, pork, mutton, and so on) without any weapons to
protect herself against the competition of her partners.

The decline of farm incomes and investment

The fall in farm incomes is the most obvious result of the crisis. The
terms of trade between agriculture and agro-industry have deteriorated sharply under the impact of the crisis at a time when modernised
agriculture had become more closely integrated in inter-sectoral
transactions. Thus farmers are having to absorb increasingly higher
input costs. Whereas input costs amounted to 20 billion francs in
1970, roughly a third of total income, these have risen to 120 billion
francs or 45 per cent of farm income. Indeed since 1973 the cost of
agroindustrial inputs has risen at a faster rate than GDP. Conversely,
farm product prices have fallen since 1973, although admittedly this
was a record year. In 1986 farm prices on average were 20 per cent
lower than 1970 levels, and 69 per cent below 1973 prices. This trend
can in part be explained by productivity growth. But it also reveals
that the policy of market regulation is no longer effective: the 'fixed'
prices are no longer observed, nor, therefore, the rules-of-the-game
in which productivity gains are shared between the farm sector and
the cost of living. Moreover, the strategies of the food industries and
large distribution chains ensure, with government blessing, that the
full burden of lower prices is passed back on to the farmers. Thus
average farm income in real terms declined to its 1972 level in 1986,
lagging 25 per cent behind the average income of wage-earners and
12 per cent behind that of the self-employed outside agriculture.
However, these averages calculated from national income data con-
ceal wide income disparities and social differences.

According to recently published 1978 data, disparities in farm
incomes are of the order of one to 35 (CERC, 1985). However, these
disparities must be seen in the context of farm *household* incomes,
which range from one to 3.5. In 1978 25 per cent of all farmers had
annual agricultural earnings of 3700 francs (roughly 7500 francs at
1987 prices), but the total average income of these households was
46 000 francs (95 000 francs at 1987 prices), thanks to off-farm
earnings, retirement pensions and investment income. On the other
hand, 10 per cent of farm families had net agricultural incomes of
46 000 francs (95 000 francs at 1987 prices) and household income of

90 000 francs, exceeding that of middle-rank business executives. Furthermore, 3 per cent of farm families had a higher standard of living than senior business executives, with 129 000 francs in agricultural earnings and total household income of 166 450 francs (275 000 francs at 1987 prices). In fact, farming is the main source of income for only 15 per cent of farm families. More recent studies by the Assembly of the Chambers of Agriculture confirm this trend: some 100 000 farmers, roughly 10 per cent of the total, account for 50 per cent of marketed output, and 350 000 or one-third of all farmers supply 75–80 per cent (Chambres d'Agriculture, 1985).

It is difficult to determine whether these upper-ranking households have experienced income losses as great as those suffered by average income farm families. This higher income group includes producers enjoying differential rent, as in the case of owners of the great vineyards, (Mallet, 1985), or the benefits of selective stock-breeding. For the most part, the fall in cereal and dairy prices has had only relatively limited impact on their incomes: since they are the largest suppliers, they are the first to benefit from price support (Blogowski et al., 1983).

More than the fall in average farm incomes, the highly unequal distribution of income undoubtedly accounts for the rigidities of the French agricultural production system and its reproduction difficulties. By tying agriculture to only two production systems, cereals and dairying, the price regime hinders the diffusion of technical progress in other sectors. These two systems provide the highest profits: they are therefore the enterprise model preferred by young farmers. Above all, the development of strong cereals and dairying industries is the key element in the modern agro-industrial complex in France. These industries benefit directly from the price support system to the extent that it is the products they produce (cereals) or manufacture (milk powder, butter) which are bought in order to maintain prices.

The form of price support in other sectors (a uniform guarantee whatever the volume sold) seriously distorts any assessment of real profitability and the social value of farm holdings. Unit production costs can be higher on large farms than medium-size farms, while subsidy costs can be lower if the product is processed, as in the case of milk into cheese. Nowadays, OECD experts recognise this perverse effect of agricultural policy, indicating that in all advanced industrial countries a reduction in subsidies would strike hardest at the incomes of the most capital-intensive holdings (*Le Monde Diplomatique*, 15 May 1987). A perverse effect indeed since price supports transform

Marshallian innovation rents created by the modernisation efforts of individual producers into permanent advantages (*rentes de situation*), which are maintained by official support policy and slower rates of innovation.

This process, whereby advantages already acquired under the price support policy become virtually permanent, is reinforced by the withdrawal of State investment subsidies. Within the framework of the CAP, governments retain control of these subsidies by virtue of the national specificities of production systems. In France, efforts to restrict budget expenditure have concentrated on this facet of agricultural policy. Within the agricultural sector budget, leaving aside social grant expenditure which represents over 50 per cent of the total and administrative costs of under 10 per cent, the share of investment subsidies has fallen from 15.5 per cent to 6.9 per cent in the years 1975–86, and that of interest subsidies from 20.5 per cent to 11.1 per cent. A comparison between the 1986 and 1987 budgets reveals that this trend is continuing under the new Conservative governments, with a 15.5 per cent fall in investment subsidies, 17.2 per cent in interest rate subsidies, and 34.2 per cent in State investment expenditure (irrigation works, and so on). This reduction in investment subsidies has completely transformed the direction of agricultural policy. Rather than the policy adopted in the 1960s to modernise agriculture and the agrofood system, it has increasingly favoured the concentration of production, benefitting well-established producers and helping them to restore the financial losses sustained in the crisis.

This decline in investment subsidies has combined with falling incomes to reduce farm-capital formation. Since 1982, national income data for agriculture indicate that depreciation has exceeded investment. Lower outlays on machinery and equipment are accompanied by the depressed agricultural land market. Property transactions have diminished with the restricted access to subsidised loans, while land prices have fallen inversely as interest rates have risen. Property sales are now 40 per cent lower in volume than ten years age, while land prices have fallen in real terms since 1978 and in nominal terms since 1983.

The marked decline in the numbers entering agriculture at the very time when nearly 40 per cent of the land in farms is being 'liberated' by the retirement of old farmers is due less to the demographic crisis than the socio-economic and political context. The number of new farms established has declined strongly from around 50 000 per year between 1963 and 1970 to only 31 500 in 1980, of which 13 500 farms were operated by farmers under 35 years of age. Ministry of Agriculture data suggest that the annual number of young farmers who entered the industry in the period 1980–85 was 10 000, and these for the most part set themselves up in cereals and dairying. In any case, these new entrants are unable to take up all the available farm land: one hectare in five in 'the garden of French agriculture', recently coveted so fiercely in property disputes, now risks being abandoned. These trends raise the prospect of French agriculture being organised around some 300 000 farms whose reproduction could be 'perpetuated', to borrow the term used by the Ministry of Agriculture.

THE IMPOSSIBLE RETURN TO CORPORATISM

The crisis has provoked major conflicts of interest at the heart of French agriculture. These conflicts are revealed in divisions on the left, between the MODEF,[5] the worker-peasants of the CNSTP and those of the FNSP, although in 1987 the latter two movements united in the Peasants Federation. Splits have also appeared on the right between the FFA and the FNPA.[6] This dissension also finds expression in the trade union movement as a whole, in the increasingly autonomous statements by product associations (the General Association of Wheat Producers [AGPB] denouncing the influence of the milk lobby) and in conflicting regional interests (the anti-MCA committee in Brittany; the silent struggle between regions over milk quotas, etc.). Under these conditions, one can understand the disarray of the big organizations ('majority' trade unionism, APCA, CNMCCA) which, like the FNSEA and following its lead, seek to preserve unity, either by restricting debate or by adopting a rhetoric of political opposition.[7] This discourse was ably used by François Guillaume first against Raymond Barre and then, in a more popular forum, against Edith Cresson and the Left in power. This silence, though in fact only relative, now takes the form of analytical academic studies on the state of agriculture and the international situation.

The questions facing farmers are brutal and simple: what rules should be established to divide up subsidies which henceforth will at best remain constant if not decline? How should markets, which also are limited, be shared between producers and according to which criteria? What is at stake undoubtedly is *who* will be able to continue farming. The answer depends first of all on the ability of different types of producers to conceive strategies in response to the crisis and put these into practice. (Coulomb and Delorme, 1985). Also at stake is to decide who *should* be allowed to stay in farming. Given the crisis of intensive production models and the distorted economic conditions created by unequal access to the system of price supports and investment assistance, it is hard to distinguish which producers are the most profitable and which are of most value to the community. It follows that the struggle also is ideological. Faced with this 'breakdown' of the technological and economic model, some producers will aspire to be 'entrepreneurs', others to be 'workers', and many more to be 'peasants'. But what kind of peasant? A 'real' peasant working full-time in agriculture, a 'rural producer' who diversifies his holding, or a 'mixed' peasant with several occupations?

In the future, unlike the situation in the agricultural crisis of 1953–65, conflicts will no longer be between social classes organised in the hierarchical order of agricultural production. They are now between social strata competing for access to a system of Community and state support. Each is conscious that its fate depends on politics and therefore each one makes its appeal to society as a whole. Hence the fierce battle of 'communication' to 'get the farmers' message across'. As François Guillaume declared at the 1986 FNSEA Congress in Brest, 'I can assure you that there is a battle of communication just as there is a battle of production and a marketing battle.' The CNJA means to 'convince' people, as it stresses in the report 'The Way Ahead' presented at its 1985 Conference. Worker-peasants see the future of agriculture as 'a choice' or 'concern' which society as a whole must face.

Links with European and International Markets?

Everyone today believes that there is no salvation outside Europe, despite the recent declaration by the new president of the FNSEA, Raymond Lacombe, that 'the Common Market is no more, we are moving toward a free trade area. We must return to national policies. Anyway, everyone is doing it!'. (*Le Monde*, 22 January 1987). Roughly 95 per cent of agricultural products depend upon markets managed at the Community level. Producers' organisations, even those that have long been anti-European like MODEF, are aware today that the European market and EEC support for exports to third countries are essential to French agriculture. Nevertheless, although withdrawal from the CAP is no longer on the agenda, producer organisations hold widely divergent views on links with the European and international markets.

For the cereal growers represented by the General Association of Wheat Producers (AGPB), the ideal solution would be to return to the original plan of a great European market for animal feed. They thus denounce the invasion of the European market by grain substitutes and, to undermine soybean imports, they support the production subsidies for European oilseed crops which have been in operation since 1977. But the European market with its guaranteed intervention prices is also seen as the platform for developing export markets in third countries. The AGPB affirms the need for a 'European cereals policy'. It argues that 'the EEC must not be allowed to turn in on itself by restricting production to what would satisfy internal needs'. On the contrary, it must 'equip itself with the commercial weapons necessary to withstand the increasingly active competition between the world's five leading producers', that is the US, Canada, Argentina, Australia and the EEC.

This conception of European protectionism also explains the anger of corn producers over the January 1987 agreement with the United States and Argentina, which was negotiated to compensate these GATT trading partners for the accession of Spain and Portugal to the EEC. Under this agreement, import levies will be reduced on 2.3 million tonnes of cereals and by-products from the US and Argentina for a four-year period. (Delorme, 1986). However, this protectionist conception does not suit many other groups of producers, ranging from livestock farmers to wine-growers, who find themselves up against either saturated European markets or more competitive rivals. These groups turn to international markets, and first to the US. Thus at the time of the 'corn crisis', the president of the CNJA, M. Teyssedou, declared that it is 'better to reach an agreement with the United States because we can sell them brandy, cheese, and wine. We cannot try to protect ourselves against imports if we wish to continue to export outside the Community' (*Le Monde*, 28 June 1986).

For these modern wine-growers and livestock producers, the aim is to export 'value added'; that is, products developed through the hard work and skill of farmers who are prepared to innovate. For the most highly modernised and intensive livestock producers, much greater free trade is seen as the answer to Dutch competition. Also, freer trade with world markets will expand exports of processed products and luxury items to the rich countries. The CNJA is thus encouraging agricultural cooperatives to reorganise and, in collaboration with private enterprise, to create more dynamic commerical structures.

But should everything be staked on exports? Can we not return to an agriculture more closely centred on European needs? Many farmers, only loosely organised and often elderly, are now reaching the conclusion that after its successive enlargements the EEC is likely in future to be harmful to their efforts to retain their holdings. This analysis comes above all from the 'Worker-Peasant' movement which, 'in the name of the right of all peoples to feed themselves', regards imports of soybeans and other basic foodstuffs as the pillaging of the Third World, as a kind of 'land imports' taken from food-producing cultures. They also regard exports and food aid as obstacles to the development of these countries (FNSP, 1986). By declaring that they belong to 'the other agricultural Europe' and are united within a 'coordinated European peasantry', they claim also that they are 'weaving links between European farmers as partners rather than rivals' (*Le Travailleur paysan*, 59, January 1987).

Do Supply Controls Inevitably Result in Concentration?

Lower prices, quotas, set-aside: the choice of instruments to control or master the expansion of production is not neutral and again reveals divisions among producers. These, first of all, are between one sector and another but, at the heart of each sector, there are divisions between those who intend to continue growing by eliminating others and farmers who, on the contrary, are seeking ways of sharing markets more evenly among all producers.

This division can be seen in the publications of the AGPB, and undoubtedly explains the change in leadership in 1986 when Henri de Benoist replaced Philippe Neeser. The 1986 General Assembly of the AGPB presented an apparently unanimous view when denouncing 'the greater decline in cereal producers' income since 1979' (when compared with other producers) and 'the levelling down of incomes'. In order to bring some short-term improvement in cereal producers' incomes, the Assembly called for the gradual elimination of indirect levies, which it regarded as being less useful 'at a time when the European co-responsibility levy is being introduced'. This position challenges the solidarity that had developed with other sectors over the financing of agricultural development policy (ANDA) and agro-industrial investment (Unigrain funds). It also involves a partial dismantling of the Cereals Office (ONIC). This could be a risky gamble at a time when one can observe a certain renationalisation of agricultural policy instruments, and when France's main competitor in intra-EEC markets, Holland, is on the contrary expanding its products bureau (*produktshap*). The 'wildcat' strike over the payment of additional indirect taxes that the AGPB embarked on in September 1986 gives a clear indication that the immediate concern of rank and file producers is to maintain their incomes (Grall, 1986).

But this is not perhaps the attitude of the large-scale cereal producers. Forced to choose between two evils, they would undoubtedly prefer lower prices to the possible creation of cereal quotas, which would freeze conditions in national markets and favour the maintenance of small cereal sectors in the strong-currency countries. This seems to be the positon of the former president of the AGPB, Philippe Neeser. A controlled and limited reduction in European prices might indeed enable the larger producers to exploit their structural advantages and reconquer the European market, and to dominate new outlets opened up by the use of cereals as industrial raw materials (ethanol, product fractioning, and so on). They hope therefore to pursue a 'modernization of (their) agriculture . . . based on structures more conducive to investment' (Neeser, 1984).

A second reason for the preference expressed by the large cereal producers is linked with international competition. Production quotas would constitute a static limitation on European output. Moreover, the price guarantees that quotas might entail would reinforce the use of imported grain substitutes as livestock production expanded, unless a complete Community preference is imposed with strict and inflexible import quotas. An acreage withdrawal scheme would present the same risks and above all reduce the financial resources allocated to exports.

Despite the noisy condemnation by François Guillaume in his political campaign against the Socialists, milk quotas now are seen by the large intensive producers as offering the protection necessary to achieve modernisation by concentrating production in 'profitable workplaces' (Coulomb and Delorme, 1987). By virtue of their low profit margins per litre, these producers, and above all the young farmers undergoing expansion, would have been placed in considerable difficulty by the strong price reduction originally envisaged by Brussels as an alternative to quotas. The problem for these intensive producers is to maintain their productionist dynamic by creating new areas of growth through the elimination of other producers. But which ones, and how is this to be done?

The ideal for intensive producers would have been an individual quota system providing each farmer with the right to produce X thousand litres. The resale of quota rights would then have ensured the rapid concentration and relocation of production, comparable to the developments seen in Quebec in the 1970s (Gouin and Hairy, 1988). However, France preferred to allocate the quotas by dairies. Now this system makes concentration more difficult. The principle, which has so far been respected, is that quotas, which become available in a given dairy catchment area due to the withdrawal of farmers from production, are redistributed in that same area. The concentration of production can therefore only occur locally under the watchful eye of other producers, and also under the control of both private and cooperative processors. There is a national reserve managed by *L'Office du Lait* which allows some redistribution of quotas (10 per cent of the quotas given up by farmers leaving the industry in 1985, and 20 per cent in 1986) but this is insufficient as the basis of 'a real policy of restructuring nor even of redistribution in favour of young farmers'.

The voluntary consent of farmers to give up milk production so far has limited tensions between dairy producers. Old farmers with no one to succeed them have welcomed payments to 'stop milk production' because they offer the possibility of early retirement. In Savoie and Haute Savoie, farmers' unions are concerned that the exodus of elderly small producers will lead to an excessive fall in production. On the other hand, older farmers in Brittany are under strong pressure to give up milk production in favour of younger operators. Quota payments were welcomed also by farmers with the possibility of changing their specialisation – to cereals in Poitou-Charente, beef cattle in Limousin, etc. More than 50 000 milk producers thus disappeared voluntarily thanks to the compensation payments made in 1984 and 1985. The continuation of this process in 1986 and 1987 should reduce the total number of producers from 350 000 in 1983 to 275 000 in 1987.

But what will happen once this 'dairy exodus' of older farmers and producers who can convert to other activities is complete? Already the unequal decline of production in different regions, departments and, above all, the catchment area of dairies is arousing 'jealousies'. That is, between farmers who can exceed their quota without penalty and other producers who, though often neighbours of the former, supply a different dairy and are heavily penalised because of a collective surplus in this particular catchment area. As yet, there is not open warfare between different regions, but mistrust is widespread. Some regions have unused quotas as in Poitou-Charente, for example, where production has fallen, and these are coveted by neighbouring departments, such as Vendée. Others fear the dairy expansionism of the West, as in the case of Rhone-Alpes, and seek to hold on to their milk quotas.

By bringing the growth of production to a halt, milk quotas have completely changed the socio-economic conditions governing the concentration of production. Since it is now impossible to assist all producers, it is necessary to choose which can stay in the industry and to cut out the rest. Until 1983, growth was accompanied by concentration as herds with less than 30 cows declined and those with 40 or more increased. In this period, when there was no limit to production growth, change came about gently, and the expansion of the larger farms did not imply the disappearance of the others. With the quota system, this is no longer the case. A herd of 40 cows yielding more than 200 000 litres per year is still the ideal model in technical terms for the CNJA and the intensive producers. This size permits good working conditions and provides a reasonable return to the technical skills of the modern dairy farmer. With this model as the norm, less than 120 000 herds would be needed to meet the French quota. That is, less than half of the 275 000 herds that are expected to remain by the end of 1987, despite the payments made to farmers to withdraw from production. This degree of concentration also would imply the geographical relocation of production around a smaller number of dairies, and thus a major restructuring of the industry. In short, it would give the green light to concentration in mechanised or automated milking-sheds.

At its 1986 Congress in Brest, the FNSEA – and this was later echoed by the new minister, François Guillaume – had declared its opposition to this outcome. However, in 1987, FNSEA inaugurated the 'second stage of the silent revolution' and offered to oversee the concentration of production within the framework of structural policy, announcing that it favoured 'an active policy of cutting back production'.

This proposal allowed the FNSEA to denounce the bureaucratic red tape and statism of the products bureaux, while reaffirming that it stood for 'responsible' trade unionism. But would most farmers today accept intervention by the large unions in production structures, with only minimum control by the State? This is doubtful, at least in those departments where intensive livestock production is most highly developed. This stratum of producers is behind the unionism of the FDSEAs and the CDJAs and controls the joint commissions which administer farm structure and investment policy at the departmental level. Tensions are often most acute in departments where this is the case.

In the West, 'ill on its own milk' (*Ouest-France*, 21 August 1986), there is open conflict between the big producers (200 000 litres and over) and medium-size producers (around 100 000 litres), who fear they will gradually be eliminated by the former's social and political power. For a long time now, union divisions (in Loire Atlantique, Mayenne, Finisterre), the estrangement of certain departmental branches from the FNSEA (Morbihan, and earlier Mayenne and Finisterre), or the growth of the worker-peasant movement (Côtes du Nord), have revealed how sharp these differences are.

This mistrust has strengthened the belief of medium-sized farmers in the legitimacy and, above all, the credibility of the smaller unions, which during the 1970s had sparked off the social debate on the intensification of production.[8] The 'minority unionism' of the CNSTP or the FNSP advocates regulation of concentration by the State. They condemn the themes of 'modernisation' or 'restructuring' put forward by the CNJA because they see these as the expression of the desire for greater concentration. Against this they argue for equal rights to work, and for the redistribution of the right to produce by limiting the farm size.

In order to restrict supply, these unions favour a policy of differentiated prices (quantum), which would provide better support for the incomes of medium-sized producers and restrict the built-in advantages (*rente de situation*) enjoyed by the largest operators. For all that, can they mobilise support among the majority of peasants who fear exclusion from dairying and livestock production? The demonstrations about the '100 000 litres', which were frequent in 1987 and often organised around these unions, clearly reveal their growing influence. But is this true for the country as a whole and for all products?

The crisis of small and medium-size holdings is reinforcing, in many diverse ways, the polyvalence (*multiactivité*) of peasant households and their integration in a rural milieu increasingly less dominated by agricultural activity. Action through trade unionism is no longer in their eyes the principal way of mediating their links with local or global society. Today, what counts as much, if not more, is direct understanding of the contradictions of wage-earning society, which their own families will henceforth experience in many diverse social situations. This may in part explain why this large body of farmers finds trade union pluralism legitimate, supported its recognition in 1981, disapproved of François Guillaume's ostracism of the minority unions, is delighted to see a farmer in control of things but is becoming itself less unionised. We can thus understand how, in this identity crisis, the union struggle, in its new diversity, is becoming largely an ideological struggle around a truly social issue: what should the farmer of tomorrow be? A businessman, a worker, or always a peasant?

Farmers' Future Socio-economic Status?

According to a recent poll by the FNSP published in January 1986, only 4.5 per cent of farmers call themselves 'businessmen'. Nevertheless this is the term used by the mainline unions and associations in their proposals and discussions on the future of agriculture. The question is to determine whether this term has the same meaning for all these organisations and, above all, whether it has the same economic significance as industrial entrepreneur.

Representatives of large-scale farming have long demanded 'parity' between agriculture and industry; that is, parity in terms of the rate of return on invested capital. As far as these farmers were concerned, protectionism on the one hand and support for many small farmers on the other, allowed them to take advantage of high price levels and so secure a true entrepreneurial profit. In this respect, the CAP in 1962 must have seemed ideally suited to meet their interests. Today, however, the steady erosion of this policy is convincing them that it is no longer desirable to squander the price support budget on the maintenance of a large number of farms. On the contrary, resources should be concentrated on the 350 000 farmers who account for 75 per cent of marketed output since this group is on the 'technological frontier' and represents the 'best in Europe' (*Le Producteur Agricole Française*, December, 1984, 7). To be sure, 'a minimum rural population mainly engaged in agriculture' must be maintained, but this must be supported by 'social assistance payments . . . under careful control' (ibid.).

This resurgence of corporatist demands, implying the heavy concentration of resources on a small number of large producers, has preoccupied the FNSEA. Its opposition to this revival is couched in tortuous phrases and meaningful repetitions: 'Must we conclude that the fewer farmers there are, the higher will be each one's income? The FNSEA condemns such an approach. Indeed, this Malthusian theory was held by many economists before the war. It was based on

selfishness which denied fair shares or, more simply, rewards for
effort. History has not judged kindly these theoreticians who advocated turning in on oneself. Let us not fall back again into this
unhealthy Malthusianism' (FNSEA Congress Report, 1986).

In fact, the FNSEA has taken up the analysis presented by the
CNJA in 1985 in favour of an 'agriculture of entrepreneurs' (CNJA
Conference Report, 1985). According to the CNJA, if 'farmers are
basically businessmen, this ideal conceals a certain moral code or
ethique . . . A businessman is not necessarily someone who, according to the picture presented by industry, controls tens, hundreds or
thousands of workers. Being a businessman is the result of a *conscious decision* and not of the size of the enterprise'(ibid.). In 1986,
the FNSEA spoke out even more plainly, 'Let no one set against our
condemnation of large-scale farming the familiar argument that
peasants can advance by becoming wage-earners' (FNSEA Congress
Report, 1986).

For both the FNSEA and CNJA, the main objective is to preserve
the technological model which, through mechanisation and now
computerisation, confers on the 'work-place' the same dignity which
tractors brought to their fathers and 'running water' to their mothers,
The CNJA's position is clarified by its proposition that 'we do not
rule out the prospect of a French agricultural sector of 700, 800, or
900 000 operators but with half the present number of farms' (CNJA
Conference Report, 1985). But are we talking then of relaunching
cooperative farming?

This conception of the 'businessman', who 'constantly questions
his own behaviour' (ibid.), is indeed a 'moral' discourse. As the title
of the 1985 CNJA report puts it, now is the time to 'understand,
imagine, convince' after having pursued the Christian Young Farmers' motto to 'see, judge, act'. The aim is to restore the confidence
of young farmers who are disorientated by the collapse of the intensive model. In future, individual initiative should be brought to the
fore. Of course, collective practices essential to the marketing and
processing of mass consumption products should not be neglected,
but it is necessary to encourage the diversification of methods of
production and selling.

Working-class norms inspire the 'social project' of the worker-
peasants. Yet, although the ideological point of reference, from
white-collar to blue-collar, clearly is oppositional, is the final objective so different? Is it not a question in both cases of solving the same
problem: of saving the 'career-farmer' (Remy, 1986) by ensuring the
reproduction, from one generation to the next, of the technological

model built up by the present generation? Nevertheless, the two currents part company over social aims and the tactics to adopt.

This divergence can be seen clearly in the case of tenant farming. Both the CNJA and FNSEA, like the worker-peasants, regard tenant farming as the most desirable means of access to the land, and recommend vigorous solutions to revive it. However, none of them wishes to see an increase in rents to the extent that property investment becomes as profitable as other investments. Similarly, these movements are also opposed to the revival of the social power of land owners as regards the management of farm holdings. But the two currents diverge over methods of action. Thus the FNSEA and CNJA have revived the solutions proposed by the large-scale corporatist farmers in the inter-war period (Coulomb, 1978). In order to attract new 'investors' in landed property they have proposed that the State should abolish the various taxes now weighing heavily on landlord-proprietors. The CNSTP, for its part, returns to the Walrasian solution of state ownership of land. In order to 'put an end to forced capitalisation', the CNSTP supports the formula of 'career grants', whereby the farm would be considered as a place of work occupied by the farmer during his professional life. 'The capital assets of agriculture must remain collective social property. In order to achieve this, the State, if it finances directly the instruments of production, must ensure that it retains this financing (. . .) We propose that the farmer should have a grant at his disposal which he will repay at the end of his career . . . The State, rather than financing the individual acquisition of capital, will finance the effective modernisation of production' (FNSP Congress Report, 1985).

The same agreements and disagreements re-emerge on the question of part-time farming. While the FNSEA admits that 'in difficult rural areas . . . farmers go beyond agricultural activity in the traditional sense and perform other services', it reaffirms strongly its preference for 'agriculture as a profession' (FNSEA Congress Report, 1987). For the CNSTP, 'the defence by the public authorities' of part-time farming (*pluriactivité*) is a 'palliative that is very convenient for the system', but which is 'too facile and unacceptable because . . . there will be even greater underpayment of industrial and agricultural labour' (CNSTP Conference Report, 1985). This 'professional' orientation partly explains the difficulties encountered by the CNSTP in trying to extend its influence among ordinary farmers. As a militant of this current in the Doubs declares, 'we, the Worker-Peasants, are regarded as large producers' (*Le Travailleur-Paysan*, 39, May 1985).

The FNSP – many of whose analyses are close to those of the CNSTP – sees itself as being more representative of the diversity of farmers and agricultural sectors. Its hopes for the rebirth of 'a living rural community' are based on the construction of 'peasant solidarity'. With this goal, the FNSP has advocated 'regionalised statutes' for part-time farmers. Above all, the FNSP hopes that a better distribution of economic assistance (neither 'abnormal' nor 'debasing') will bring out 'the real value of farm holdings' by 'treating the illness rather than its symptoms' and instead of 'further increasing the concentration of production' (*Pays, Paysan!*, 25 March 1986).

But do the CNSTP and the FNSP really embody the aspirations of this disparate collection of people which forms the majority of farmers? In many agricultural regions, their views are well-received by the young who intend to live and work in the area. Does this also apply to the mass of 'ordinary' farmers who can still be considered the majority? But these are also the oldest as they include the larger part of the 520 000 farmers due to retire between 1983 and 1993, and almost all of the 240 000 retiring with no heirs or where the succession is in doubt.[9] This body of farmers also includes the highest proportion of part-timers (Delord and Lacombe, 1984). The full-time farmers in this group often have adopted modern practices but their production systems also retain agronomic characteristics typical of mixed arable-livestock systems. This is notably the case of dairy and livestock farmers who use the full variety of traditional breeds of cattle (Bonnemaire and Vissac, 1988).

The political position of these 'ordinary' farmers is also extremely varied. Having participated little in the race towards technological progress, they may be passive union members of the FNSEA. They may also be linked, according to regional traditions, with old but now modernised union movements: right-wing unionism, like the FFA, the republican unionism of the MODEF or of the old CGA (*Confederation Generale de l'Agriculture*), which was created at the time of the Liberation and still exists officially. Certain branches of the FDSEA in the South-West, allied to old socialist currents, still belong to the CGA.

These 'ordinary' farmers all 'vow to remain peasants'. But what sort of peasants? The cooperative peasant and citizen of the MODEF? The peasant of the FFA, victim of 'state parasitism', the 'nationalisation of activity', and of 'hatred of our native soil'? In reality, few of these farmers have much sympathy for militant trade unionism. When they have mobilised in the last 30 years it has been around precise demands that concerned them directly (a momentary crisis in local markets, for example, or questioning state procedures), rather than behind the banners of those wanting to 'liven up the struggle' (Coulomb and Nallet, 1972). This behaviour explains their strong mobilisation at the time of the States General of Agricultural Development in 1983, as well as local actions to facilitate the taking over of holdings by young farmers. The heterogeneous nature of this group also may explain the difficulties experienced by Edith Cresson in 1981 when she sought the support of the smaller minority unions, as Michel Debré had done in 1959–60 with the CNJA.

CRISIS OF POLICY OR POLITICAL CRISIS?

The creation-reconstruction of advantage is the motivating force in modern agricultural policies which are all, by their very nature, protectionist. These policies depend on the insulation of the domestic market, which is essential in order to maintain relative prices (between agricultural products and between agriculture and industry), thus allowing production to develop but at the same time supporting agricultural incomes. For this very reason, these policies are expansionist and it is necessary to manage the rising floods of exports. Caught in this contradiction, the advanced industrial states resort to all the weapons of their economic and political power to confront their rivals, and so transfer to the developing countries the instability generated by the fluctuations in their surpluses.

In these political power struggles, for ever overtaken by market forces, matters have reached an impasse: in each country (rich or poor), as well as between them, trends in production, consumption, and trade are becoming divorced from each other, resulting in a general crisis. This is manifest after 1981 in the collapse of world prices and the increasing cost of agricultural policies.

The anarchy in world prices, that is being transmitted increasingly to domestic markets, may revive corporatist defence reflexes among those farmers who have profited most from agricultural policies and their subsidies. But is not this anarchy at the same time ruining these vague desires? The destabilisation of prices in all the major agricultural blocs (the EEC, US, Oceania, and so on) compels all producers, and above all those who benefit most from present policies since they are more closely integrated than the rest, to change their costs in order to survive and rediscover the way back to profitability. Market movements could thus lead to the appearance of new forms of production, in the industrial countries as well as developing countries.

This instability also raises doubts about political relationships as the markets constantly modify the positions of different groups whose alliance conditions the definition of a new compromise, redistributing incomes between States, various types of farmers and between the other agents of the agro-industrial complex.

In this battle, and French experience in Europe shows this, natural trump cards derived from climate and soils count less than comparative advantages created by a strong currency, an efficient industry, a powerful commercial apparatus, and a well-organised agriculture under a state pledged to develop it. Between ruinous free-tradism and the revival of protectionist corporatisms, agricultural policies based on the authority of the State remain the only possible means of mediation. In this sense the agricultural crisis is indeed a *crisis of policy* but it can also develop into a *political crisis* to the extent that the systems of power, legitimation, and domination are called into question.

Notes

1. As regards cereals, the market price in France was regularly above the intervention price until 1984. In 1984–85 and 1985–86 the market price plunged below the intervention price, and then only regained this level with difficulty in 1986–87. In the case of milk, the support system operates through the processed products (milk, powder, butter) and the price is guaranteed to the manufacturer, who should pass it on to the farmers. The price the farmers receive, however, is on average always less than the recommended price for milk fixed in Brussels.
2. The preference shown to the United States is reflected in the tariff systems: soybeans and soybean meal enter duty free, while other oilseeds and meal carry a 2 per cent duty. In the same way, corn gluten enters duty free, whereas manioc is taxed at 6 per cent and subject to an 'export limitation agreement'.
3. These export subsidies can take the form of subsidies in kind: this is the case of the BICEP programme which, for every tonne exported, allows a certain quantity of the product to be withdrawn from federal stocks, which may amount up to 50 per cent of the total exported. This programme applies mainly to cereals, but can include dairy products, poultry, and other products. Planned for eight Middle Eastern countries when it was launched in October 1986, this programme was extended in 1987 to the Soviet Union and China.
4. 'Budgetary discipline' was established by the agreement reached in Dublin in December, 1984 to limit agricultural expenditure. It is intended to ensure that the increase in these outlays must be less than that of 'own

resources' (*ressources propres*); that is, of the VAT revenues allotted to the EEC budget. Exceeding this barrier gives each State the right to veto when agricultural prices come to be fixed.

5. MODEF (*Mouvement de Défense des Exploitants Familiaux*) is a union movement which has taken up again the tradition of pre-war unions in Southern and Central France. In departments where it is in the majority it may not always appear to be in control of the FDSEA. The CNSTP (*Confédération nationale des syndicats de Travailleurs Paysans*) was created during the 1970s by splits in the CDJA but also through the break away of individual FDSEAs. The FNSP (*Fédération nationale des Syndicats paysans*) represents the regrouping in 1982 of the left-wing militants of the FNSEA in the West, the Rhone-Alpes and others. In 1987 the CNSTP and FNSP organised a 'Peasants Conference' to which they invited the MODEF (which refused to attend) with the aim of forming a single union: *la Confédération Paysanne*.

6. The FFA (*Fédération française de l'agriculture*) is a right-wing union (and sometimes extreme right) which originates in part from the *dorgérist* populist movement. The FNPA (*Fédération nationale de la propriété agricole*) claims to defend the interests of 'property'.

7. Four organizations constitute the domain of 'majority' union representation. Two of these are trade unions: the FNSEA (Fédération nationale des syndicats d'exploitants agricoles), and the CNJA (*Confédération nationale des jeunes agriculteurs*.) The third is the CNMCCA, a confederation of unions, mutual aid and credit agencies, and co-operatives. Finally, the Chambers of Agriculture (consular establishments) are represented by the APCA (*L'Assemblée Permanente des Chambres d' Agriculture*). These 'four big ones' take part in an annual Conference and are received by the minister on the first Tuesday of each month.

8. Compare the impact of Bernard Lambert's book, *Less Paysans dans la lutte des classes* (Paris: Le Seuil, 1970).

9. It is difficult to be precise about production structures and the number of holdings in 1987. The last general census of agriculture (RGA) dates from 1980, although a new RGA is in preparation. Agriculture is also experiencing a 'demographic crisis'. The many farmers who started farming at the time of the crisis of the 1930s and Second World War are now retiring. Many have no heirs: these are those who 'resisted' the drift from the land but whose sons left. On the 'end of the rural exodus', see the presentation by Pierre Coulomb 'L'exploitation familiale en question' to the book by Nicole Eizner, *Les Paradoxes de l'Agriculture Française*, (Paris: L'Harmattan, 1985).

Bibliography

Bonnemaire, J. and B. Vissac (1988), 'Races bovines et modèles de développment' in M. Jollivet (ed.), *Pour une agriculture diversifiée* (Paris: L'Hermattan).

Blogowski, A., J. P. Bompart, V. Durieux and V. Desambre (1983), 'Repartition des aides publiques aux exploitations agricoles adhérentes du RICA en 1979', *Cahier de statistique agricole*, 66, november-décembre.

The International Farm Crisis

Bertrand, J. P. *et al.* (1984) *Le monde de soja* (Paris: La Découverte).

Chambres d'Agriculture (1985), Projet pour l'agriculture demain. juin (supplément.)

Coulomb, P. (1978), 'Systèmes fonciers et politiques foncières' in P. Coulomb, H. Nallet and L. Servolin, *L'élaboration de la politique agricole* (Paris: INRA).

Coulomb, P. (1985), 'Derecho de propriedad, Derechos de la explotacion: La mutación de las relaciones sociales en el crecimiento agrícolo francés', *Agricultura y Sociedad*, 35, avril-juin.

Coulomb, P. and H. Delorme, (1981), 'La France: les difficultés d'une réussite', *Etudes internationales*, mars.

Coulomb, P. and H. Delorme (1985), 'L'agriculture, les agriculteurs et la crise', *POUR*, 102, septembre-octobre.

Coulomb, P. and H. Delorme (1987), 'La politique agricole' in *L'Etat de la France et ses habitants* (Paris: La Découverte).

Coulomb P. and H. Nallet (1972), 'Le syndicalisme agricole à l'épreuve de l'unité', in *L'Univers politique des paysans* (Paris: A. Colin).

Coulomb, P. and H. Nallet (1980), 'Le syndicalisme moderne et la création du paysan modèle' (Paris: INRA-CORDES).

CERC (Centre d'étude des revenus et des coûts) (1985), *Les agriculteurs et leurs revenus* (2 vols.) (Paris: La Documentation française).

Delord, B. and P. Lacombe (1984), 'La multiactivité des agriculteurs, conjoncture ou structure?', in *La Pluriactivité des familles agricoles* (Paris: ARF).

Delorme, H. (1978), *Les paysans de Bruxelles* (Paris: IEP).

Delorme, H. (1986), 'Le poids de l'allié américain dans la CEE: treize à table', *Le Monde diplomatique*, novembre.

Delorme, H. (1988), 'Y a-t-il un marché international des produits laitiers?', in H. Franquen (ed.), *Agriculture et politiques agricoles* (Paris: L'Harmattan).

FNSP (1986), 'Nord-Sud: une seule planète', *Pays-Paysans!*, fèvrier.

Gouin, D., and D. Hairy (1988), 'Les quotas laitiers au Quèbec et au Canada: un équilibre menacé?' in H. Franquen (ed.), *Agriculture et politiques agricoles* (Paris: L'Harmattan).

Grall, J. (1986), 'Le torchon brûle entre M. Guillaume et les organisations professionnelles', *Le Monde*, 19 septembre.

Mallet, M. (1985), 'Le label pour rendre compte de la diversité'. Rapport au colloque, *Diversification des modèles de développement rural*.

Neeser, P. (1984), 'Moderniser l'agriculture', *Le producteur agricole francais*, 361, décembre.

Remy, J. (1986), 'Profession: agriculteur' (Paris: INRA).

Viau, C. (1984), 'La politique agricole commune et l'union economique et monétaire: du traité de Rome au sommet de Brême', in *Politique agricole commune et construction communautaire*, (Paris: Economica).

5 The Farm Crisis in Britain

Graham Cox, Philip Lowe
and Michael Winter.

In some ways it seems misplaced to talk of a farm crisis in Britain. Agriculture continues to hold a privileged position in the national polity and culture. Through the EEC's Common Agricultural Policy it enjoys a high degree of protection from the full rigours of world market forces and, even during eight years of Conservative monetarist policies, agriculture has received fairly mild treatment at the hands of a government intent on curbing public expenditure. Moreover few of the more extreme signs of agricultural depression, such as Britain experienced at the end of the last century and between the wars, are yet in evidence. Despite constant speculation about acreages thought surplus to requirements little land has fallen out of production: on the contrary, reclamation continues at an alarming rate. Recent survey work by the Countryside Commission and the Department of the Environment, for example, shows that the annual rate of hedgerow removal in England and Wales accelerated between 1980 and 1985 to 4000 miles a year compared with 2900 miles a year between 1969 and 1980 (Countryside Commission, 1986).

Production of most basic commodities is still rising. The political reaction of farmers to the various threats directed at the industry has been pained rather than ferocious and there has been little of the militancy which the industry experienced, albeit in piecemeal fashion, as recently as the late 1960s and early 1970s. Fundamentally, however, the industry faces a crisis far deeper than anything experienced in those relatively prosperous times. The lack of farmer militancy is, perhaps, indicative of an underlying acceptance on the part of both the farming lobby and government officials, that fundamental change is needed. More than that though, it speaks of deep confusion as to how it might best be brought about. This paper examines the extent of the current farm crisis, the nature of its deepening impact, and the political responses to crisis in terms of both substantive policy and ideology. Our broader concern, however, is to attempt an assessment of the relative importance of the political, economic and ideological elements of the crisis.

113

CHANGE IN BRITISH AGRICULTURE[1]

Agricultural policy formed a significant component of the post-war programme of reconstruction undertaken by the Labour Government elected in 1945. The 1947 Agriculture Act offered a new deal to British farmers. With prices and markets assured, the industry was encouraged to adopt a long term perspective in planning its role in the expansion of the nation's capacity for producing food. As the memory of food shortages receded the emphasis of policy shifted from output to efficiency. The Conservative governments of the 1950s retained a commitment to support policies but, as the position of world food supplies improved, they sought to contain the costs of such support. The drive to efficiency was two-pronged, and continued to entail an important facilitative role for the state. First, the government directly financed agricultural research and education, and a state advisory service. Particular emphasis was placed on the development and promotion of new technologies and plant and animal varieties. Second, support policy was orientated towards encouraging farmers to adopt the new technologies. This was done directly through capital grants and input subsidies, and indirectly through a ceiling on the annual increase in guaranteed prices.

Thus the 1957 Agriculture Act enshrined the principle that the annual price award would not reimburse the farmer for all the increases in his costs of production. It was expected that a proportion of the costs would be absorbed by the farmer through increased efficiency. For many farmers this was a powerful incentive, not only to adopt new techniques to boost production but also to cut costs through releasing labour or enlarging the size of their holdings, and to borrow the money to finance land purchase and capital projects. This cost-price squeeze lies at the heart of the current crisis and the contradictions characteristic of the industry. Public money has been poured into it, resulting in massively increased output; yet the number of farmers has steadily declined and a farm income problem remains.

No sector of agriculture has been exempt from the processes of change. In arable farming, yields of cereal crops have trebled in the post-war period. Between 1950 and 1985 the total volume of wheat harvested in the UK expanded fivefold. Grassland yields have improved allowing an increase in the number of cattle in the UK from 10.5 million in 1945 to nearly 13 million in 1985. Land has been brought into more intensive production, even in the less favourable agricultural areas. For example in a poor farming region of West Devon the area of rough grazing halved in 25 years (Winter, 1986). The increased production has occurred mainly on the larger and more specialised farm units with a greater dependence upon external inputs and the availability of credit and they, disproportionately, have been the recipients – though not always the ultimate beneficiaries – of the public money flowing into agriculture.

The structural changes in the industry have certainly strengthened the dominance of this group at the expense of both smaller farmers and hired workers. The number of small farms has declined dramatically since the 1950s after a decade in which the number of holdings remained relatively static. Between 1955 and 1975 the proportion of the crops and grass area of England and Wales in farms of over 300 acres rose from 27 per cent to 43 per cent (Britton, 1977). The total number of holdings in the UK has halved since 1950 and the number of whole-time farmers has declined by one third to 199 000 in 1985. The number of whole-time hired workers in the UK declined from 717 000 in 1950 to 121 000 in 1985. Although more casual and contract labour is employed than hitherto (Errington, 1986; Ball, 1987) the picture that emerges is one of an industry in which the farmer and family members provide the major part, at around 60 per cent, of the farm labour force.

Labour's contribution to production has been substantially replaced by a massive injection of capital in the form of machinery and labour-saving buildings. Gross capital formation in UK agriculture more than doubled in real terms between 1973 and 1983. Increases in the size of holdings, to achieve the full advantage of new plant and machinery, have often been a corollary of capital expansion. Demand for land throughout the post-war period, except very recently, has been keen and land prices have grown at more than three times the general rate of price increases (Howarth, 1985). Expansion has thus become a progressively more costly process, and farmers have steadily been drawn into hitherto unprecedented credit relations. For example between 1958/59 and 1967/68 net farm income in south-western England increased by 35 per cent, gross output by 42 per cent, costs by 45 per cent and loans by 122 per cent (Davies *et al.*, 1971).

The incorporation of agriculture into wider circuits of capital has meant a diversion of financial support from farmers to the input sectors. The direct cost of public support for UK agriculture is now over two billion pounds per annum. The indirect cost – much of the

burden having shifted from the taxpayer to the consumer as a result
of entry into the EEC – is in the region of three to four billion, a
doubling in real terms since the 1950s and 1960s (Howarth, 1985;
Buckwell *et al.*, 1982). Yet, as the figures already quoted indicate,
farm incomes have by no means received all the benefit. Instead
there has been a diversion into land values and other inputs. The cost
of farm machinery, for example, increased by 30 per cent more than
farm product prices in the period between 1970 and 1982 (Howarth,
1985).

Not all farmers, of course, are equally affected by the changes in
the industry. Agriculture is clearly characterised by variety, and there
are huge disparities in wealth and income between, say, the
thousand-acre cereal producer in the east of England and the
hundred-acre dairy or livestock farmer in West Wales. Nor is the
debt burden equally shared. The farmer, of whatever size, who is
heavily in debt, faces particular problems when margins are cut. Thus
those most likely to be severely squeezed as the economic crisis in the
industry deepens are small farmers and producers with heavy debt
burdens. Neither group is well placed to mount any form of political
counter-offensive.

Small farmers have always been notoriously difficult to organise.
Nor are they well represented within the National Farmers' Union.
Although their plight may be exploited by the NFU for ideological
purposes neither the union nor the Ministry of Agriculture, Fisheries
and Food (MAFF) has shown any serious inclination to adopt policies that would discriminate in favour of smaller producers. Indebted
producers, on the other hand, cannot be clearly identified as a group,
for debt problems transcend the traditional divisions within the
industry, between arable and livestock, upland and lowland, small
and large farms. They are often the farmers who, perhaps as relative
newcomers, responded most recently and most whole-heartedly to
government incentives to enlarge production in the expansionary
climate that prevailed through the 1970s and into the early 1980s
(MAFF, 1975 and 1979). In the markedly different climate of today –
with government seeking to curb output, the cost-price squeeze
biting deeper and markets saturated – bankruptcy looms large for
many of those who were persuaded to borrow heavily. This crisis,
though, is not shared by farmers with few debts. On the contrary, as
land prices drop some of these are in a strong position to expand their
holdings at the expense of those forced to sell. Thus the response to

the crisis has tended to be individualised rather than collective, manifest in a general air of despondency in the industry and decisions to quit by some of the more hard-pressed farmers, as well as an increased incidence of bankruptcies, suicides and accidents.

THE NATURE OF THE CRISIS

The economic crisis is compounded by a crisis of political and ideological legitimation which heavily circumscribes the actions farmers and their leaders can now contemplate. Surpluses and environmental problems have eroded public sympathy for farming. Thus, though the current crisis may be deeper, it has not prompted so much political protest by farmers as during the previous crisis of the late 1960s and early 1970s. At that time they commanded much more political and public support. The strength of disquiet in the industry, then, must be understood in the context of the general economic growth and optimism of that period. It was still very much a period when the importance of government promotion of agricultural expansion was almost unquestioned. Nevertheless, real aggregate net farm income had declined during the 1960s in the face of a sustained cost-price squeeze. But for many individual farmers this was more than offset by increases in farm size as smaller and elderly farmers left the industry. The consequence of considerably fewer farmers sharing a slightly smaller cake was that the income of a full-time farmer increased in real terms by a modest 14 per cent between 1956 and 1968 (Howarth, 1985). Repeatedly, though, MAFF and the NFU failed to reach agreement in the annual price review necessitating, thereby, a government-imposed settlement. This had never happened before 1956. But between 1958 and 1971 the NFU formally dissociated itself from eight of the fourteen annual settlements.[2] It seems the political disquiet which did exist arose both from comparisons with other sectors where incomes were improving more rapidly, and annoyance with a government policy which continually emphasised agricultural productivity whilst, in successive annual reviews, expecting the industry to assume a growing share of the burden of financing its own growth through efficiency and productivity gains. Thus exchequer support remained more or less static for the industry over this period, so that by 1970, it contributed, through price guarantees, just 14 per cent to farming's net income (ibid.).

The political disquiet abated fairly abruptly around the time of Britain's entry into the EEC. Indeed notwithstanding grave apprehensions about the Common Agricultural Policy within the farming lobby, it soon became apparent that British agriculture was entering upon a new phase of expansion. The transition to CAP support coincided with the world oil and commodity crises of the early 1970s, and major technical breakthroughs promised greatly increased yields in temperate foodstuffs. 1973 in particular was an outstandingly successful year for the industry, which registered a dramatic increase in farm incomes. However, the boom was short-lived. Incomes dropped back again the following year – accompanied by renewed farmer protests (Wormell, 1978) – but although they remained at a higher level than the sixties for a few years a further sharp decline occurred in 1979/80. Discontent over the drop in incomes was given particular emphasis in the vigorous NFU campaign for devaluation of the Green Pound (Grant, 1981). Howarth (1985) estimates a real drop in incomes for full-time farmers of 35 per cent between 1970 and 1980. But as he includes all farms over 15 acres in his calculation this figure must be treated with some caution. During the same period the cost of support trebled, at current prices, with much of this money being diverted from farmers' pockets into the input sector and, especially, into land prices. The story in the 1980s has been one of partial recovery followed by further decline so that incomes in 1985 were barely three-quarters the level, in real terms, of 1980 and only half the levels of a decade earlier. Although there was an increase again in 1986, in February 1987, following a vote of no confidence in Government policy for agriculture at the NFU's annual meeting their President claimed farmers had experienced two years of the lowest net farm income since the war, and he later argued that a further 15 per cent reduction was in prospect as a result of the EC Council of Ministers decisions on farm prices for 1987/8.

However, published income figures, especially those relating to Net Farm Income (NFI), must be treated with considerable circumspection for four main reasons.[3] First, they exclude income from non-farming activities, yet Inland Revenue sources indicate that this amounts to over 40 per cent of farmers' incomes (Hill, B. 1984). Second, returns from the farm to members of the farm family other than the farmer and spouse are excluded. Third, no account is taken of capital growth and the gains accruing from borrowing under inflation (Hill, B. 1982; Hill, G. P. 1984). Fourth, NFI excludes interest on loans and assumes that rent is paid. Thus, as the National Audit Office makes clear, NFI has tended 'to overstate the incomes of farmers who had to borrow working capital, and to understate the incomes of owner-occupiers whose mortgage interests (if any) and other landlord type outgoings were less than the notional rent in the NFI calculations' (National Audit Office, 1987). A closer analysis of farm incomes, therefore, lends further support to our contention that the effects of the crisis are uneven. Aggregate figures mask the continued prosperity of many and the severe problems of the in-debted and those who have little or no opportunity to earn sup-plementary income.

Land prices provide another indicator of agricultural prosperity and confidence. In the mid 1980s land values have suffered a sus-tained fall for the first time since before the Second World War. Prices were just about static in 1980 and 1981, increased again up to mid-1984, and then under the impact of, first, milk quotas and, then, the more general uncertainty surrounding the CAP, fell sharply in the second half of 1984, 1985 and the first half of 1986. June 1986 saw the lowest land prices, even in current terms, since 1978. In real terms prices had roughly halved. In order to finance land purchase and other productive investment, farmers increased their borrowings and in the last ten years bank borrowing has increased by nearly two and a half times in real terms (Johnson, 1986). While land values were rising land provided collateral for such extensive loans. But banks are now understandably becoming more wary of this strategy and in 1985 gross capital formation in UK agriculture fell to its lowest real level since 1956 (ibid.). A further indicator of the present crisis is that borrowing to service the trading account has become increas-ingly common. The share of farm business income absorbed by interest payments on outstanding debts increased from 9 per cent in 1976 to 31 per cent in 1985 with an estimated marginal recovery to 25 per cent in 1986 (ibid.). However it must be emphasised that debt liabilities are still only at 15 per cent of total assets – a low percentage compared to many sectors of industry. Nor is there cause for much public concern over the impact such indebtedness might have on the banking sector since agriculture makes up just 7 per cent of sterling advances to the private sector from the large clearing banks (ibid.).

Of greater significance to the emergence of a sense of crisis in the 1980s has been a dawning realisation, both within the industry and amongst the general public, that agricultural support is not only costly but actually contributes to surpluses in a number of commodities. This is what lies behind declining land values and it is an almost unprecedented experience for British farmers in recent times. Occasional overproduction of liquid milk, potatoes and eggs had, of course, previously exercised policy-makers and farmers' leaders. There were even government proposals, successfully resisted by the farm lobby, for a milk quota as early as 1961 and acreage quotas for potatoes and sugar beet were introduced in 1955 and 1936 respectively. Hops had been subject to quota since 1928/32. But such supply problems tended to be temporary and fluctuating and, especially in the case of sugar, had more to do with the costs of support and overseas trading commitments than with genuine overproduction. Such restrictions were a far cry from the structural surpluses which confront the industry today. Contemporary surpluses have to be seen within a European context, where cereals, milk and beef are all in considerable oversupply. But even within the UK increases in yields mean that the country is now more than self-sufficient in a number of commodities, notably wheat, barley, oilseed rape and beef. Long self-sufficient in liquid milk, Britain was even approaching self-sufficiency in butter, with an increase from 50 per cent to 87 per cent in just seven years up to 1985, before the attenuation which followed the imposition of milk quotas. Meanwhile butter stocks in the Community stand at 830 per cent of the volume of annual butter exports from the EEC (Pooley, 1986).

Table 5.1 shows the growing level of self-sufficiency in certain of the major agricultural commodities which is at the root of the crisis in the CAP, and Table 5.2 the corresponding increases in intervention stocks.

TABLE 5.1   *Self-sufficiency ratios in the EEC* (%).*

	Total Cereals	Sugar	Butter	Beef
1973/74	91	90	98	95
1981/82	106	144	122	103
1984/85	127	125	129	106

* Excluding Spain and Portugal.

SOURCE   Commission of the European Communities. *The Agricultural Situation in the Community*, annual.

TABLE 5.2　*Intervention stocks, EEC and the UK ('000 tons).*

		Wheat	Barley	Butter	Beef
1975	EEC	1 799	523	71	252
	UK	0	0	0	0
1980	EEC	4 914	1 086	128	302
	UK	91	529	19	26
1985	EEC	11 580	2 151	879	606
	UK	2 971	976	134	50

SOURCE　National Audit Office, 1985.

The Community has so far responded to the surpluses with a combination of measures. In cereals, for example, a co-responsibility levy coupled with fairly modest price restraint has so far done little to contain the problem.[4] For dairy produce the imposition of quotas in 1984 only eased the sector's difficulties and in 1987 a further cut in quota proved necessary. There is, however, little enthusiasm within the Commission for the extension of quotas to other commodities and the long-term solution to the problems of surplus production remains uncertain. Moreover, even with a declining level of support, there is every likelihood that anticipated yield increases in the coming years will further bloat the surpluses in store unless radical steps are taken to restrict production. The United States Congress Office of Technology Assessment, for example, has predicted a likely doubling of milk yields in America in the next 15 years as a result of biotechnology and information technology advances. US yields are already 10 per cent above those in Britain which are, themselves, higher than elsewhere in Europe. With regard to crops, moreover, continuing research on nitrogen fixation in cereals, disease and pest resistance, and photosynthetic efficiency all point to huge potential improvements in productivity.

It is above all, however, the uncertainty and apprehension regarding steps that may be taken to curb production which has engendered the crisis feeling in the industry. It is an uncertainty which has been compounded by public disquiet on environmental issues, animal welfare, diet and health, and so forth. Whilst it is not the purpose of this paper to give attention to these wider issues it is important to emphasise the way in which they heighten farmers' fears and provide the farming lobby with yet more evidence of the critical political climate which it faces. The crisis is thus as much one concerning political and ideological legitimation as economic or social change and we continue by focusing on one particular instance of the crisis which illustrates such political, as well as economic and social, aspects: the impact of quotas in the dairy sector.

MILK QUOTAS

On 31 March 1984 the Council of Ministers approved the immediate introduction of milk quotas. The reaction of the industry was one of surprise and horror. In a letter to UK producers the Ministry of Agriculture described the decision as a 'seismic shock'. However there had been warning signs. Some sort of quota policy had been on the Commission's agenda since the mid-1970s, and when the time came the existing regulations for the co-responsibility levy did actually provide the legal basis for the imposition of quotas (Tsinisizelis, 1985). Production quotas were first mooted publicly in a Commission report of September 1978, although the report's favoured option was price restraint (COM 78). In both 1980 and 1981 the Commission proposed a supplementary levy to apply to milk supplied above a reference level of production (COM 80; Howe, 1985), but the Council of Ministers rejected the proposals. The co-responsibility levy, introduced for milk in 1977, acted as a kind of 'covert price reduction' (Hill, B. E. 1984) or added cost which farmers were expected to absorb as a contribution towards the costs of storing surplus production and, supposedly, towards measures that might increase the size of the market for dairy products. The failure of the Council of Ministers to set the levy high enough to have an impact upon production levels is a root cause of the need for quotas.

In 1982 a temporary decline in surplus stocks coupled with a sharp drop in farm incomes persuaded the Commission to propose a 9 per cent increase in the target price for milk in the 1982/83 year. In the event the Council adopted a 10.5 per cent increase and a 2.33 per cent increase the following year. At the same time a guarantee threshold based on 1981 milk production levels plus 0.5 per cent was adopted in an attempt to limit further increases in production, but with no clear policy for penalising those who might transgress this threshold the policy was doomed to failure. In fact all it did was to reduce slightly the overall level of prices. Milk output continued to increase. With the failure of this measure, quotas provided the only alternative to massive and politically unacceptable price cuts. Whereas with hindsight the inevitability of milk quotas might seem obvious it was not at the time so apparent to producers, their representative organisations or indeed, it seems, the Ministry itself.

It has usually been assumed that the Ministry and the farming bodies have been adept at monitoring, and even shaping, developments in Brussels. However, on this issue the House of Commons Agriculture Committee (1984) has strongly condemned them for a lack of foresight:

> We believe that the problems which the United Kingdom's dairy farmers now face were exacerbated by the inexplicable lack of foresight of those who should have guarded their interests. It is quite evident to us that few British officials believed that the Council of Ministers would adopt a policy of quotas in 1984; and the Ministry, the National Farmers' Union and the Milk Marketing Boards were not prepared for negotiations in Brussels on the basis of quotas, and in this regard have failed the farming industry.

The information gathered by the Committee, however, provides only limited evidence to support such a conclusion. Oral evidence was received only from Michael Jopling, the then Minister of Agriculture, accompanied by two officials, and the putative 'lack of foresight' by the NFU or the Milk Marketing Boards (MMBs) can only be obliquely inferred from his evidence. It is not surprising then that the Ministry, the NFU and the MMBs all responded sharply to the Committee's criticisms. Both the Board and the NFU provided evidence of actions taken in the months immediately prior to quota imposition. It is important to note, however, that these mostly involved behind-the-scenes negotiations and information gathering. The NFU and the English and Welsh MMB avoided public debate on quotas. The publicity given to the possibility of quotas by the three Scottish Milk Marketing Boards provides something of an exception to this pattern.

The crisis atmosphere engendered by the sudden imposition of quotas was therefore exacerbated by the ignorance of producers and their lack of forewarning of what was to be visited upon them. In consequence much of the initial furore was directed at the NFU, the Ministry and the MMBs for their apparent lack of preparedness, and accusations of betrayal and incompetence abounded. The speed with which quotas had to be implemented appeared to confirm such indictments, though the same organisations acquitted themselves remarkably well in establishing the detailed administration of the quotas, notwithstanding a number of contentious issues. The crisis was principally one of legitimation. The NFU and MMB had been proceeding along well-established corporatist lines.[5] No doubt, in time, the NFU, in particular, would have begun the process of selling a particular package to its members, or, of explaining to members the concessions which the Union had won in the light of inevitable restrictions on members' freedom. However the uncharacteristic speed with which the Council of Ministers acted precluded such a carefully orchestrated presentation and the Union and Ministry were left in the unenviable position of having to explain a retrospectively applied policy, which at first sight seemed to pose such intolerable burdens as to threaten the very survival of UK dairy farming.[6] Small wonder that farmer protest groups sprang up all over the country and with particular vigour in Wales and the West. The Farmers' Union of Wales vehemently condemned the speed and manner of imposition and bitterly lamented the likely consequences for West Wales dairy farmers – the smallest producers in the UK outside of Northern Ireland which was accorded special treatment under quota regulations. Even a number of local authorites, notably Devon and Dyfed, though lacking specific responsibilities in this field since the outset of the Second World War, entered the fray.

The worst fears of the farmers' groups concerning the economic consequences of quotas proved to be unfounded, although further rounds of cuts in quota might have more drastic affects. For one thing, producers showed some alacrity in implementing the changes in farm management necessary to cope with quotas. The special cases procedure, for all its inadequacies, also ensured sensible adjustments in quota allocations for a number of really hard-pressed producers, and the first Outgoers Scheme offered relatively generous compensation. None of these ameliorative arrangements was available either for hired farm workers or for businesses and their employees in the ancillary sectors. To cope with quotas farmers were encouraged to limit their inputs of bought-in feedstuffs and to take a careful look at all their costs, including labour. Thus farm workers, the manufacturers of compound feed and milking machinery, and workers in the dairy processing industry all suffered. The number of those employed in the compound feed sector declined from 16 to 12.5 thousand between 1983 and 1987 (BBC Radio: Farming Today, 23 November 1987). A survey of dairy farms carried out by the MMB showed that the number of full-time hired farm workers declined by 7 per cent between 1983 and 1985. There was no change in the number of full-time farmers and family workers, although the survey did not cover dairy producers who had gone out of dairying.[7] To some extent then, the crisis was diverted away from the farmers to other sectors of the rural economy or class groupings in agriculture. Michael Jopling was continually and unsuccessfully pressed by Labour members of the House of Commons Agriculture Committee to provide compensation for workers in these other sectors.

In a more complicated manner the crisis has also been diverted even within the farming sector away from the well-established dairy farmers to the less well-endowed and, particularly, to those wishing to enter milk production. One of the main concerns of economists and of the industry has been the means by which quotas might be transferred. Quota trading has been accomplished in two ways in the UK, both of which appear technically to be outside the terms of the European Commission regulations, which permit transfer of quota between farmers only through the purchase or secure leasing of land to which quota is attached.[8] In this way any notional market-value of quota would have been confined to the premium paid for land which carried a quota allocation. This went against the economic efficiency arguments of economists in the UK (Burrell, 1986; Harvey, 1984; Hubbard, 1986) and it soon became clear that attempts to circumvent these conditions would be sought. The first type of trading loophole developed was through an 'official' annual leasing scheme; the second, which, though not administered by the MMBs, has received their sanction, and has been through the direct sale of quota.

Under the EEC and UK regulations the MMBs were given a significant responsibility in the administration of quotas: one of the concessions written into the regulations for which Michael Jopling claimed credit. Even more importantly, the Ministry delegated further government responsibilities to the Boards, for which the Board receives payment from government. As one official of the English and Welsh MMB explained to us, 'we were keen to do it, if we were paid, so as to get the best deal for the producers.' The Board has undoubtedly seen one aspect of achieving a good deal as ensuring the greatest possible freedom for quota transfer. The role of the

MMB in policy implementation has clearly involved shifts in policy content away from the original spirit of the regulations. This is no mere technicality but has considerable ramifications for the restructuring of the industry creating what one observer has called a 'Fat Cats Club' (Croft, 1986). By countenancing relatively free quota transfer, and thus the establishment of a market for quotas, the MMB is undoubtedly serving the interests of its larger members. Superficially this development also allows for first-time purchases, but it actually makes entry into the industry considerably harder, for the high market value of quota is a formidable additional barrier to new entrants. Johnson has estimated that milk quotas, at current prices, are worth $3 billion ['billion' here and hereafter is equal to 1000 million in English usage] on the UK agricultural balance sheet, which is equivalent to one sixth of the value of all land and nearly half of the total value of all livestock (Johnson, 1986). Moreover the market for quotas has fatally compromised the second Outgoers Scheme, where the payments offered do not begin to compete with market value for quota. Thus the Ministry's half-hearted intention to use released quota for new entrants has foundered on the rock of the MMB's particular interpretation of self-interest. These arrangements are in sharp contrast to those adopted in France, where formally no quota trading is permitted, and where a comprehensive outgoers scheme has allowed some quota reallocation which has been administered through local farmer committees. One country, therefore, has established a social and administrative mechanism for reallocation; the other, a market mechanism.

Turning now to the producers' response to quotas, the main advice initially followed by most producers was to sacrifice high yields per cow for more efficient production of less milk. MMB and MAFF advisers recommended a reduction in the use of bought-in high protein concentrated cake and better utilisation and management of grassland. In the event the response of producers was immediate: the average cake use per cow dropped by 30 per cent in nine months and, more significantly, margins actually improved. This gave farmers more confidence and in the second year after quotas were introduced (1985/86) concentrate use recovered somewhat. Margins per cow, per hectare and over concentrates all increased significantly in the year ending Spring 1986 (Poole et al., 1986). Increases in overheads, however, eroded some of the benefit of these achievements, and profits – although returning to the levels of 1980–81 – were significantly lower, in real terms, than in the late 1970s (ibid.).

The response of producers was by no means uniform from farm to farm, however. Clearly such sudden changes of management required technical and managerial skills and capacities not possessed to the same degree by all producers. Holdings also varied in their adaptability. The MMB survey shows how smaller producers (0–50 cows) were slower to respond to the recommended changes in farm policy than the medium (50–100 cows) or large (100 + cows) producers. For example, whereas 67.5 per cent of large producers altered their purchases of feeds, only 40.6 per cent of small producers did so. In addition 19.5 per cent of large producers modified the size of their hired labour, force compared to only 4.1 per cent of small producers. Higher proportions of smaller producers were producing below quota and were contemplating ceasing milk production altogether.

By 1986 milk producers had much to be thankful for, especially in comparison with some of the difficulties faced by other sectors of agriculture. The profitability, and with it confidence, engendered by two years' experience of quotas is reflected both in the keen market for leasing or purchasing of milk quotas and in the relative buoyancy of the price of land with quota compared to the slump in land prices generally. Few would have predicted in April 1984 that milk quotas would be seen as such a success story so soon after their imposition. Significantly, in Devon – the county with the greatest number of dairy farmers and the largest NFU membership – the county NFU branch produced a policy paper in March 1986 arguing for a Central Agricultural Authority, with producer and government representation, to administer production controls on all commodities.

Consideration of the need for controls on the output of other commodities was hastened by the ramifications of milk quotas, particularly in the phenomenon of a rolling surplus as affected farmers switched to beef, sheep and arable cropping to sustain their incomes. The MMB survey, comparing 1983/84 with 1985/86, found that a degree of enterprise diversification had taken place among dairy farmers. Cereal acreage, for example, had increased by 5.4 per cent, a particularly notable growth considering that dairy farmers were also responding to the need to place more emphasis on grassland production, and that the total area farmed only increased by 1 per cent. But the main growth came in the livestock sector. Whereas the number of dairy cows declined by 2.9 per cent the number of beef stock was up by 18.3 per cent, sheep by 16 per cent, pigs by 28.3 per cent and poultry by 22.3 per cent. The figures demonstrate the dangers that single commodity solutions pose with regard to knock-on problems of overproduction in other sectors. Most of the growth in pigs and poultry occurred on farms with existing pig and poultry enterprises, particularly on the mixed farms of the West Midlands. Unfortunately the survey sought no information on non-agricultural forms of diversification. While such activities are likely to be very limited at present it would have been interesting to have had some indication of attitudes from such a large sample of farmers. The long term implications for land use and the rural economy of efforts to curb overproduction – not only dairying but in other commodity sectors as well – are increasingly concentrating the minds of policy makers.

CONCLUSION: CHARACTERISING THE CRISIS

We began by saying that in some ways talk of a farm crisis in Britain is misplaced. And yet it might reasonably be thought that the considerable catalogue of evidence we have presented more than warrants just that terminology which we were initially reluctant to use. We must now seek to resolve this apparent contradiction. Not surprisingly, perhaps, our assessment focuses particularly on the contradictory ways in which the economic, political and ideological elements of agriculture's present disquiet are articulated one with another.

The crisis, fundamentally, is an economic one. It is the escalating public cost of agricultural support necessitated, not least, by the expenditure entailed in accumulating, storing and disposing of surplus production, which is at the heart of the industry's difficulties. At the level of the farm enterprise, meanwhile, the squeeze on farm incomes, falling land values and disturbing trends in indebtedness speak similarly of severely straitened economic circumstances. But because agriculture has, for so long, been an extensively supported industry the present crisis presents itself in the form of – to use Claus Offe's term – a 'crisis of crisis management' (Offe, 1984). Crises issue from unresolved steering problems and their defining feature, as both Offe and Habermas (1976) have argued, follows from the way in which actual or prospective structural change threatens social identity. We have argued elsewhere that the farm crisis is also a crisis for the representative structures in agriculture (Cox *et al.*, 1987) and it is to such considerations that we must now turn. For the crisis is at once political and ideological as well as economic and its resolution may demand nothing less than a new relationship between farmers and the state.

Making sense of the farm crisis demands an appreciation of the contradictions both within and between the dominant Thatcherite political philosophy in Britain and the strongly productionist ideology which has prevailed within the agricultural industry during the post-war period. The profound antipathy between 'New Right' thinking and corporatist politics[9] is readily apparent and this has meant, most notably, the exclusion of producer interests and especially, organised labour from a strategic role in macroeconomic policy-making. The resilience of corporatism at the meso, or sectoral, level should not be underestimated however. Such arrangements have survived and, in some cases, even flourished reflecting in part the strength and conti-nuity of government–industry links in particular sectors. Elsewhere, as Alan Cawson's study of teletext shows, international competitive pressures have prompted the development of such links (Cawson, 1986a, 1986b). Some aspects of Thatcherite reform can themselves serve actually to promote meso-corporatism at the sectoral level as the emphasis on 'rolling back the frontiers of the state' and asserting the primacy of the market leads to the development of self-regulatory mechanisms which embody corporatist relationships. Thus, as we have seen, the introduction of milk quotas strengthened the role of the Milk Marketing Board, itself a classic corporatist agency. Whilst in the sphere of land use politics the promotion of voluntary co-operation and self-regulation as the solution to the problems of the relationship between agriculture and conservation has further ex-tended corporatist relations.

Thus, although it is evidently the case that at the level of rhetoric Thatcherite pronouncements are often deeply uncongenial to the agricultural industry, other contradictions within present day Tory-ism limit the scope for the sort of onslaught on agriculture that has been visited upon other traditional industries in which the state had become deeply involved, such as steel, ship building, coal mining and car manufacture, though such a fate was envisaged by some when John MacGregor, previously a Chief Secretary to the Treasury, became Minister of Agriculture in June 1987. Agriculture and the countryside have long occupied a special place in the pantheon of traditional Tory values and, at the level of symbolism certainly, rural areas remain emblematic of the Tory heartland. But the impulse to relax planning controls and force farmers increasingly to accept the dictates of the market to survive finds little favour among middle-class Conservative voters who have moved to the countryside and are invariably keen on rural preservation. In other ways, too, shire paternalists find themselves radically at odds with right-wing free marketeers. Ideolgical and electoral considerations, therefore, place bounds on the impact neo-conservative radicalism might have on agriculture.

In addition, the EEC context of policy-making greatly constrains the possibilities of autonomous action in this field by member states and it must be emphasised that Britain is locked into a strongly corporatist form of decision-making on farming issues within the European Community. So, although extensive farm support remains a matter of considerable embarrassment to the Government as they are continually attacked by right-wing backbenchers and think-tanks for their bearing on food surpluses, public expenditure levels and the liberalisation of world trade, the scope for manoeuvre is seldom more than limited. The Thatcherite offensive has, in short, had the effect of diminishing the legitimacy of agricultural support without seriously compromising established corporatist arrangements.

If there are notable contradictions within contemporary Toryism the fissures within the dominant agricultural ideology are no less readily apparent. The farmers' preferred self-image as individualistic entrepreneurs has arguably constrained the agricultural lobby's efforts to mount a vigorous collective defence of state support and protection for agriculture. The industry's identity, moreover, has in the post-war period been associated with the dominance of a productionist ideology much encouraged by the state. Accordingly the indicators of success – its yield and productivity performance, market responsiveness and contribution to import substitution – to which it typically draws attention reflect the hegemonic status of big farm efficiency arguments. Welfare and conservationist arguments have traditionally, by comparison, been conspicuous only by their absence.

The recent sustained attention directed at the excesses of agricultural policy has greatly undermined the plausibility of this productionist ideology though. The farming and landowning lobby has reacted to this attrition by working to embrace alternative ideologies and demonstrate a commitment to rural welfare and conservation. But adjustment is not easy and the effort is handicapped by the legacy of the productionist ideology ingrained as it is in the outlook and behaviour of most farmers.

The difficulties of effecting such fundamental change in basic orientation are evidenced by the NFU's initial reaction to the introduction of milk quotas which was to suggest that small dairy farmers be removed from the industry. It was not long before fitful efforts were being made to develop a policy for small farmers but, somewhat indicatively, progress was stymied by definitional disputes as to what constitutes a small farmer. The Union's ambivalence towards welfare considerations has been evident in its opposition to the extension of production quotas to other commodities and preference for the flexi-quotas which are much less likely to discriminate against big producers and which constitute less of a constraint on the market pressures within the industry. It is evident, as well, how the agricultural lobby's relentless redefinition of the farm crisis in terms of set-aside and surplus land for the most part avoids addressing the social dimensions of the problem. Meanwhile, the assiduous promotion of alternative crops and new markets itself helps to refurbish the productionist ideology (Cox *et al.*, 1986).

Thus, although there is widespread recognition within the industry that fundamental change is unavoidable and an increasingly evident resignation that the post-war identity of British agriculture cannot be sustained, it can hardly yet be said that the agricultural world has been 'turned upside down'. Rather, as we have indicated, the net effect of a range of contradictory pressures has been to generate a somewhat piecemeal and opportunistic approach to reform and remedial measures. Not surprisingly, therefore, present trends are themselves quite contradictory with greater reliance on free market mechanisms in some areas accompanying extensions of corporatist relations in others and stronger state intervention elsewhere.

Such incoherence is, perhaps, symptomatic of the loss of a broad social rationale and consensus for agricultural support and that, in turn, accounts for the chronic uncertainty and apprehension within the industry. The crisis is one which presents itself first and foremost as a crisis of crisis management and that is why spokesmen for the industry are calling, principally, for a clear sense of direction. Speaking at a pre-election meeting, John Norris, President of the Country Landowners' Association, called for Government to give a clear lead to agriculture and some indication of a longer term strategy was one of three priorities for action by Government communicated to the new Minister of Agriculture by the NFU on the 16 June. Most pointedly indicative of such concern, though, was the way NFU President Simon Gourlay sought to explain the background to the vote of no confidence in Government policy for agriculture at the Union's February AGM:

It was not a vote that there isn't enough taxpayers' money being spent on agriculture. It was a vote of unease that so much is being spent that is doing so little good. It was a vote that Government –

and the EC Commission – have no cohesive longer term strategy to surmount today's and tomorrow's acute problems. (NFU Press Release, 17 February 1987)

Notes

We gratefully acknowledge the support of the ESRC for the research on agricultural policy on which this paper is based.
1. The figures used in this section are drawn from three sources: MAFF, 1986; Britton *et al.*, 1980; Burrell *et al.*, 1984. Unless otherwise stated the figures are derived from one of these sources.
2. These were the reviews for 1958, 1960, 1962, 1963, 1965, 1969, 1970 and 1971. In addition, the NFU merely 'noted' the 1968 price review.
3. Useful critiques of conventional farm income figures and alternative suggestions are contained in the following: Hill, B., 1982; Hill, B., 1984; Hill, G. P., 1984; Lund and Watson, 1981; National Audit Office, 1987.
4. A co-responsibility levy is a payment made by producers on each tonne of grain sold to commercial outlets. The measure was introduced in time for the 1986 harvest. Repayments of levy have been made to smaller producers in the UK.
5. On corporatism in British agriculture see Cox *et al.*, 1985, 1986, 1987; Grant, 1983.
6. It is perhaps significant that, while British farmers' leaders somewhat lamely and vaguely blamed Brussels and the Council of Ministers for the quota decision, farmers' leaders in other EEC countries deflected criticism to Margaret Thatcher and the British Government's insistence on a budget rebate and constraints on CAP expenditure. See, for example, Evans, 1987.
7. A summary of the findings from the MMB survey was presented in *Milk Producer*, September 1986, pp. 24–5. We are grateful to the Board for releasing further details of this survey to us.
8. According to the regulations quota is initially allocated to producers and is then ascribed to the holding.
9. We use corporatism as a middle-range theory not to characterise whole societies or state forms, but to refer to a distinctive style of interest intermediation in which the state operates in conjuction with representative organisations based on the division of labour within society. What distinguishes corporatism, therefore, is the salience of producer groups and their capacity to regulate their own constituencies and reach bargained agreements with state agencies. The achievement of a degree of representational monopoly is clearly also crucial.

Bibliography

Ball, R. M. (1987), 'Intermittent labour forms in U.K. agriculture: some implications for rural areas', *Journal of Rural Studies*, 3 (2), 133–50.

Britton, D. K. (1977), 'Some explorations in the analysis of long-term changes in the structure of agricultre', *Journal of Agricultural Economics*, 28 (3), 197–209.

Britton, D. K., A. M. Burrell, B. Hill and D. Ray (1980), *Statistical Handbook of UK Agriculture*, Wye College.

Buckwell, A. E., D. R. Harvey, K. T. Thompson and K. A. Parton (1982), *The Costs of the Common Agricultural Policy* (London: Croom Helm).

Burrell, A. (1986), *Milk Quotas in England and Wales: Under- and Over-Quota Production in 1984 and the Scope for Quota Leasing*, Wye College: Discussion Paper in Agricultural Policy 86/1.

Burrell, A. M., B. Hill and J. Medland (1984), *A Statistical Handbook of UK Agriculture* (London: Macmillan).

Cawson, A. (1986a), 'Meso-corporatism and industrial policy: the anatomy of a success story', *ESRC Corporatism and Accountability Newsletter*, 4, 1–3.

Cawson, A. (1986b), 'Hostile brothers: the role of firms in the politics of industry sectors', Paper presented to the XI World Congress of Sociology, New Delhi.

Commission of the European Communities (1978), *COM (78) 430 final*.

Commission of the European Communities (1980), *COM (80) 800 final*.

Commission of the European Communities (1981), *COM (81) 608 final*.

Countryside Commission (1986), 'What really is happening to the landscape', *Countryside Commission News*, 23, 4–5.

Cox, G., A. Flynn, P. Lowe and M. Winter (1986), 'The alternative land-use debate: where are the conservationists?', *Ecos*, 7 (3), 16–21.

Cox, G., P. Lowe and M. Winter (1985), 'Changing directions in agricultural policy: corporatist arrangements in production and conservation policies', *Sociologia Ruralis*, 25 (2), 130–54.

Cox, G., P. Lowe and M. Winter (1986), 'From state direction to self regulation: the historical development of corporatism in British agriculture', *Policy and Politics*, 14 (4), 475–90.

Cox, G., P. Lowe and M. Winter (1987), 'Farmers and the state: a crisis for corporatism', *Political Quarterly*, 58 (1), 73–81.

Croft, A. R. (1986), 'Address', Tenant Farmers' Association Regional Conference, *Quotas, Finance, Rent*, Taunton.

Davies, G. D. D., W. J. Dunford and S. T. Morris (1971), *Aspects of Farm Financial Structure*, University of Exeter Agricultural Economics Unit, Report No. 185.

Errington, A. (1986), 'Employment', in G. M. Craig, J. L. Jollans and A. Korbey (eds), *The Case for Agriculture: An Independent Assessment*, 59–100. Reading: Centre for Agricultural Strategy.

Evans, E. S. (1987), 'Protest and representation among French mountain-zone dairy farmers', *Sociologia Ruralis*, 27 (2) 149–65.

Grant, W. (1981), 'The politics of the green pound', *Journal of Common Market Studies*, 19 (4), 313–29.

Grant, W. (1983), 'The National Farmers' Union: the classic case of incorporation?', in D. Marsh (ed.), *Pressure Politics* (London: Junction Books).

Habermas, J. (1976), Legitimation Crisis (London: Heinemann Educational).

134   *The International Farm Crisis*

Harvey, D. R. (1984), 'Saleable quotas, compensation policy and the reform of the CAP', in K. J. Thomson and R. M. Warren (eds), *Price and Market Policies in European Agriculture* (University of Newcastle) 191–204.
Hill, B. (1982), 'Concepts and measurement of the incomes, wealth, and economic well-being of farmers', *Journal of Agricultural Economics*, 33 (3), 311–24.
Hill, B. (1984), 'Information on farmers' incomes: data from Inland Revenue sources', *Journal of Agricultural Economics* 35 (1), 39–50.
Hill, B. E. (1984), *The Common Agricultural Policy: Past, Present and Future* (London: Methuen).
Hill, G. P. (1984), 'Measuring farm income under conditions of inflation: the gains from borrowing', *Journal of Agricultural Economics*, 35 (1), 51–60.
House of Commons Agriculture Committee (1984), *The Implementation of Dairy Quotas*, First Report Session 1984–85, C 14 (London: HMSO).
Howarth, R. W. (1985), *Farming for Farmers* (London: Institute for Economic Affairs).
Howe, K. (1985), 'Quotas for Milk: Causes and Consequences', *Countryside Planning Yearbook*, 6, 35–252.
Hubbard, L. J. (1986), 'The price of dairy quotas in England and Wales'. Paper presented to Twelfth European Seminar of Agricultural Economists, Helsinki.
Johnson, C. (1986), 'Counting the farmers' assets', *Lloyds Bank Economic Bulletin* No. 95.
Lund, P. J. and J. M. Watson (1981) 'Agricultural incomes: a review of the data and recent trends', *Economic Trends*, 338.
MAFF (1975), *Food from Our Own Resources*, Cmnd. 6020 (London: HMSO).
MAFF (1979), *Farming and the Nation*, Cmnd. 7458 (London: HMSO).
MAFF (1986), *Annual Review of Agriculture 1986*, Cmnd. 9708 (London: HMSO).
National Audit Office (1987), *The Measurement of Farming Incomes*, Report by the Comptroller and Auditor General (London: HMSO).
Offe, C. (1984), 'Crises of crisis management: elements of a political crisis theory ', In *Contradictions of the Welfare State* (London: Hutchinson) 35–65.
Poole, A. H., J. A. Craven and S. J. Mabey (1986), *An Analysis of Farm Management Services Costed Dairy Farms 1985–6*, Milk Marketing Board FMS Information Unit Report No. 50. Thames Ditton.
Pooley, P. (1986), 'UK Attitudes towards the CAP – the view from Brussels', *Midland Bank Farm Management Lecture*, Seale-Hayne College, Newton Abbot, Devon.
Tsinisizelis, M. (1985), *The Politics of the Common Agricultural Policy: A Study of Interest Group Politics*, Ph.D. Thesis, University of Manchester.
Winter, M. (1986), *The Survival and Re-Emergence of Family Farming: A Study of the Holsworthy Area of West Devon*. Unpublished Ph.D. Thesis, Open University.
Wormell, P. (1978), *Anatomy of Agriculture* (London: Harrap).

6 Approaching Limits: Farming Contraction and Environmental Conservation in the UK

Clive Potter

European agriculture is finally encountering limits which have been anticipated for years, but inevitable for decades. The European Community's Common Agricultural Policy (CAP) faces two separate but related crises, one budgetary, the other technological and economic. The first of these has long exercised the minds of policy-makers, as farm spending has continued to outpace any expansion in the Community's 'Own Resources'. Yet this is merely a symptom of a deeper crisis, a crisis which has arisen because, in a fundamental sense, European agriculture is in long-term decline. The industry faces a level of consumer demand which is static or even declining for long term rather than cyclical reasons (Duchene et al., 1986). The fact is that despite an annual increase in output of up to 2 per cent since the early 1970s, internal consumer demand for most farm products has grown by a sluggish 0.5 per cent over the same period (EC, 1987). The CAP, by guaranteeing a market for everything farmers could produce, has effectively disguised this secular over-capacity beneath a dynamic of expansion. At considerable and mounting cost to consumers and taxpayers through intervention buying and export subsidies,it has artificially stretched the limits. Yet at the same time it has accelerated technological change in the industry by financing research and development, and furnishing a climate of security which has encouraged farmers to adopt highly productive farming techniques and new plant and machinery. The resulting boost to farm output has only served to exacerbate the overproduction problem and the costly build up of surpluses. Farm spending has rapidly inflated as structural surpluses, the most visible indication of overcapacity, have increased.

The budgetary crisis means that, for the first time, this disguise is being stripped away. There is the stark realisation that, without new frontiers for expansion within the European Community and, in a long-term sense, on world markets, European agriculture finally faces insuperable limits. The expectation is for reductions in farm support, accompanied by longer-term policies aimed at restructuring. Regarding the latter, there is agreement that if the problem of overcapacity is to be remedied, then land, labour or capital will need to be moved out of the industry. More controversy surrounds which of these should be given priority. Howarth (1985), for instance, expresses the opinion that the problem ultimately reduces to a problem of demand and supply for farmers, rather than for farm products. Others support the withdrawal of land through programmes of land diversion on the American model (Potter, 1986a). What is becoming increasingly clear is the profound implication of any such long term process of restructuring, whether achieved directly through the Community's structural policies or indirectly through its market policies, not just for the farming community but also for the role of the farmer in society and the future evolution of the European 'countryside'. Of particular significance in the UK is the coincidence of this approach to limits with an upsurge in public concern about the rural environment and its conservation. This paper considers how agricultural restructuring promises to transform this important debate, with the attempts being made by policy-makers to resolve conflicts between agriculture and the environment becoming increasingly bound up with, and conditional upon, solutions to the macroeconomic problems facing European agriculture. It shows how farming contraction could alter the appearance and ecology of the British countryside and, more significantly in the context of a policy analysis, change the framework within which the debate itself will be conducted.

THE UK COUNTRYSIDE DEBATE

A little thought confirms, of course, that the crisis of overcapacity and the rise of concern surrounding agriculture and the environment are merely two sides of the same coin; related and inevitable features of the economic growth process. The same rising real incomes which had led to a levelling-off in the income-inelastic demand for farm products has also heightened demand for income-elastic 'positional goods' such as unspoilt countryside, quietness, space and privacy (Hirsh, 1978) and encouraged individuals, through membership of environmental pressure groups, to articulate an 'option demand' for beautiful landscapes or particular recreational experiences (Bishop, 1982). Indeed, this growing concern with rural conservation has been described by one commentator as 'probably the most important movement of public feeling since the second world war' (Thomas, 1983, 15). Lowe and Goyder (1983) demonstrate how an upsurge of environmentalism has been reflected in expanding membership of environmental groups and an increasingly effective articulation of 'green' issues in local and national politics.

There is therefore some irony in the fact that the CAP should have perfected the ability of farmers to increase the output of surplus farm products, often at the direct expense of those same countryside qualities (amenity, landscape and wilderness) which the public now value so highly. By dint of culture, history and geography, the United Kingdom was the first member state in the EEC to recognise a new contradiction to add to those already facing capital intensive agriculture; namely that between the increasingly effective quantitative production of surplus farm products and the progressively less effective qualitative 'production' of countryside. As will be shown, this was to become significant given the role of rather different Community perceptions and institutions in shaping future policy in this area.

Indeed, the agriculture and environment debate, seemingly a European phenomenon of the 1980s, dates back in the UK to the early 1960s, when public attention was alerted to the 'chemical revolution on the land' that was by then well in progress. Concern was expressed by ecologists about the long term and cumulative ecological effects of persistent pesticides in agriculture. Studies from the government's agency on nature conservation, the Nature Conservancy, revealed dramatic declines in the populations of top predators, like the peregrine falcon, due to the use of organo-chlorines (Hooper, 1984). By the early 1970s this concern had broadened to the loss of habitat like moorland, heathland and ancient woodland due to agricultural intensification and reclamation. The issues became more politicised as influential pressure groups like the Council for the Protection of Rural England (CPRE) publicised the irreversible nature of these losses. Long-running controversies such as the ploughing of moorland in the Exmoor National Park (MacEwen and MacEwen, 1982) meant that the problems of conflicting land use began to receive more attention than environmental pollution or contamination from intensive farming practices. A general concern with amenity and the loss of traditional agricultural landscapes in the wider countryside was another peculiarly British feature of the debate at this time. In 1974, the Countryside Commission published its 'New Agricultural Landscapes' study which showed how agricultural intensification and land improvement was sweeping away many of the features of the farmed landscape, particularly the landscape of lowland England (Countryside Commission, 1974). Hedges, woodland and hedgerow trees were all being removed at an accelerating rate as farmers shifted away from the mixed farming systems which justified their existence. Later, in 1977, the Nature Conservancy Council underscored the extent of habitat change, concluding that existing policies which emphasised site safeguard, rather than integrated land use, were inadequate to stem the tide of damage and loss (Nature Conservancy Council, 1977). Despite this, the Wildlife and Countryside Act 1981, itself largely a response to the public outcry about habitat loss, furthered the trend towards protecting conservation sites rather than the wider countryside (Adams, 1986). By 1984 the Nature Conservancy Council could reveal that, *inter alia*, only 3 per cent of the lowland neutral grasslands which had existed in 1945 had been left undamaged by agricultural intensification and that ancient lowland woodland had been reduced in extent by between 30 and 50 per cent (Nature Conservancy Council, 1984).

It is particularly significant in the context of the present discussion that the public debate about these changes should have developed during a period of steady farming expansion. An expansionary climate has influenced the debate in several important respects, imposing constraints on the scope for policy reform and affecting the attitudes and perceptions of conservationists and interest groups such as the National Farmers' Union (NFU) and the Country Landowners' Association (CLA). With agriculture in the ascendancy, conservation agencies like the NCC and national park authorities found themselves retreating from the objective of achieving an integrated use of land in the wider countryside to a more defensive role linked to the designation of conservation sites and sensitive areas. Retaining a privileged status as 'permitted development', agricultural operations remained beyond the reach of the planning system throughout this period of rapid agricultural change. On the Nature Conservancy Council's own admission, nature conservation policies had by 1984 been 'compressed into a narrow responsibility for the protection and management of wild flora, fauna and physical features' (NCC, 1984,

49). This was far removed from the broad and spatially unrestricted vision of resource conservation intended by the founding fathers of British nature conservation in the 1940s. The debate became polarised as advocates of a voluntary approach to settling countryside conflicts were ranged against radical conservationists, who were concerned to regulate the actions of individual farmers (Lowe, *et al.*, 1986).

Nevertheless, by the mid 1980s the focus of the debate had begun to shift from farmers and sites to the agricultural policies which were identified as driving the intensification process. Influential commentaries such as those by Bowers and Cheshire (1983) argued that the problem of habitat loss was inextricably bound up with reform of the CAP. Cheshire makes the point well when he comments that 'the problem is not one of ill will and ignorance but of a system which systematically establishes financial inducements to erode the countryside, offers no rewards to offset market failures and increases the penalties (by way of foregone profits or higher net costs) on farmers who may want to farm in a way which enhances and enriches the rural environment' (Cheshire, 1985, 15). This marked an important breakthrough in perception, promoting the conservation problem to the status of a policy issue, and specifically, an agricultural policy issue. It was a breakthrough which would not be made until much later by other member states in parallel debates about agriculture and the environment. According to Nowiki (1985), for instance, the role of the CAP in fuelling the arterial drainage of wetlands in France in the last decade had until recently been ignored or disregarded. Unlike environmental groups in the UK, those in France do not perceive the crucial connection as being between agricultural change and environmental damage, preferring to identify national agencies and the techniques of land re-allocation as the main culprits of habitat loss.

Despite this advance, the fact that British farming was still on an expansionist path meant that the opportunities for remedial action and reform were still necessarily restricted and incremental. The attention of countryside reformers was constrained at this stage to arguing for improved incentives for investments by farmers and in lobbying for a diversion of funds away from environmentally damaging operations and into 'conservation-friendly' ones. An experimental scheme was set up in the Peak District National Park, for instance (Parker, 1984), which provided reward payments to farmers who undertook to carry out habitat management tasks. There was a particular emphasis placed on the implementation of community policy, particularly structural policy directives, by national agriculture departments and the scope for improving the management of the countryside through a more liberal and environmentally-orientated interpretation of these same directives.

The Ministry of Agriculture's (MAFF's) interpretation of Less Favoured Areas Directive (268/75) was roundly criticised by certain conservationists (MacEwan and Sinclair, 1983) for its narrow, productionist slant. Farmers within areas subject to a 'permanent natural handicap' are eligible for payments on each of their cows and sheep (headage payments) and benefit from preferential rates of capital grant on new investments. Unlike other member states, notably France, MAFF chooses to set headage payments at a fixed rate, regardless of natural handicap (Smith, 1985). This means that the system has tended to favour large scale farmers who had improved and reclaimed land while also providing powerful incentives for all farmers to overgraze upland habitats. Together with the system of premium payments under the Community's 'Sheepmeat regime', LFA policies have been criticised for intensifying the pressures for farm amalgamation and depopulation, contrary to the social and environmental rationale of the Less Favoured Areas Directive (MacEwan and MacEwan, 1982). At the same time, the Ministry's capital grant schemes were also being condemned for being restricted 'to the purposes of an agricultural business' and proposals were made to broaden their application (Potter, 1983). This phase of the debate came to a head in 1984 when new Structures Regulations were published by the European Commission, which placed more emphasis on environmental protection, cost reduction and energy conservation. It was regarded as a small but significant advance for conservationists, though as Revell (1985) commented soon after, the environmental measures seemed unlikely to receive the funding from member states that they deserved.

It was at this point that more powerful forces for change began to impinge on the debate, creating new opportunities for reform but also making the debate itself more complex and less self-contained. The mounting surpluses problem, particularly in the dairy sector where intervention stocks had continued to increase, meant that market policy would now also be subject to adjustment. The imposition of milk quotas in 1984 (See Cox *et al.*, this volume) and the agreement on budgetary discipline reached later the same year, appeared to signal a new resolve to come to grips with the budgetary crisis of the CAP. Nicholl (1986) comments that the Council decision on a quota system for milk was a new departure for the CAP, indicating as it did an intention to limit Community liability at the legislative end of the CAP.

Meanwhile, discussions within the EC about the longer term future for the CAP culminated in publication of 'Perspectives for the CAP' (EC, 1985b), a trenchant consultation paper which argued that agriculture, like any other sector in the economy, 'should be subject to the laws of supply and demand'. Optimism that this marked a turning point was admittedly tempered by the knowledge that the EC had already published no less than four other reform plans during the previous twelve years (EC, 1968; EC, 1973; EC, 1975; EC, 1982), all of them stressing the urgent need to bring farm spending under control by reducing farm output. 'Perspectives' though was more forthright in its vision of a more market-orientated CAP and a new set of relationships between farmers and society.

Despite this promise of reform, it seemed unlikely, even at this point, that the set of policy reforms in prospect would radicalise the options of conservationists. Many were by this time nonetheless lobbying for countryside conflicts to be resolved by reforms to market policy under the CAP, as well as to the nationally implemented structural schemes (CPRE, 1985). According to Griffen and Stoll (1984) a 'fundamental policy change' can be distinguished from an incremental one in terms of its ability to 'provide for new patterns of action and momentum' based on basic societal innovations (Griffen and Stoll, 1984, 36). By 1985, with discussions continuing in the wake of the 'green paper', it was becoming clear that the sort of CAP reform in prospect would fall short on this definition. As Fennell (1985, 274) comments, because of 'the overriding concern with budgetary costs, attempts to modify the CAP have concentrated on adjustments to the machinery through which it functions and have not dealt with fundamentals'. In support of this, Ritson and Fearne (1984) point out that more attention has focused on the instruments of policy and the way these are implemented than on the fundamental reformist question of 'what should the policy achieve for the people of the European Community?' (213). For thoughtful commentators like Baldock (1984), expeditious changes in the area of market policy came to be regarded as factors which would influence the nature of countryside change from outside the debate.

Nevertheless, the likelihood of such 'first round' adjustments to the CAP and their consequences in terms of farming contraction had already influenced the conduct of the British countryside debate in a number of decisive ways. It stimulated discussion and research about the desirability of retrenchment as a conservation strategy in its own right. Moreover, it meant that rural conservation issues could be linked for the first time to the long-standing problem of agricultural restructuring, with land use shifts and alternative land use emerging as serious possibilities. The proposition that farming contraction would be generally beneficial for the rural environment was one which was promoted strongly by commentators such as Bowers and Cheshire (1983). They reasoned, logically enough, that since the CAP had to a large extent fuelled the post-war loss of habitats, the dismantling of farm support should remove many of the economic incentives behind wetland drainage, woodland clearance and so on. The farm lobby was anxious to refute this, maintaining instead that the conservation of rural landscapes and habitats actually depends for its success on a prosperous agriculture (NFU, 1984). An interesting debate ensued about the relationship between farming prosperity and rural conservation and the sustainability of rural communities.

A simplistic standpoint, which was at first adopted by the farm lobby, was that only prosperous farmers invest in conservation management and that farm profitability must be sufficient to justify the expenditure incurred. In the words of the NFU, 'Conservation costs money and will inevitably receive a low priority unless the industry is in a satisfactory financial position . . . a farming community with extremely depressed incomes cannot be expected to meet the environmental goals of society at large' (NFU, 1984, 3).

The chief flaw in this argument is that it associates conservation with spending and investment and ignores the fact that inefficient and run-down farms are often reservoirs of conservation value. A more sophisticated standpoint, and one which appeared to be shared by conservationists and agriculturalists alike by the mid-1980s, was that the British countryside is essentially a managed countryside which must be farmed if it is to retain its interest and diversity in the form of 'arrested' climax vegetation and man-created landscapes (Countryside Commission, 1984). An important seminar convened by the Institute of European Environmental Policy and the CPRE early in 1985 considered these and other arguments in an attempt to answer the vexed question: 'Can the CAP fit the environment?' The response appeared to be a qualified 'yes', provided price cuts or direct production controls were accompanied by more direct measures aimed at managing farming change (Baldock and Conder, 1985). The seminar participants, who included civil servants and representatives from other member states, warned against complacent symmetrical reasoning concerning the respective environmental impact of farming expansion and farming contraction. The mere fact that high levels of price support had, by general agreement, contributed to that environmental damage in the past did not mean that simply reducing prices would put the process into reverse (Potter, 1985).

NEW PROCESSES OF COUNTRYSIDE CHANGE

Considered in more detail, the environmental effects of reduced farm support to British and European farmers are many and various. Environmental damage in the past has been linked to changes in both the structure of agriculture (in terms of the number and types of farmers) and to the pattern and methods of production – specifically, the degree of specialisation and intensification. Price cuts, the option favoured by the Commission to reduce surpluses, would affect both sets of factors in a number of ways to produce new processes of countryside change. Changes to the farming profile due to some farmers leaving the industry and others retaining and even increasing their land holding, is perhaps the most obvious way in which structural change, accelerated by price cuts, could affect the ecology and appearance of the countryside. Many commentators believe that real price cuts in the order of 30–35 per cent may be necessary to persuade farmers to reduce output and so alleviate the surpluses problem in the cereals sector (Thomson and Neville-Rolfe, 1984).

Under this scenario of falling product prices and their corollary, declining land values, several types of farms would become vulnerable, notably those facing high land finance changes in terms of rent, mortgage and bank loan repayments. Coleman and Traill (1984) make the ironic observation that any reversal of policy would lead to great financial problems for precisely those young, dynamic, high investing farmers who have been responsible for most of the recent capital investment which has contributed most to the industry's output growth. It has been estimated (House of Lords, 1985) that something like 10 per cent of 'main occupation' farmers could be faced with severe liquidity problems and even bankruptcy in these circumstances. At the same time, farmers without successors and nearing retirement could decide to give up farming altogether at this point. Either way, voluntarily or involuntarily, land will change hands, either in parcels or as whole farms. What is critical in environmental terms is the destination of this land. Within arable heartland areas, it is perfectly conceivable that land placed on the market by retiring or bankrupt farmers would be bought by better-placed and expansionist farmers, able and willing, even within a low price regime, to improve the land and rationalise the landscape. In the case of retirees, these transfers could involve parcels of land which had previously been extensively farmed and therefore possessing high conservation value. In the upland countryside, it is expected that land sold by farmers will often be purchased by private forestry companies, with damaging consequences for open habitat like moorland and heathland as areas are planted to conifers.

Alterations to the profile of the farming community due to new patterns of exit and entry created by policy retrenchment, will also have implications for the rural environment. It is the view of commentators like Cheshire (1985) that by inducing a strong growth in capital values, the CAP has encouraged a systematic transfer of management to individuals and financial institutions least sympathetic to conservation. This trend could be arrested with falling land values. At the same time, many family businesses with an interest in stewarding the land can be expected to survive in large numbers, particularly 'low-geared' owner occupiers. Part-time farmers are also expected to increase in number, cushioned by their other income sources (Gasson, 1985).

Changes to the pattern of agricultural production brought about by policy changes will have considerable environmental side-effects. It is widely accepted that even at world prices, few specialist producers in heartland areas would withdraw from cereal production. Indeed research conducted by the Centre for Agricultural Strategy for the Department of the Environment (CAS, 1986), suggests that a removal of price support under a 'free trade' scenario would have the perverse effect of increasing the cereal area, due to an improvement in returns to cereal production relative to lowland livestock enterprises. Meanwhile, at the opposite extreme, commentators expect continued support for farmers in the marginal upland countryside under the Community's Less Favoured Areas (LFAs) policy, given a social and environmental rationale for maintaining farmers on the land (Capstick, 1985). Consequently, many predict that it is within 'middle countryside', on land of medium suitability for arable production along the fringes of arable heartland areas in the English

Midlands, that most shifts in land use connected with enterprise changes can be expected. It is still unclear whether on balance these would be damaging or beneficial for the rural environment.

New processes of countryside change, linked more directly than before to movements of land between holdings and shifts between enterprises and land uses, can be expected if the European Commission is successful in pursuing a rigorous pricing policy. There is agreement that the pattern of environmental gains and losses will be complex and that the mediation of crude policy changes by individual farmers will make accurate prediction difficult (Potter, 1986b). At the level of farming practice, for instance, it is difficult to predict which farmers will react to price cuts by reducing their utilisation of capacity, by cutting back on the use of inputs such as fertiliser and concentrates, and which will react by making inroads into capacity itself by withdrawing land, labour and fixed capital from production. Weinschench and Kemper (1981) suggest that farmers with well-managed businesses might be expected to react to price cuts by giving up a farm enterprise or retiring land rather than reducing the intensity of production per hectare by altering their use of variable inputs. The behaviour of farmers who find they are no longer able to achieve expected income targets will be a particularly important determinant of future countryside change.

A NEW AGENDA

Perhaps more significant than the literal impact of policy change on the countryside is the effect the 'approach to limits' is already having on the scope and content of the countryside debate itself. The necessarily crude nature of 'first round' adjustments to market policy is now appreciated by many environmental groups and commentators (Baldock, 1984). Attention is focusing instead on the opportunity for managing change under the guise of the Community's structural policies. Environmental concerns are increasingly linked to the complicated debate surrounding agricultural structures and 'rural life', with land use shifts and the emergence of new farm structures beginning to seem likely and desirable. A consequence of this is that the debate is becoming increasingly Europeanised, with agriculture and environment problems being articulated within a European as well as a national arena. The relationship between market and structural policy, and in particular the balance between 'guarantee' and 'guidance' expenditure, is now therefore a crucial factor determining the future course of the agriculture and environment debate.

The European Commission has already argued for a linked reform of market and structural policies, clearly regarding the latter as a catalyst which can be used to 'assist a process of change' (EC, 1985b). As a minimum, action on prices will demand new schemes of assistance to farmers worst affected by retrenchment or least able to make the necessary adaptations. There are signs that the protection and management of the rural environment is being seized on as a way of legitimising these aids, with the diversion of land into non-agricultural uses being favoured as a central policy mechanism (see below). Certain generic features of structural policy suggest that this linkage will not be easy to achieve. Barbero and Croci-Angeline (1984) for instance, note certain fundamental differences between the decision-making structures of market and structural policy respectively, pointing out that it has always been easier to work up a consensus for the level of price guarantees than to reach agreement about a common policy for agricultural restructuring. Price policy affects all producers and, once agreed, can be implemented more or less autonomously. Structural policies, by contrast, must discriminate if they are to succeed, either between target holdings or between geographical areas.

The Mansholt Plan of 1968, for instance, was based on a recognition of the need for long term restructuring through farm amalgamation and the removal of small and part-time farmers from the industry. The intention was to foster the conditions – an industry of large, efficient 'production units' – under which support prices could be brought down without causing widespread bankruptcy and distress. Guidance expenditure would be phased up as a prelude to phasing guarantee expenditure down. The onus was on rationalisation and simplification, with long term targets which were set in terms of an optimum combination of farm types and styles and a balance of land uses. The Plan suggested that 5–6 per cent of the cultivated land of the EEC be removed from cultivation and converted to forestry and recreation parks (Mansholt, 1969). It was bold but also extremely controversial. It proposed a common policy on land use and agricultural structures, at a time when member states were anxious to maintain their traditional autonomy in such matters. Moreover, it proposed speeding up the exit of farmers and farm workers from agriculture when a majority of member states were passionately committed to keeping people on the land for cultural and ideological

TABLE 6.1   *Guarantee and guidance expenditure under the CAP* (million
ECUs)

	1982	1983	1984	1985	1986	1987[1]
FEOGA Guarantee Expenditure:	12 405	15 811	18 346	19 744	22 744	22 153
FEOGA Guidance Expenditure:	650	728	676	719	785	955

NOTE 1   Draft 1987 budget accepted by Council on 9.9.1986.
SOURCE: EC (1987).

reasons (George, 1986). As Harrison observes, structural policies
were and have since remained 'strongly nationalistic, displaying a
remarkable readiness to interfere with the operation of market forces
and identifying strongly with the aims and ideals of the family farm'
(Harrison, 1982, p. 163).

In the event, the structural directives which finally emerged in 1972
to shape policy for the next decade were a pale reflection of the
Mansholt Plan, allowing considerable national autonomy in interpretation and implementation. Discrimination between holdings was
kept to a minimum through voluntary and (poorly funded) schemes
of farmer retirement and capital aids, which aimed to help all holdings to increase their economic size through land saving investment
and intensification. Guidance expenditure continued to be dwarfed
by its guarantee counterpart (Table 1).

In retrospect, it is unclear whether either measure significantly
influenced the restructuring process. Revell (1985) comments that
the impact of structural policies during the 1970s was heavily influenced and often deflected by prevailing economic circumstances:
inflation and rising interest rates meant that the income targets set
under the farm modernisation schemes become harder to achieve,
while rising unemployment discouraged farmers from participating in
the cessation of farming schemes and threw doubt on their economic
and social validity. This failure forced the Community still further
away from the Mansholt ideal, developing a scheme under the Less
Favoured Areas Directive to maintain farming activity within areas in
danger of depopulation. Policy became still more regionalised with
the Mediterranean Programme, introduced in 1978 and the Integrated Development Programmes. New regulations introduced in
1984 (EC, 1985a) appear to signal a further evolutionary phase, with

TABLE 6.2   *Projected agricultural employment for 1997*

	Employment 1997 (thousands)		Decline 1977–1997 (per cent)	
	A	B	A	B
Italy	1 635	1 370	48	56
Spain	1 700	1 370	34	47
France	1 130	970	44	52
West Germany	940	825	43	50
Portugal	590	470	39	52
Greece	540	440	40	51
UK	598	534	19	27
Netherlands	222	211	31	34
Ireland	160	150	32	36
Denmark	115	110	47	50
Belgium	80	70	39	47
EC–12	7 710	8 520	40	50

NOTES:
A: assumes that the 14–24 year old persons employed in 1987 will form
   same proportion of labour force as in 1977.
B: assumes that 14–24 age groups in agriculture will decline at same rate
   as corresponding parent generations have done.
SOURCE: ILO (1977), in Duchene et al. (1986, p.169).

the onus on cost reduction, energy conservation and environmental
protection.

The most recent discussions about structural policy in the wake of
the green paper show few signs that a Mansholt mentality is about to
resurface. Yet a safe prediction, given reliable demographic predic-
tions (Table 6.2), is that the drift from the land is likely to continue in
all member states, albeit at differing rates, with the rate of decline
being rather faster in the 1990s than in the 1980s (Duchene *et al.*,
1986). The question which now arises is whether this inevitable
process can and should be speeded up or slowed down by the
Community's structural policies. Given its new and direct linkage
with agricultural restructuring, the answer to (or indeed failure to
answer) this question bears powerfully on the future direction of the
agriculture and environment debate in Britain.

In fact, the British countryside debate is only now beginning to
reflect the relationship between farm structures and environmental
change. The initiative taken by the British Ministry of Agriculture in
1985 to insert a new title within the Structures Regulations which

allows state aids to be paid to farmers within 'environmentally sensitive areas' (ESAs) is undoubtedly the clearest and most radical indication of this. According to the enabling legislation (EC, 1985a), ESAs are to be designated by agriculture departments of member states where 'the maintenance or adoption of particular agricultural methods is likely to facilitate the conservation, enhancement or protection of the nature conservation, amenity or archeological and historic interest of an area'. The role of British agriculture departments in initiating ESAs signals an acceptance of the need for husbandry solutions to land use conflicts, with part of the farm support budget being used for the first time to support what might justifiably be called 'environmentally strategic farmers'. ESAs are built on the radical notion that specific tracts or pieces of countryside can only be effectively conserved by perpetuating the systems and styles of farming which lie behind them.

Participants must agree to comply with management guidelines and notify the authorities of an intention to convert or intensify production. Table 6.3 shows the areas and rates of payment which will apply within the six ESAs already designated within the UK. A recent agreement by the Council of Ministers will now allow this national expenditure to be eligible for reimbursement from Community funds. The UK government has already committed £6 million to finance these schemes and has recently announced additional funding of some £7 million.

TABLE 6.3   *Environmentally sensitive areas in England and Wales*

Designated ESA	Area (has)	Rate of payment per hectare (£)
Norfolk Broads	29 870	125 and 200
Pennine Dales	15 900	100
Somerset Levels and Moors	26 970	82 and 120
South Downs	26 600	35 and 160
West Penwith	7 200	60
Cambrian Mountains	22 800	30 and 45

NOTE:
Higher rates of payment in Broads and Somerset Levels available to farmers who enter into more restrictive management agreements. Higher rates in South Downs available to farmers who convert from arable to grass. Low rate in Cambrian Mountains for semi-natural grassland management and higher rates for woodland management.

Outside the ESAs, however, the relationship between farm structures and environmental protection is less precise and, more to the
point, less well identified in the public debate surrounding agriculture
and the environment. There is no obvious consensus regarding just
how 'environmentally strategic' particular types, styles and sizes of
farm actually are. Research conducted by Munton *et al.* (1987), for
example, suggests that the assumption, long held by some commentators, that small and part-time family farms will necessarily prove
better guardians of the rural landscape than large commercial business may now need to be re-examined. A less 'strong' argument is
that *changes* to the structure of farming within an area are often
detrimental to landscapes and habitats. A further depopulation of
less favoured areas, coinciding as they do with all the national parks
in the UK, is seen as undesirable on environmental as well as social
grounds, because it would lead to an abandonment of land and a
'ranching' of upland landscapes. The MacEwans, for instance, believe that 'hill farming is integral to the traditional upland landscape'
(MacEwan and MacEwan, 1982, 104). The prospect of widespread
afforestation resulting from the sale of non-viable hill and upland
farms is particularly feared. This commitment to maintaining farmers
on the land is shared by most conservation groups and official
conservation agencies, as was confirmed by a recent House of Lords
select committee enquiry, which concluded on the basis of the evidence received that 'conservation should generally be achieved
through farming and not instead of farming' (House of Lords, 1986,
33).

It is a viewpoint which coincides in certain essential respects with
the preoccupations of other member states in the field of structural
policy. The French commitment to preserving rural life by preventing
'rural desertification' and the West German belief in 'a healthy
mixture' of full-and part-time farming activities in the countryside
suggest potential areas of common ground here. The scene is set for a
number of environmentally orientated schemes of assistance to farmers,
implemented under the umbrella of sociostructural policy.

Recent proposals from the European Commission (EC, 1987)
suggest that the need to maintain farmers on the land will continue
to guide structural policies. The EC is clear in its rejection of an
agriculture based on the model of the USA 'with vast spaces and few
farmers' (EC, 1985b). The emphasis will instead be on a diversion of
land by those farmers who are maintained on the land. The recently
agreed 'extensification scheme', for instance, will encourage farmers

to reduce the output from their holding by at least 20 per cent, in return for an annual hectarage payment. Farmers are expected to achieve this reduction by converting land under surplus products to non-surplus products and/or diverting the land to forestry or some other non-agricultural use. A pre-pension scheme, although not agreed at the time of writing, was also under active consideration early in 1987. Farmers in the 55–65 age bracket would be eligible for annual payments and hectarage payments where they agree to cease farming parts of their holding for a specified period (not less than five years). The land is to be either abandoned altogether or diverted into a non-agricultural use, such as forestry. It is expected that about 55 000 farmers will be drawn into such a scheme. In addition, a direct income aid scheme is now under discussion.

The principle of land diversion which is common to these schemes and to 'national' schemes about to be implemented by member states agriculture departments (MAFF, 1987) has obvious appeal to policy makers as a direct and visible means of reducing productive capacity, providing income support to worst affected farmers, and achieving environmental improvement. For conservationists in the UK, however, such a linkage could be disadvantageous, resulting in ostensibly multi-purpose schemes which are actually tailored to meeting income support and supply control goals. The targeting of the new schemes of assistance exemplifies this danger. According to Griffen and Stoll (1984), 'targetting epitomises fundamental decision making because it requires explicit regard of social (and environmental) objectives' (Griffin and Stoll, 1984, 37). To be efficient in achieving environmental goals, land diversion needs to be targetted at land or pieces of countryside (Burnham *et al.*, 1986). With the notable exception of the ESA initiative, the EC schemes are very clearly targetted at farmer groups. The pre-pension scheme is a case in point, being directed towards a definite farmer target group: 'those elderly farmers who are no longer in a position, either physically or financially, to adapt their farms to the new situation' (Dessylas, 1987, 5). The extensification scheme, by dint of the levels of payment which have been set, is similarly directed at marginal producers. The implication, and it is an important one for those wishing to see longer term environmental guidance of farming change, is that 'the successful applicants will be distributed geographically in a way which is not likely to coincide with the areas of greatest environmental need' (House of Lords, 1986, 16). Clearly, a generalised identification of environmental issues with the long standing European concern with

farm structures and 'rural life' promises to introduce new and compli-
cating factors into the agriculture and environment debate.

CONCLUSIONS

Triggered by crude adjustments to levels of public support, farming
contraction in Britain and Europe promises to alter both the processes of environmental change in the countryside and to recast the
policy framework within which they can be managed. A new dynamic
of farming adjustment will have profound implications for the public
debate about agriculture and the environment which has raged in
Britain since the late 1960s. Opportunities for promoting landscape
and nature conservation in the wake of farming contraction are
already being discussed, typically in terms of the visualised land
surplus which will provide scope for conservation to emerge as an
alternative land use, as a means of earning a farming living in the
future countryside. There will also be more subtle 'psychological'
opportunities as farmers begin to adjust their income expectations
and become more receptive to conservation aid schemes.

Countryside change itself will become more situationally defined,
producing a more direct linkage between environmental concerns
and the vexed issues of agricultural restructuring and rural society.
The debate will consequently become less self-contained, but also
more unmanageable in terms of the policy tools which will be available. With attention therefore focusing on the structural arm of the
CAP, it is becoming increasingly clear that a coincidence of interest
between the mainly European concern with preserving farm structures and the specially British concern with conserving farmed landscapes, could hold the key to the successful emergence of a 'common'
structural policy framework. This is already evident regarding the
ESA initiative, which allows 'environmental strategic farms' to be
maintained on the land through a system of state aids. Using farm
support under the CAP to perpetuate the 'particular character' of
farming in an area has become a legitimate policy goal. Other recent
initiatives suggest however that the coupling of income support and
environmental protection may mean that environmental objectives
are not properly built into the design of schemes of assistance to
farmers. The targetting of schemes towards farmers or land is a
particularly important, if controversial, aspect of policy design. The
environmental guidance of farming change must recognise other,

predominantly social, concerns if it is to operate at a truly European
level.

Bibliography

Adams, W. M. (1986), *Nature's Place: conservation sites and countryside change* (Allen & Unwin).
Baldock, D. (1984), *The CAP Price Policy and the Environment: An Exploratory Essay* (London: IEEP).
Baldock, D. and D. Conder (eds) (1985), *Can the CAP Fit the Environment?* Seminar Proceedings (London: IEEP/CPRE).
Barbero, G. and E. Croci-Angelini (1986), 'Towards a better structural policy', *European Journal of Agricultural Economics*, 11, 245–54.
Bishop, R. (1982), 'Option Value: An Exposition and Extension', in *Land Economics*, 58.
Bowers, J. and P. Cheshire (1983), *Agriculture, the Countryside and Land Use* (London: Methuen).
Burnham, P., B. Green and C. Potter (1986), *A Set Aside Policy for the UK*, Set Aside Working Paper No. 3. Department of Environmental Studies and Countryside Planning, Wye College, University of London.
Capstick, C. (1985), 'Future CAP Price Policies — What are the Environmental Implications?', in D. Baldock and D. Conder, (eds), *Can the CAP Fit the Environment?* (London: IEEP/CPRE) 19–27.
Centre for Agricultural Strategy (1986), *Countryside Implications for England and Wales of Possible Changes in the Common Agricultural Policy*. Main Report, CAS, Reading.
Cheshire, P. (1985), 'The Environmental Implications of European Agricultural Support Policies', in P. Baldock and D. Conder (eds), *Can the CAP Fit the Environment?* Seminar Proceedings (London: IEEP/CPRE) 9–19.
Council for Protection of Rural England (1985), Memorandum in House of Lords (1985). The Reform of the CAP, HL 237, (London: HMSO).
Countryside Commission (1974), *New Agricultural Landscapes*, Countryside Commission, Cheltenham.
Countryside Commission (1974), *A Better Future for the Uplands*, CCP 162 Countryside Commission, Cheltenham.
Coleman, D. and B. Traill (1984), Economic Pressures on the Environment, in A. Korbey (ed.), *Investing in Rural Harmony: a critique*, Centre for Agricultural Strategy, Paper 16 (Reading: CAS) 30–41.
Dessylas, M. (1987), Commission of European Communities Press Release, September, Brussels.
Duchene, F., E. Szczepanik and W. Legg (1986), *New Limits in European Agriculture, Politics and the Common Agricultural Policy* (London: Croom Helm).
European Commission (1968), *Memorandum on the Reform of Agriculture in the European Community*, Com(68) 1000, Brussels.
European Commission (1973), *Improvement of the Common Agricultural Policy*, Com (73) 1850, Brussels.

European Commission (1975), *Stocktaking of the Common Agricultural Policy*, Com(75) 100, Brussels.
European Commission (1982), *Reflections on the Common Agricultural Policy*, Com(80) 800, Brussels.
European Commission (1985a), *Structures Regulations*, Com(85)797, Brussels.
European Commission (1985b.) *Perspectives for the Common Agricultural Policy*, Com(85) 333, Brussels.
European Commission (1986), *Proposals for a Council Regulation amending Regulations on Agricultural Structures*, Com(86) 199, Brussels.
European Commission (1987), *Agricultural Situation in the Community*, 1986 Report, Brussels.
Fennell, R. (1985), A Reconsideration of the Objectives of the Common Agricultural Policy, *Journal of Common Market Studies*, 23(3), 257–75.
Gasson, R. (1985), *Gainful Occupations of Farm Families*, Wye College, University of London.
George, S. (1986), *Politics and Policy in the European Community* (Oxford: Clarendon Press).
Griffin, R. and J. Stoll (1984), 'Evolutionary Processes in Soil Conservation Policy', *Land Economics*, 60, 30–9.
Harrison, A. (1982), Land Policies in the Member States of the European Community, *Agricultural Administration, 11, 159–74.*
Hirsch, F. (1978), *Social Limits to Growth* (London: Routledge).
Hooper, M. (1984), What are the main impacts of agriculture on wildlife?, in D. Jenkins (ed.), *Agriculture and the Environment* (Cambridge: ITE).
House of Lords (1985), *The Reform of the Common Agricultural Policy*, 17th Report (1984–85), HL (London: HMSO).
House of Lords (1986), *Socio-Structural Policy in Agriculture*, 20th Report (1985–86), HL 242 (London: HMSO).
Howarth, R. (1985), *Farming for Farmers?* Hobart Paperback 20 (London: IEA).
Lowe, P. and J. Goyder (1983), *Environmental Groups in Politics* (London: Allen & Unwin).
Lowe, P, G. Cox, T. O'Riordan, M. MacEwen and M. Winter, (1986), *Countryside Conflicts: the Politics of farming, forestry and conservation* (London: Temple Smith/Gower).
MacEwan, A. and M. MacEwan (1982), *National Parks: Conservation or Cosmetics?* (London: Allen & Unwin).
MacEwan, M. and G. Sinclair (1983), *New Life for the Hills* (London: Council for National Parks).
Mansholt, S. (1969), *Le Plan Mansholt — le rapport Vedel* (Paris: Seclaf).
Ministry of Agriculture, Fisheries and Food (1987), *Farm Woodland Scheme: a consultation paper* (London: MAFF).
Munton, R. and T. Marsden (1987), 'Farmers' Response to an Uncertain Policy Future', in *Removing Land from Agriculture — the Implications for Farming and the Environment*. Seminar Proceedings (London: CPRE/IEEP).
Nature Conservancy Council (1977), *Nature Conservation and Agriculture* (London: NCC).

Nature Conservancy Council (1984), *Nature Conservation in Great Britain* (London: NCC).

National Farmers' Union (1984), *New Directions for agricultural policy: the way forward*.

Nicholl, W. (1986), 'From Rejection to Repudiation: EC Budgetary Affairs', in (1985), *Journal of Common Market Studies*, 25, 1, 31–49.

Nowicki, P. (1985), 'Where is the CAP in the debate in France on agriculture and the environment?' Unpublished paper.

Parker, K. (1984), *A Tale of Two Villages* (Bakewell: Peak District National Park Authority).

Potter, C. (1983), *Investing in Rural Harmony* (Godalming: WWF).

Potter, C. (1985), 'The Environmental Impact of CAP Reform at Farm Level', in D. Baldock and D. Conder (eds), *Can the CAP Fit the Environment?* (London: IEEP/CPRE).

Potter, C. (1986a), *Environmental Protection and Agricultural Adjustment: lessons from the American Experience*, Set Aside Working Paper No. 1, Department of Environmental Studies and Countryside Planning, Wye College, University of London.

Potter, C. (1986b), 'Processes of Countryside Change in Lowland England', *Journal of Rural Studies*, 2 (3): 187–95.

Revell, B. (1985), *EC Structure Policy and UK Agriculture*, Centre for Agricultural Strategy, Study 2, CAS, Reading.

Ritson, C. and J. Fearne (1984), 'Long term goals for the CAP', *European Review of Agricultural Economics*, 11 (2): 207–16.

Smith, M. (1985), *Agriculture and nature conservation in conflict: the less favoured areas of France and the UK* (Langholm: Arkelton Trust).

Thomas, K. (1983), *Man and the Natural World* (London: Allen Lane).

Thomson, K. and E. Neville-Rolfe (1985), *Cereal Supply Control in the European Community*, Agra-Europe Special Report 25 (London: Agra-Europe).

Weinschenck, G. and J. Kemper (1981), 'Agricultural Policies and their regional impact in Western Europe', *European Review of Agricultural Economics*, 8, 251–81.

7 The Restructuring of Spanish Agriculture, and Spain's Accession to the EEC

Miren Etxezarreta and Lourdes Viladomiu

INTRODUCTION

The word 'crisis' is frequently used in relation to Spanish agriculture; indeed, it has been used constantly to describe the situation since the end of the Civil War (1936–39). In the first place, because of the primary sector's inability to achieve pre-Civil War levels of production, a situation which resulted in an insufficient supply of food and consequent rationing. Since the beginning of the 1950s, the term has referred to the problems accompanying the transformation of traditional agriculture into modern productive units. At the present time, the 'crisis' is felt in some subsectors of the food industry, in relation to Spanish membership of the EEC. In fact, Spanish agriculture has already survived more than fifty years of permanent 'crisis'. Clearly, it is important to examine more precisely what is meant by the expression and the circumstances that surround each concrete manifestation of the 'crisis'.

What does 'agricultural crisis' mean? Does it refer to the fact that farmers obtain low incomes, that production is low, or that the rural exodus has risen and rural communities are disappearing? The term is ambiguous and frequently difficult to accept if one analyses the principal variables of the sector (production, productivity, changes in the composition of output, the utilisation of modern means of production, etc.) Can one talk about an 'agricultural crisis' when production in real terms has risen from a base of 100 (in 1970) to 166 in seventeen years and productivity from 100 to 277, while for the economy as a whole it has only reached 189, and agricultural exports

156

have risen from 100 to 216 in the same period? Does the crisis situation extend to agriculture as a whole or only specific parts of the sector? Should we refer to a process of 'crisis' or to constant adaptation of the productive apparatus to market conditions? In this article, we refer to the restructuring of the productive apparatus, which can occur with or without crisis, and we will use the term 'crisis' to refer to the inability of the agricultural community to reproduce itself and its productive units without traumatic changes and/or the help of external institutions, particularly the public sector. In the pages that follow we will examine both meanings of 'crisis'.

The present situation of Spanish agriculture is the result of a vast process of change which was initiated in the 1950s and which accelerated rapidly in the 1960s. During this period, Spanish economy and society underwent an intense process of modernisation, industrialisation and urbanisation that, naturally, also brought important changes in agriculture, notably the transformation of traditional agriculture into modern units of production. This evolution was at the same time closely articulated to the integration of Spanish agriculture within the international agro-industrial system and the principal agricultural markets of the world. The process continued during the 1970s, becoming increasingly affected by the general world economic crisis, particularly acute in Spain and, even more, by the significant restructuring of Spanish agriculture imposed by membership of the EEC in the 1980s, which has occurred within the setting of the world agrarian crisis. These basic elements — modernisation, internationalisation, the general economic and agrarian crisis, and the integration with the EEC – have subjected Spanish agriculture, in the last 30 years, to a profound and rapid transformation. This transformation occurred over many more years in other countries which passed through similar processes during earlier historical epochs. These are the elements that make up the present situation of Spanish agriculture and determine the principal lines of its development in the near future.

THE TRANSFORMATION OF TRADITIONAL AGRICULTURE

At the beginning of the 1960s, 42 per cent of the employed population of Spain was still agricultural, producing 23.6 per cent of Gross Domestic Product (GDP). The utilisation of chemical fertilisers was very limited,[1] most agricultural inputs were produced within the farm itself, machinery was scarce – only 35 000 tractors for the 2 900 000 farms – technology was very traditional and productivity very low. Nevertheless, external payments equilibrium depended greatly on the primary sector as 60 per cent of Spain's exports came from this sector, as against 27 per cent of imports. In short, at the beginning of the 1960s, Spain was still an agricultural country with a traditional agriculture.

This situation changed rapidly. Already in 1953 several agreements with the US produced a significant change in the general economic context. This had particular effect in the agrarian sector, given that half the external assistance was channelled through PL 480, in the form of agricultural products, particularly soya oil and cotton, together with smaller quantities of wheat and dairy products. Also, by the middle of the decade hybrid breeding stock began to be imported from the USA heralding changes in poultry and pig production, and initiating a system of cattle production clearly linked to foreign firms. These methods still lacked quantitative importance, but nevertheless revealed the pattern that would condition the evolution of the sector in the following decade. After 1957, the external sector of the Spanish economy was progressively liberalised, and this was accompanied by a Stabilisation Plan in 1959. These measures led to a phase of strong growth in the economy throughout the 1960s. This process was based on an intense industrialisation effort, which brought considerable expansion of industry and the concentration of population in industrial and urban centres. The interest and enthusiasm of political and economic decision-makers for industrialisation ensured that the requirements of the agricultural sector were practically ignored in this period.

Nevertheless, industrial growth profoundly affected the Spanish countryside in various ways: on the one hand, the increase in urbanisation and incomes brought an increase in the demand for food, and especially changes in the composition of the diet. The traditional diet was being abandoned in favour of more dairy products, meat, vegetables and fruit. This promoted changes in agricultural output, even if they were not sufficiently rapid to avoid the need to import more of these products, in order to reduce inflationary pressures. Demand also changed as a result of the growth of tourism during this decade, again increasing the consumption of non-traditional food items. It should also be remembered that the new industrial workers had come from the countryside. They were agricultural workers or small producers who had abandoned agriculture as soon as they could obtain employment elsewhere. Similarly, the industrial 'boom' in Western Europe absorbed an important number of Spanish workers, most of them from the countryside, from where they were being expelled as external trade liberalisation made available imported agricultural machinery. Mechanisation was also stimulated by the rise in agricultural salaries associated with the same process of migration. From an economically active agricultural population of around four million people, more than a million left between 1964 and 1974, and many others had left before this date. It is estimated that the active agricultural population diminished between 35 and 50 per cent in the 1960s, the migrants being, in general, the most youthful and the most enterprising members of the rural community.

This process, nevertheless, did not depend only on factors internal to agriculture, nor on factors peculiar to the Spanish economy. As we have suggested, the gradual liberalisation of Spain's external trade provided an incentive for foreign capital to enter the country to exploit the opportunities offered by a strictly controlled labour market and ever-widening product markets. In this period, international capital made a great effort to occupy the Spanish market, increasing the dependence on imported goods and, by means of investment policy, establishing productive enterprises for a market which still relied on foreign technology and means of production. The process of agricultural modernisation was thus promoted by the dynamic of the domestic economy and the aggressive sales methods of foreign enterprises. The 1960s constituted the 'first wave' in the internationalisation of Spanish agriculture. A sector starved of technology, faced with growing and changing demand, and with a declining labour force was, at the end of the day, directed by large transnational enterprises. These enterprises acquired added importance from the fact that the Spanish Government gave little attention to agricultural technology. In the absence of alternative policies Spanish agriculture was remodelled in the image of other industrialised countries, but without achieving their level of productivity.

The result of this process was the modernisation of Spanish agriculture and its progressive articulation within the agro-industrial system throughout the 1960s, at the same time as this system was becoming internationalised. It stimulated technological change, the absorption of new inputs and new productive systems, and strongly increased the level of mechanisation.

This served to increase the financial requirements of agriculture, as much for investment as for current expenditure. The process of modernisation was accompanied by the intensification and specialisation of production which brought important increases in productivity. This also meant an advance in the forms of capitalist organisation in the Spanish countryside. The new productive system intensified the production of goods for exchange, requiring that a surplus be generated for accumulation, integrating producers more closely into the capitalist system. Despite the complexity which capitalism presents within family-based agriculture, the transformation of the sixties significantly strengthened capitalism in the Spanish countryside.

In studying the articulation of Spanish agriculture within agro-industry, it is necessary to distinguish between the integration of agriculture/industry, on the one hand, and the international character of this process on the other. The gradual integration of agricultural production in the agro-industrial system occurred in practically every facet of activity, while internationalisation was much more selective, affecting the diverse elements of the system in distinct ways. The process of internationalisation had an asymmetrical character, revealed through the industrialisation of the means of production ('from above') rather than through the absorption of the product ('from below'). In the 1960s, internationalisation was brought about mainly through the industrialisation of the means of production that incorporated the new technology and by the aggressive diffusion of this technology. This led to the wider use of chemical fertilisers, improved seeds, pesticides and, above all, machinery, bought under specific and preferential credit terms that could be more easily obtained than for other components of agrarian modernisation. Also, and importantly, agro-industrial integration was introduced through systems of livestock production, especially for poultry and pigs, in which animal feed firms undertook huge programmes to stimulate production, principally through integrated contracts and by disseminating technological information using commercial channels. It was the representatives of animal feed companies who suggested the dietary requirements of livestock. The new methods brought about a spectacular increase in the scale and volume of production concentrated on increasingly specialised farms. It also altered the location of productive capacity, which moved closer to centres of consumption.

In addition, the system provided meat products at cheap prices to industrial workers as demand increased. For large livestock (beef cattle) the change was less revolutionary. Although animal feed systems had changed radically, and improved livestock strains were used, the scale of production increased much more slowly, probably because in addition to technical difficulties, the economic capacity of the farms did not allow the rapid process of accumulation necessary to substantially increase the number of animals. Even today the majority of farms that keep cattle rear few animals, and the processes of integration are considerably weaker. If we take the consumption of compound feeds as an index of levels of integration in the new systems, the situation is illustrated by the fact that in 1974 cattle consumed only 14.3 per cent, compared with 37.4 per cent for pigs and 41.8 per cent for poultry.

The situation is more complex in terms of the processing and marketing of agricultural production. In this respect, with the exception of the integrated contract production of poultry and pigs, national companies maintained a fundamental role during most of the decade. Only at the end of the 1960s did the transnational enterprises occupy positions in the production of high 'value added' foods destined for high income urban groups. Milk provides an interesting illustration of this dynamic. At the beginning of the 1960s, foreign capital in this sector was represented only by a few firms which were established in Spain before the Civil War, and geared to domestic consumption, such as Nestlé and Suchard. In the 1960s, a considerable increase occurred in the commercialisation of milk through modern dairy processing plants, many of which were established as the result of legal measures which prevented the processing of milk by other means. However, these were national firms and, in many cases, they were co-operatives formed by the dairy farmers themselves which, given the increase in milk production, needed to improve the marketing and processing of their product. It was only in the early 1970s that transnational enterprises began to acquire significance by transforming milk into other products (yoghourt, chocolate, desserts, flans and other processed foods). Agricultural exports were also undertaken largely by enterprises of national origin, which were basically traditional in character.

The integration of Spanish agriculture within the agro-industrial system was accompanied by a growing incorporation in international markets for primary products. Spain has traditionally been an agricultural exporting country, but the type of products exported, with the exception of oil, were not important in world markets. The process of modernisation, and especially the diffusion of methods of animal nutrition based on compound feeds, converted Spain into an important importer of agricultural products, particularly soya and maize. Imports of agricultural products, if we take 1964 as the base year (100), increased to 181.2 in 1970 and 259 in 1974, while imports of products for livestock feed reached 193.2 in 1970 and 313.3 in 1974. Furthermore, imports of basic grains for animal feeds were closely related to imports of specially selected animals, drugs and all those elements that make up the technological package which defines intensive livestock production. Its introduction in Spanish agriculture governed not only the volume of imported primary products, but also shaped a type of technological dependency.

> In the first instance it is the rigidity of this dependency which establishes one of the fundamental characteristics of Spanish live-stock development and which will make its reconversion difficult in the future.   (Soria and Zuñiga, 131)

At the end of the 1960s, Spanish livestock development had become consolidated into a system of meat production unconnected with agroecological conditions, which required permanent imports of animal feed. From then onwards, the Spanish livestock system was closely linked to world primary product markets and technologically dependent on the outside world. At the same time, new consumption habits and the expansion of international tourism, necessitated imports of certain products – milks, eggs and meat – to cover the inadequate supply and mitigate inflationary pressures. Nevertheless the volume and the irregular character of these imports ensured that their impact on agriculture and external trade was considerably less than that of imports of basic grains destined for animal consumption.

As was to be expected, this transformation accelerated the process of rural differentiation. Not all farmers had the same resources available to undertake the necessary modernisation and adopt the new techniques. This technology reinforced the advantages of scale economies favouring the largest farms and those with greater economic capacity. As the modernisation of agriculture advanced, so the differentiation of the farming population could be observed in terms of its capacity to undertake innovation. In this period, farmers with fewer resources, without the capacity for modernisation, were abandoning the sector while those who remained became integrated in a process which forced them towards growing and permanent accumulation, leading to a situation of great instability. This differentiation, initiated in the 1960s, became increasingly accentuated as capital accumulation in agriculture proceeded. The same dynamic transformed the social structure of rural areas, following the same course seen in other countries which had experienced agricultural modernisation. As is well known, it consists basically of the drastic reduction of the rural population, the deterioration of small nuclear settlements – villages and hamlets – starting a process which eventually leads to the abandonment of wide areas of territory, and the domination of the city and modes of urban life. It is the typical process associated with modernisation and need not detain us further.

It is worth emphasising that the broad process of transformation that we are describing was brought about with only limited administrative support. As has been suggested already, during the years in which the Spanish economy grew rapidly, agriculture was never considered as a significant contributory element in this growth except as a labour reserve, and, consequently, it was ignored in economic policy. The obstacles which the lack of agrarian development presented for rapid industrialisation were addressed through imports or by conceding considerable scope for initiatives to the transnational companies. In fact no clear policy on the structure or profitability of the agricultural sector was adopted. Furthermore, the principal function of agricultural price policy was to foster rapid industrial growth, which usually implied that the agricultural sector had to face international competition or that paradoxical situations occurred, such as the subsidising of imported products.

Despite this important modernising period, Spanish agriculture at the beginning of the 1970s was still far behind that of the most advanced countries in so far as technology and productivity were concerned. The 1960s involved the intense modernisation of Spanish agriculture but it by no means achieved the levels of productivity of the industrialised countries.

ECONOMIC CRISIS AND THE FIRST PROPOSALS FOR ENTRY INTO THE EEC

The early 1970s do not display any special features in the evolution of agriculture. The process initiated in the 1960s was consolidated and deepened, continuing the same general trends without any substantial change. Nevertheless, it is worth drawing attention to some elements that would later have an impact on the crisis of the agricultural sector.

The crisis in primary products in 1972–73 preceded the energy crisis, and its strong repercussions on the world markets for basic agricultural products had important consequences for Spain, both in terms of prices and external provisioning. The international short-ages in primary products led to direct intervention in the agricultural sector to correct pressing problems. Thus programmes of agricultural import substitution were introduced in order to limit the dependence on external supplies by diversifying domestic sources of animal feeds, which had been exclusively centred on maize and soya. Conse-quently, the production of barley and oats was stimulated at the expense of wheat, and the cultivation of vegetable oils was begun in Spain. Cattle production also attracted official support. Nevertheless, these programmes, like other agricultural policy measures taken in this period, had a rather limited impact and failed to bring significant changes in the general lines of development.

At the same time, in order to mitigate the effect of rising food prices on inflation during the 1970s, the previous policies were continued, notably agricultural imports, consumer subsidies and concessions to the activities of transnational firms in the sector. These measures also failed to introduce significant changes in agriculture. As the decade advanced, the growing economic crisis became more perceptible, although its full impact was considerably delayed for political reasons. Although agriculture was one of the activities least affected by the crisis, which was basically industrial, it made itself felt in the following ways:

First, the crisis provoked a slowdown in consumer demand, with negative growth in the demand for certain products, which provoked growing competition in the market and reinforced the adverse effects of the lower prices. Concomitantly the recession also brought in-creased competition in world markets for Spanish agricultural pro-ducts.

Second, the rise in the price of inputs, which from the earliest year of the crisis the Administration had sought to avoid, finally occurred, increasing the prices of fuel, fertilisers and other inputs of foreign origin. To these increases in price, one has to add the rise in the level of interest rates, which contributed to higher financial costs, es-pecially for those farms which had undertaken major modernisation.

Third, this produced an important deterioration in agricultural profitability. At first, the rise in costs was absorbed by means of increased agricultural prices, but the situation had changed radically by the end of 1977.

Thenceforth the struggle against inflation became the principal objective of economic policy, which implied drastic measures to control agricultural prices, making it difficult for farmers to pass on their increasing costs via higher product prices. After 1978, relative price movements led to a growing differential between agricultural incomes and those in other sectors. Prices and incomes deteriorated especially for arable producers, a significant change from previous periods.

The reduced profitability of agricultural activities, a consequence of the inability to transfer the rise in costs to final prices, stimulated a growing rationalisation of farming operations, especially among producers that used wage-labour, typically the larger farmers. This process lies behind the rapid growth of unemployment in agriculture, notably in the least developed regions of Spain, Andalucia and Extremadura, where the number of agricultural workers is still high.

This situation was aggravated by the profound deterioration in the non-agricultural labour market which was brought about by the crisis. The growth in the general level of unemployment in the economy put a brake on the migration of agricultural labour, which throughout the whole process of modernisation in the 1960s had siphoned off surplus labour. With the onset of the crisis, agricultural workers and small farmers found themselves in great difficulty and, in many cases, rather than abandon agriculture altogether they had to make up for their low incomes by staying in rural areas and diversifying their activities. The crisis also led to the return of many rural migrants, both from the unemployed in Spanish cities and from abroad, the latter prompted by special programmes established in their host countries. In this period, the agricultural sector was no longer able to adapt to decreasing employment opportunities through the mechanism of migration, further depressing general labour markets in the areas where agricultural workers were concentrated.

In this context of crisis and difficulty, Spain was obliged to prepare itself for entry to the European Economic Community, which had been considered imminent since 1978. Administrative intervention in agriculture had from that moment a double objective: to equip the sector to meet community norms and to accelerate agricultural modernisation to improve its competitiveness.

The position of Spanish agriculture in the light of EEC integration is complex. Prior to membership this had been anticipated with some optimism, suggesting that an important part of the agricultural sector would be a net beneficiary of the process. Agriculture was considered one of the better prepared sectors for incorporation in the European

Common Market. This view was based on the demonstrated capacity of Spanish agricultural exports to penetrate European markets. It was also felt that the competitive position of Spain would benefit significant segments of agricultural production. This referred especially to typical Mediterranean products, such as wine, olive oil, vegetables, certain fruits and flowers.

Furthermore, incorporation in the Community's agricultural policy meant an increase in many of its 'regulated' prices, since European prices were higher than those in Spain, with the exception of milk products, sugar beet and some cereals. This led to the expectation of better returns for farmers. Monetary tendencies were likely to reinforce this position. These factors suggested that Spanish agriculture would obtain, within a few years, favourable prices for its products which would help in the complicated process of adjustment demanded by membership of the community. It was expected, at the same time, that the incorporation of Spain and Portugal would strengthen the block of 'southern' countries and that this would force the Community to extend its protection of Mediterranean products in relation to those of the 'northern' countries.

Over and above price effects, positive repercussions were anticipated for the agriculture of many zones of the country as a consequence of the Community's socio-structural policy. Especially for the stratum of less viable farms located mainly in the less developed areas of Spanish territory, membership was contemplated like the arrival of a gigantic Father Christmas, laden with subsidies and assistance for farmers in difficulties.

As the first analyses of EEC integration indicated, not everything was going to be advantageous. Integration led to an increase in the level of agricultural prices that affected domestic consumption negatively, aggravating inflationary pressures at a time when the rate of inflation in Spain was already considerably above that of the Community. For the agricultural sector as a whole, although competitiveness improved owing to the disappearance of existing protection, certain products could only take advantage of the new situation successfully if Spanish agriculture greatly improved its levels of productivity. The list of sensitive products, headed by those whose production was likely to be problematical – sugar beet, milk – was widened. Furthermore, evaluation of the positive and negative effects of integration became more difficult to carry out since the probability of a drastic reform of the Common Agricultural Policy was evident, but its concrete form was unknown. To this one should add doubts about such questions as exchange rates for 'green money', monetary compensation amounts, and other arcane issues of Community policy.

In fact, what was at issue was participation without protection in a market subjected to strong tensions created by an excess of productive capacity. Spanish agriculture had to find a space within an economic environment that was strongly competitive. Except in certain cereals, fruits, cotton and tobacco, the EEC is self-sufficient and needs to export to equilibrate its markets. In this context, Spanish agricultural production not only has to consolidate and extend its previous position in EEC markets, it also needs to maintain itself in its own domestic market. Nevertheless, different studies agree that incorporation in the EEC is in the interests of Spanish agriculture, in spite of the possibility that the advantages might prove partial and transitional if current levels of competitiveness are not improved.

During the 1970s Spanish agriculture was forced to intensify the process of modernisation initiated in the 1960s. This new stage in the transformation of Spanish agriculture can be seen as a continuation, a deepening of the process already begun, which was accelerated by the need to incorporate Spain within the EEC. Spanish agriculture had to correspond as quickly as possible to the model of European productionist agriculture, which was presented as the only viable route. Competitiveness is the key word. At that time no perception of the crisis of modern agriculture seemed to exist, but the premise which governed debate was that the increase in efficiency would resolve the unsettled problems of Spanish agriculture. According to this view, the agrarian crisis could only be resolved by means of the growth in productivity and production.

As might be expected agriculture strengthened its articulation with agro-industry in this period, but with some interesting modifications. The presence of transnational enterprises increased, but detailed observation of this process suggests that they withdrew from certain segments of the productive apparatus and increased their participation in others. The production of compound feeds is among the sectors abandoned by foreign capital, giving autonomous local enterprises a larger role in the production, distribution and organisation of contracts with livestock farmers. Foreign capital henceforth concentrated on importing feed grains and supplying genetically improved breeding stock and other services. This did not mean, of course, that the model was not consolidated:

The importance of the phenomenon of complete integration during the seventies has been growing. Even when its quantitative evaluation is difficult, diverse writers agree in saying that today almost all poultry production is undertaken under integrated systems, and estimates of integrated pig production lie between 50 and 70 per cent.   (Soria and Zuñiga, 134)

At the same time, cattle cake made up of soya and cereals, particularly maize, already constituted the basis of animal production. It can be argued that once technological dependence had been established, in animals feeds as in the genetic base, then the process could be left to develop internally, in the knowledge that it will have to depend on external supplies.

As can be anticipated, imports of soya and maize increased strongly in this period, and those of soya cake diminished once the processing plants had been established within the country. In 1980, 4 533 000 metric tons of maize was imported, compared with 4 103 000 metric tons in 1974, while imports of soya reached 3 214 000 metric tons in 1980 compared with 1 588 000 in 1974. Spain was being converted into a major importer of these products, and wheat, barley and sorghum, while imports of milk products remained stable, and other food products were of minor importance (Table 7.1). As a result of the substantial increase in the imports of basic grains, the agricultural trade balance, traditionally in surplus since the 1960s, moved into deficit of some US $10 442 million for the period 1965–83. This made Spain into a 'client state' for the advanced and 'surplus-ridden' agricultural sector of the United States.

The internationalisation of Spanish agriculture was strengthened from the other 'side' of the food system as transnational enterprises gradually came to dominate food processing and the most dynamic segments of the markets for agro-food products. A series of particular circumstances favoured this control. The small size of most existing food-producing firms made it very difficult for them to meet new market requirements and absorption within a multinational enterprise was seen as the only possible way to survive. Furthermore, due to the growing influence of Neo-Liberal economic policy in the public sector, the state sold some food firms it previously owned and also abandoned the project to create a strong food division within the public sector.[2] In the recession years, the banks also sold their industrial interests including important enterprises in food manufacturing. Taking advantage of these circumstances, the transnational enterprises gained control of the modern food sector in Spain.

These multinational enterprises penetrated the Spanish economy, or broadened and diversified their existing activities, basically by supplying the internal market and without immediate plans to export. With the exception of a few nationally-owned firms making canned foods, the food companies with foreign capital meet internal demand, directing their products towards the highest income groups, and seeking to develop demand for sophisticated products (drinks, frozen food, pre-cooked dishes and new products). These firms direct their production principally at three subsectors of demand: (a) the population with higher than average earnings, (b) drinks, and processed foods for children (fancy food); (c) collective demand (schools, hospitals, canteens) and 'fast food' outlets. So far there are no signs that these companies have plans to develop significant export capacity. Their objective at this stage is not to take advantage of cheap local raw materials as the basis for processed food exports but rather to concentrate on the internal market. As a matter of fact, total exports from the agro-food sector declined from 1970 to 1975, when they reached the same level as in 1965.

It is necessary to note here the way foreign interests have bought up national companies involved in the processing and marketing of agricultural products, principally wine and oil. Without ignoring the export dimension, there are indications that these acquisitions are linked to processes of market rationalisation, and that they are motivated by strategies to establish a single market in the EEC for the products of multinational companies. In this respect, one can mention the case of the international cooking-oil chain, Lessieur, which has made inroads in Spain. The exception to the tendency indicated above is, therefore, more apparent than real.

Foreign capital does not appear to be interested in penetrating directly into the area of agricultural production. This has been left in the hands of national producers, linked at both ends of the food system by companies providing inputs and transforming the product. In addition to the important influence of these companies, there are other sources of internationalisation of the productive apparatus which originate elsewhere. In particular, the export possibilities for fresh products on the European market, which have grown rapidly in recent years and whose prospects have improved since Spain's accession to the EEC. Spanish producers are trying to take maximum advantage of the opportunities offered by European markets for vegetables, flowers and high value products, especially non-seasonal varieties. Largely in the last 15 years, the agriculture of south – east Spain has experienced an intense transformation linked to the adoption of new production technologies using greenhouses and the highly developed use of water technology in the production of vegetables and fruit. These water technologies were developed by Dutch and Israeli industrial companies and rapidly adopted in the south of Spain. The spectacular transformation of Almeria, previously a desert area, achieved by the great expansion of plastic-covered 'greenhouses' growing unseasonal products, is a well-known example of this process. However it is not confined to Almeria province alone, but extends to the whole eastern part of Spain and some other regions of the country (Rioja and the Valley of Guadalquivir, for example). These have also developed traditional vegetable and fruit production in new directions, benefitting from their comparative advantage for European markets. This process, in national hands, nevertheless requires international inputs of production, which increases the external dependence of the productive apparatus as sales increase. Thus the way that the market for export products is constituted, and the variety and preparation of fresh products, ensures an adaptation to the demands of foreign markets. This in turn brings greater integration between areas of major agricultural expansion and the habits and requirements of consumers in other countries.

In addition, another form of international contract exists which, although of only marginal importance in quantitative terms, suggests a tendency worthy of attention. Companies based in the north of Europe enter into contracts with farmers from north – east Spain and the Levant, to raise ornamental plants and cactuses requiring high temperatures and intensive care in the early stages of their growth. These plants, once germinated in northern Europe, are transported in lorries or by plane to the hotter climates of Spain and, when they mature, are sold on the European market, paying the Spanish contractors a price for each unit produced. The process of raising and caring for the plants is under the technical control of their foreign owners, who make savings in heating costs, are able to benefit from the low wage-levels and take advantage of the know-how of Spanish farmers. With the exception of this ingenious system, there is no other tendency to internationalise agricultural production directly.

THE PRESENT CONTEXT OF SPANISH AGRICULTURE IN THE 1980s

Spanish agriculture in the 1980s bears little relationship to the position of 50 years ago when the transformation began, even if tradition has served to influence the direction of this change. In 1981 the economically-active population in agriculture was still more than two million workers, 16.2 per cent of the working population. Furthermore, more than 65 per cent of this population was over 40 years of age. Irrigation only covered 17.3 per cent of cultivable land and with the exception of the northern coast, the Spanish drought is very severe. Despite the important improvements achieved during the last 20 years, the productivity per worker in Spanish agriculture is considerably less than for the EEC as a whole. It is not surprising, then, that this 16 per cent of the economically active population only contributes 5.8 per cent of the Gross Domestic Product.

If we consider the main components of agricultural production, the basic features remain the same, although cattle-raising has made a considerable advance. The importance of cereal production (barley, wheat and – much less important – maize) and sugar beet is worth noting. Among tree crops there are olives and grapes, which are highly concentrated geographically (Andalucia produces 60 per cent of the former and Castille – La Mancha some 45 per cent of the latter). As far as agricultural exports are concerned, which constitute 18 per cent of total exports, the principal products are vegetables, citrus fruit, olive oil and wine. Livestock production, accounting for 39 per cent of sectoral output, is almost entirely for the domestic market. Although in connection with Spain's entry to the EEC attempts have been made to minimise the extent to which Spanish agriculture is dependent on Mediterranean products, this is still the predominant pattern.

Nevertheless macro-economic figures, as is often the case in economics, do not provide all the necessary information. Average figures can actually provide a very distorted picture of the real situation that they are supposed to reflect. Spanish agriculture is not made up of homogenous units of production and the process of modernisation that has taken place since the 1960s has been based on a considerable increase in differentiation. In order to understand the agrarian economy in the second half of the 1980s, it is essential to distinguish between the diverse situations and the distinct types of farm.

TABLE 7.1 Spanish agriculture: trade balances

Product	Imports (Tm)			Exports (Tm)		
	1970	1975	1980	1970	1975	1980
Wheat	934		304 917	414 176		239 928
Oats	6 403		554 108	20 427		377
Rice	3		1 711	70 186		56 476
Maize	1 971 898		4 532 545	7 196		804
Sorghum	184 261		666 164	40		11
Soya (seed)	1 229 652		3 213 607			369 400
(oil)	2 602		9 962	85 581		14 619
(flour)	25 001		57 325	100		25 678
Sunflower	6 400		40 092	1 205		
Meat (fresh)	102 494	84 387	43 592	4 746	6 171	16 630
(prepared)	6 282	7 108	11 021	308	1 365	3 664
Citrus fruits	NS	NS	NS	1 518 437	1 509 402	1 548 059
Grapes	NS	NS	NS			129 736
Vegetables	NS	NS	NS	454 487	546 160	746 503
Milk (fresh)	37 559	172 764	8 826	490	81	213
(conc.)	8 271	6 289	5 251	193	54	1 312
(powder)	67 262	32 206	52 782	64	436	312
(butter)	1 846	1 893	3 287	1	2	74
(cheese)	7 698	12 712	20 700	67	332	1 545
Wine	NS	NS	NS	326 499	515 538	574 146

SOURCE: Manual Estadisticas Agrarias 1982.

It is possible to classify agricultural units in the 1980s in terms of three distinct types although, as always, the precise limits of each category are often difficult to establish. First, there are the large commercial (very modern) farms, situated mainly in the centre or the southern half of the country. Most of these large farms have come about as the result of the transformation of the old *latifundios*, although large farms are also found in other areas of the country. Frequently they are the property of old families or, if created more recently, belong to people who have been involved in other sectors, particularly successful professional people or industrial entrepreneurs who live in the cities. In these cases, the reasons for the establishment of these large farms are often very far removed from the direct profitability of the farms themselves. They include asset diversification for tax reasons, risk avoidance, or an attempt to maintain the value of an estate. Taken together they are productive units that have been intensively modernised, particularly by substituting machinery for manual labour. At the present time, they absorb very limited amounts of labour and produce large quantities for the market. They have learned how to make use of the public funds established to promote agricultural modernisation and generally they do not face serious financial difficulties. These farms constitute the cutting edge of Spanish agriculture and present major possibilities for maintaining its competitiveness in the international arena. Needless to say, they are far removed from the low productivity levels which constitute the average for the sector as a whole.

The second major category comprises smaller but modernised and intensively operated farms. These farms are worked fundamentally by family labour and have made a considerable effort to adapt their holdings to new methods of production. The farmers concerned have frequently had to resort to external finance, especially to buy machinery and construct new buildings. These farms constitute the major group of farming units, the nucleus of Spanish agriculture, with a great variety of economic levels and different sizes producing the bulk of agricultural output. Their economic situation is much more unstable than that of the large farms. Perhaps for this reason, these farmers are the most vocal and active in representing their case to the public and to politicians, and in pursuing their corporate interests through agricultural organisations and lobbies, political representatives and trade unions.

The third and last category is made up of small family producers. These include many who have actually attempted to modernise their

TABLE 7.2 *Spanish farm structure*

	No. of farms	%	Land area	%
FARMS WITH LAND	2 344 000	100	44 311 700	100
SMALL FARMS				
0.1 to 2 ha	957 300	40.8	758 800	1.7
2.1 to 5 ha	518 140	22.1	1 632 700	3.7
5.1 to 20 ha	576 485	24.6	5 664 070	13.8
MEDIUM FARMS				
20.1 to 50 ha	168 253	7.0	5 126 522	11.5
50.1 to 100 ha	61 618	2.5	4 234 150	9.4
LARGE FARMS				
100.1 to 200 ha	31 118	1.2	4 255 427	9.5
200 ha	31 098	1.3	22 640 094	51.1

SOURCE: Agricultural Census (1982)

holdings and adopt modern technology on their farms.

Table 7.2 uses data from the 1982 Agricultural Census to provide a profile of Spanish farm structure. Although 'family farmers' exist, whom we might refer to as 'peasants', they are relatively few in number, and usually confined to older people, especially in marginal areas of the country. Family farming is a misnomer for this group, since most able-bodied younger people who might have worked small farms have left in search of work in other sectors. In the first three-quarters of 1986, the economically active population in Spain fell by ten per cent, the level of unemployment exceeding 20 per cent throughout the 1980s.

In our opinion, the first category, shown in Table 7.2 of less than 2 hectares, should include most of the commercial vegetable and fruit production farms in the country. This group would be small in comparison with the very large number of farms which one could hardly describe as farms at all. Farms under 20 hectares can in fact be described as 'marginal farms', with the exception of those indicated in vegetable and fruit production. Only those farms over 20 hectares can realistically be described as functioning farms, and indeed it might be preferable to regard 50 hectares as the watershed. Once it is realised that 87.5 per cent of farms control only 18.2 per cent of the land area and that the remaining 12.5 per cent of farms actually account for 81.8 per cent of the land area in Spain, then other explanations about the dual character of Spanish agriculture are hardly necessary.

In some cases, although less often, small producers have undertaken an intensive process of investment in an attempt to reach a higher stratum, especially the young children of farmers who have not been able to abandon the farm altogether as they had planned. In the majority of cases, however, this surplus population has been forced to complement its inadequate income from agriculture with any other source of income available, usually having recourse to other types of activity such as seasonal work, self-employment, work in the black economy and multiple job holding.

The two first groups to which we referred above make up, properly speaking, the agriculture of Spain, while the last group, that of very small producers, – quantitatively the most important – constitutes in fact a marginal group from the viewpoint of production. The indiscriminate inclusion of all farms in the calculations about Spanish agriculture has tended to distort the picture. It has also led to wrong assumptions about the direction that change will probably take in the sector. Every day and with increasing clarity, Spanish agriculture becomes more and more dualistic, made up of two groups, one large group consisting of the first two categories referred to above, which is significant for its contribution to production, and the second group consisting of the smaller marginal farmers, who are effectively refugees from the agricultural production process. They stay within the agricultural sector largely because they cannot find sufficient employment within the economy as a whole.

If we consider the size of landholdings as an approximate indication of their economic capacity, something which one would want to qualify, then we should accept the following structure as outlined. We would then find that 40.8 per cent of all farms in the 1982 agricultural census had less than 2 hectares of land. Another 22.1 per cent possessed between 2 and 5 hectares of land; 24.6 per cent possessed between 5 and 20 hectares and 9.5 per cent of farms between 20 and 100 hectares. This last category accounts for 21 per cent of all the land. Only 1.3 per cent of farms possessed more than 200 hectares. Nevertheless, holdings of this size, that is very large holdings, made up over half, 51.1 per cent, of all the land available. In fact, within the category of large farms, farms over 1000 hectares accounted for 27 per cent of the total agricultural land in Spain.

THE INTERNATIONAL AGRICULTURAL CRISIS AND SPANISH AGRICULTURE

Spanish agriculture, increasingly under pressure to modernise and to increase its productivity within an increasingly dualistic structure, and at a time when indebtedness is also rising and profits are basically unstable, if not falling, also had to confront the effects of integration within the EEC. Membership of the EEC itself necessitated considerable structural readjustment, but this process was complicated by two additional tendencies. First, the continuing high level of unemployment which exceeded 22.5 per cent in 1986. This level of unemployment impeded rural migration, thus closing one avenue of adjustment. The second factor is the international agricultural crisis.

The international crisis involves increasing confrontation between the two principal agricultural superpowers, the United States and the EEC, both of which are preoccupied with expanding and maintaining their markets. The crisis assumes the form of depressed prices on the world market, as well as various attempts to subsidise agricultural production for export. Industrial countries, with relatively advanced agricultural sectors, have become increasingly aggressive in trying to maintain as well as to broaden their external markets, while defending their domestic markets.

Spain, like other countries, has been forced to confront this commercial aggression and protectionism, but in addition, through its membership of the European Community, it has lost its own autonomy in national decision-making, which is increasingly being transferred from Spain itself to the European Community under the terms of the Common Agricultural Policy. The signing, in June 1985, of the Treaty of Accession of Spain and Portugal to the EEC, initiated an important battle for agricultural markets between the United States and the EEC. When the Treaty was signed no clear compensation had been negotiated under the rules of the GATT which require that 'third' countries which are negatively affected by the Treaty should be compensated. The widening of the European tariff system and Spain's membership of the EEC had clear implications for the United States which had previously been able to regard the Iberian Peninsula as a privileged client in terms of its agricultural exports. In fact, in recent years, Spain and Portugal have been amongst the six most important countries for grain imports from the United States. Clearly, at a time when the United States was finding it difficult to place its exports on world markets, the position of Spain was quite critical. A complete crisis was averted by the end of 1986, when an agreement was reached between the United States and the EEC, enabling Spain and Portugal to import more than 2 million tonnes of maize and 300 000 tonnes of sorghum every year for a four-year period from the United States.

This agreement, which at first might seem a triumph for the United States, nevertheless, does not resolve the real problem of the present crisis. Although the EEC had deferred to the United States, the Common Agricultural Policy continues to be operative, and the European Community can continue to subsidise its exports in order to dispose of its production surpluses. The United States will thus continue to encounter on world markets the European maize that it had been able to eliminate from the Spanish and Portuguese markets. In this way, the mechanisms that have generated overproduction in agriculture continue to function. Spain is in the middle of this agricultural marketing war. The provisioning of the Spanish market has become one element in the struggle between the superpowers on the international agricultural market.

The agricultural crisis, then, has a double negative effect on Spanish agriculture. On the one hand, facing the decline in prices, a hardening of world markets and diminishing protection, Spanish producers have to increase their competitiveness not only to maintain external markets but also to safeguard their domestic market. On the other hand, the agreements reached between the superpowers over agricultural produce make it difficult for Spanish agriculture to direct its efforts towards products in which it has a deficit and whose output in recent years has tended to increase. Nor should one forget the differences in political power between countries, which place Spain in a very weak position in all these negotiations.

Nevertheless the perception in Spain of the international agricultural crisis, and the anxiety surrounding it, appears to be still rather weak. Although not ignored by political leaders and amongst the upper ranks of civil servants, the issue is not an important part of the current discussions about Spanish agriculture and the consequences of the international crisis are not clearly seen. The problems of accession to the EEC dominate all other views regarding domestic and international problems and constitute the most important elements which catalyse and accelerate the restructuring of Spanish agriculture. The consequences for Spain of the agricultural crisis in the world as a whole are seen as simply aggravating the effects of Spain's adhesion to the Community.

Within the EEC, the present budgetary difficulties have their origin in continuous conflicts between member countries, for which the Common Agricultural Policy is seen as the main culprit. But in the context of the crisis of overproduction on world markets, the surpluses that have arisen from the Common Agricultural Policy must be subsidised in order to find commercial outlets. It is a paradox of the present situation that these surpluses occur at a moment in which new liberal economic policies imply greater willingness for government to reduce public expenditure and the public budget, and to try and limit the extent to which governments are prepared to assist in the financing of the EEC.

It seems clear, then, that in this context in the next few years it is likely that the support that the EEC provides agricultural producers will decline. This tendency can already be seen in the reforms which have been incorporated in the different parts of the productive apparatus in Europe. Nevertheless these changes are not going to affect European agriculture in a unified way. In the case of Spain, it is obvious that a reduction in the level of support will affect an important part of agriculture, since it is characterised by a much lower level of capitalisation than most parts of northern Europe.

Nor will assistance in terms of the structural policy established under the EEC, rather than quota policy, affect the different levels of the agricultural production system in Spain in the same way. Structural aid in principle will be directed largely towards helping the areas in which agriculture is most marginal, whereas the deterioration of price policy is most likely to affect the areas of greatest production. Thus modernised enterprises, of medium scale, are probably the most vulnerable to changes in agricultural policy. A hardening of EEC price policy would therefore be most prejudicial to these middle commercial sectors which will not receive aid in terms of structural policy, and will find it difficult to survive.

Nor has Spain's accession to the EEC been as favourable as was anticipated in other respects. Spain's position within the EEC has been prejudiced, to a considerable extent, by the preferential agreements that have been made between the EEC and 'third countries', which have enhanced the competitiveness of these countries within the world market. Conversely, Spain's membership of the EEC has made it more difficult to export certain typically Spanish products to other markets, like the United States and Canada. At the same time, the demands for control of production arising as a result of EEC membership are also important. A number of limitations can clearly be identified in cereal production: the introduction of co-responsibility levies within the EEC together with a less favourable price policy, the limitation of intervention, the demand for greater product quality, and other aspects. In the case of vegetable oils, the free entry of soya makes it impossible to improve Spanish competitiveness in those crops, given the differential in costs between American and Spanish production. Moreover, any protective measures in this field might lead to greater problems in the oilseed market, and provoke United States' retaliation. In the case of sugar production, the great surpluses in sugar beet block any initiatives in this area.

Apart from arable crops, the situation of milk production also deserves attention. Only one year after Spain's accession to the EEC, milk quotas are already a reality, although Spain is a deficit producer in milk and dairy produce. The negotiations for entry stipulated a series of measures to benefit the dairy sector as compensation for the very unfavourable treatment of Spanish vegetables and fruit. However, the only visible results so far have been to completely freeze, if not reduce, the production of dairy produce in Spain. Furthermore, Spain has had to participate in financing the reduction and ultimate removal of all European stocks of butter which, of course, it had no part in producing. At the same time, many products which are typically Mediterranean, like wine and olive oil, no longer have a very promising future. In the first case, the complementary mechanisms for exchanging wine can have serious effects on its exports, and in the case of olive oil, problems have arisen as a result of the confrontation between the United States and the EEC. It seems quite clear that the present situation is leading towards reduced opportunities for Spanish agriculture. In this context, it is difficult for Spain to consider increasing agricultural production. In fact, all the indications are that in the near future Spanish agriculture will undergo further rationalisation rather than expand production. In most sectors, maintaining production, while continuing to absorb advanced technology, will simply lead to the concentration of production and the reduction of the number of farms and of the working population within the agricultural sector in Spain. All these elements mean that Spain's membership of the Community is being perceived increasingly by farmers as a grave problem.

In which directions can Spanish agriculture continue to grow? There are possibilities for expansion, although not particularly favourable ones in the subsector of fruit and fresh vegetables, particularly citrus fruits and non-seasonal products or products of high value. It is possible that the demand for these products will increase both in the external and the domestic market. In these products, Spain has certain important climatic advantages and, above all, a productive structure that permits low cost production in products that require intensive labour input. The low agricultural labour costs in

Spain are related both to low salary levels compared with the European Community, and to the preponderance of family agriculture in which low incomes are often absorbed by the household. All this suggests that further expansion may occur in the fruit and fresh vegetables sectors. Nevertheless, this would benefit only selected regions in Spain and, moreover, producers in other countries of the EEC are very resistant to increases in Spanish production of these crops.

As far as the productive structure is concerned, it does not appear that integration within the European Community has substantially altered the tendencies towards concentration that have been operating since the 1960s. There have been no important changes in the agrarian structure which could be attributed to the effects of the Common Agricultural Policy or to new market conditions. The process has been reinforced and accelerated by modernisation and entry into the EEC. Furthermore, concentration has been achieved not only at the level of production but also by means of new systems of marketing. The production of vegetables for the external market, for example, has required a considerable concentration in the hands of private groups and co-operatives, which have come to dominate the productive apparatus and have made family producers much less autonomous in the kinds of decisions they can take about production.

This whole process has led to increasing concentration of enterprises in agriculture both in production and marketing. A few farms, modern, efficient and profitable, are increasingly producing the major part of Spanish agricultural output with more investment and much less recourse to labour. At the same time, with high urban unemployment making it difficult to abandon the sector entirely, the number of marginal holdings and marginal farms have tended to increase. These farms each day experience greater difficulty in surviving, as the costs of production rise and agricultural policy becomes restrictive.

In reviewing the consequences for Spanish agriculture of the world agricultural crisis, and Spain's accession to the EEC, it is worth emphasising two principal aspects. First to suggest that both phenomena have meant essentially the consolidation, acceleration and deepening of the process of transformation in agriculture which was started in the 1960s and has continued ever since. This modernisation is strongly linked with agro-industrial expansion and integration at the international level. The economic crisis in Spain, the world agricultural crisis and Spain's integration within the EEC have on the one hand reinforced the tendencies to modernisation, and on the other have presented additional difficulties by reducing Spanish agriculture's room for manoeuvre and its autonomy. However, none of these processes has altered the fundamental direction taken by Spanish agriculture.

It is difficult to anticipate the reaction of farmers faced with this dynamic process. In the spring of 1987 a number of important actions were taken which suggest that farmers, principally those of medium size are increasingly protesting against the new situation. A particular area of conflict is associated with the establishment of milk quotas and one can also detect a great deal of discord among the producers of dryland cereals. Nevertheless it is difficult to predict exactly how this dissatisfaction will be articulated and what forms protest may take.

One part of the agricultural sector is constituted as a provider of agricultural goods for the European market that requires intensive labour, an abundant use of water, and certain climatic features for their successful growth. At the same time, it is also clear that Spain has gradually consolidated its position as an important market for the basic products and surpluses of the agriculture of other advanced societies, for example in cereals, soya, and milk production. The productive apparatus of Spanish agriculture is highly dependent on the world economy for technology and for basic inputs. Similarly, production for the internal market is every day more dependent on agro-industrial enterprises, most of them of transnational character. These patterns seem to correspond quite remarkably to those found in the agricultural sector of certain Latin American countries. Will Spanish agriculture become the European equivalent of Mexico, or can it be converted into Europe's California?

Notes

1. Average figures for use of chemical fertilisers: 14.9 Kg.N, 17.7 Kg. P_2O_5 and 4.3 Kg. K_2O per ha.
2. In 1980 the number of agro-food enterprises was 54 000, of which 70 per cent had less than five employees. In 1975 it was estimated that foreign capital constituted 15 per cent of the food sector, but five years later this was 29 per cent. The participation of foreign capital varied widely with the product: soft drinks (70 per cent in 1980): sweets, cakes and biscuits (50 per cent), milk products (40 per cent). In some products, such as sugar, foreign participation was practically nil.

Bibliography

Baron, E. (1971), *El final del campesinado* (Barcelona: Zero).

Bayo, E. (1973), *El manifesto de la tierra* ed(Barcelona: Planeta).

Cruz Villalón, J. (1986), *La agricultura española ante los recientes cambios políticos y económicos*. Mimeo.

García Delgado, J. L. and S. Roldán, 'Contribución al análisis de la agricultura tradicional en España: los cambios decisivos de la última década', in *Velarde et al, La España de los años 70 II La Economía* (Madrid: Zero).

García de Blas, A., 'Empleo y Rentas en el Sector Agrario', Papeles No. 16, 91.

Leal, J. L. *et al.* (1975), 'La agricultura en el desarrollo capitalista español (1940–70)' ed (Madrid: Siglo XXI).

Naredo, J. M. (1971), *La evolución de la agricultura en España* ed (Madrid: Estela).

Peréz Blanco, J. M., 'Rasgos macroeconómicos básicos de la evolución de la agricultura española 1964/82: crisis actual', Papeles de Economía Española No. 16, 4.

Sánchez, P. (1983), 'La integración de España en la CEE', Papeles de Economía Española No. 16.

Sánchez, P. (1986), 'Estructura Agraria de España: aspectos socio-económicos', in *Enciclopedia de la Economía Española* ed (Madrid: Orbis).

Soria, R. and M. Rodríguez Zuñiga (1984), 'El sector ganadero', Papeles de Economía Española No. 16.

Tarrafeta Puyal, L. (1984), 'Financiación de la agricultura española', Papeles de Economía Española No. 16, 91.

Tio, C. (1982), 'La política de aceites comestibles en la España del Siglo XX', Ministerio de Agricultura (Madrid: Serie Estudios).

Titos Moreno, A. and Giménez de Haro 'El complejo de producción agro-alimentaria' Papeles de Economía Española No. 16, Cuadro 2.

Viladomiu, L. (1985), 'La inserción de España en el complejo soja mundial, Ministerio de Agricultura, Madrid (Colección Estudios) 257.

8 Structural Dimensions of Farm Crisis in the Federal Republic of Germany

Max J. Pfeffer

INTRODUCTION

Farm crisis has taken different forms in the Federal Republic of Germany since the Second World War. Whatever the nature of the crisis, small, economically marginal farms have been of central importance. Small farms were to play a central role in overcoming food shortages in the years immediately following the war. Later, high rates of decline in the number of small farms were interpreted as a family farm crisis by the German Farmers Union (Deutscher Bauernverband, DBV). The stated policy objective of the DBV was to preserve the greatest number of farms possible.

It was argued that the loss of small farms was rooted in the inability of farmers to earn an income at parity with comparable occupational groups. It was observed that several factors such as inelasticity in the demand for food, and rising costs of production contribute to a dampening of the income-generating capacity of the farm sector. Consequently, increases in farm incomes tended to fall below those of other sectors of the economy.

The DBV promoted the introduction of price support programmes as a means of improving farm incomes and stemming the reduction of farm numbers. Price support programmes did not prevent sharp declines in the number of small farms in the 1960s and early 1970s, as economic growth offered alternative employment opportunities to operators of small farms and their families. However, during this period, farm incomes on average kept pace with comparable occupational groups, and concern over the farm income problem eased.

Over the past decade farm income has suffered a relative decline, and economic stagnation has limited alternative employment opportunities for farmers. Under these circumstances, there is cause for renewed concern with the incomes of small farms. The incomes of small and medium-sized farms have not kept pace with those of comparable occupational groups since the mid-1970s. These farms are proportionately more important in regions officially designated as 'agriculturally disadvantaged'. The economies of such areas are heavily reliant on incomes from agriculture. In these regions, the farm income problem has the quality of a crisis.

The farm crisis in agriculturally disadvantaged regions raises a variety of concerns, including, for example, rural depopulation and its social consequences. Given limited employment alternatives, individuals often have no choice but to leave these areas if they cannot secure a livelihood from agriculture. A related concern is the quality of the natural environment in these areas. It is feared that the abandonment of such areas will result in a lack of maintenance of delicate soils and the destruction of the traditional image of the countryside.

Price supports, that form the core of agricultural policy for Germany and the European Economic Community (EEC), have failed to adequately address the needs of agriculturally disadvantaged regions. The basic flaw of these policies is that they disproportionately benefit larger producers who are concentrated in regions more favourable for agricultural production. If economic stagnation and the erosion of farm incomes persist, regional differences are likely to become the main line of conflict over future developments in agricultural policy. Policy makers, aware of the shortcomings of price support policies, have already introduced policies to provide investment subsidies and direct transfer payments targeted specifically at agriculturally disadvantaged regions. These policies are in their infancy and are very limited, but they may represent an important step beyond the price support regime in the longrun.

This chapter begins with an overview of the changing structure of agriculture in the Federal Republic of Germany since World War II. The importance of small farms, the effects of changes in the structure of agriculture on these farms, and the forces behind the rise of price support programmes are discussed. This overview is followed by a consideration of the implications of the declining incomes of small- and medium-sized farms for agriculturally disadvantaged regions. It is argued that the farm income problem constitutes a farm crisis in these regions. Finally, policy alternatives for farms in agriculturally disadvantaged regions and their implications for future policy development are evaluated.

THE CHANGING NATURE OF THE FARM CRISIS

The farm crisis has been defined in several ways in the Federal Republic of Germany since the Second World War. In the years immediately following the war, farm production was unable to meet demand for food. The farm crisis took the form of a food shortage in Germany as well as the rest of war-torn Europe. The average German had consumed 3000 calories per day prior to the war. After the war the average daily caloric intake stood at 1500 and was as low as 1000 in industrial areas such as the Ruhr Valley. Food rations in the 1945–47 period averaged between 1200 and 1300 calories per day per person, or about half of what was considered a normal calorie intake (Hallett, 1973). German agricultural policy's declared objective of self-sufficiency in food production arose from this situation.

Germany's partition left the large landed estates of the German Reich which had employed wage workers in what is today the Soviet Union, Poland, and the German Democratic Republic. The Federal Republic of Germany inherited a large number of very small- and medium-sized farms (Planck, 1987). It was on the basis of this farm structure that Germany was to attempt to overcome the food shortages and achieve self-sufficiency in food production.

Small farms were of obvious importance in terms of farm numbers in the immediate post-war years. In 1949, farms of less than 20 hectares accounted for more than 90 per cent of all farms. In contrast, farms with more than 50 hectares made up less than 1 per cent of all farms (Table 8.1). Consequently, small farms were to play an important role in raising food production. But small farms were of

TABLE 8.1 *Percentage distribution of farms by size, Federal Republic of Germany, selected years*

Year	Size of farm in hectares				
	1–19	20–50	50 +	Total	Number of farms
1949	92.3	6.8	0.9	100.0	1 647 515
1960	90.0	8.8	1.2	100.0	1 385 250
1965	87.8	10.8	1.4	100.0	1 252 397
1970	83.7	14.5	1.8	100.0	1 083 128
1975	77.6	19.5	2.9	100.0	904 732
1980	73.8	22.3	3.9	100.0	797 378
1985	71.1	23.7	5.2	100.0	720 835

SOURCE: Agrarbericht, 1986.

TABLE 8.2 *Rates of unemployment, Federal Republic of Germany, 1950–84*

Years	Average unemployment rate
1950–54	7.9
1955–59	2.5
1960–64	0.6
1965–69	0.6
1970–74	1.2
1975–79	4.4
1980–84	7.9

SOURCE: *Statistisches Jahrbuch für die Bundesrepublik*, 1954, 1960, 1962, 1970, 1980, 1985.

central importance in a variety of other issues as well. For example, over 50 000 war refugees were resettled on small farms (Henning, 1978). There were few job opportunities at the time for either refugees or for farmers leaving agriculture. The unemployment rate in 1950 was still 10 per cent, and did not drop substantially until the late 1950s (Table 8.2).

As food shortages eased and industrial production expanded, farmers had less incentive to remain in farming. With unemployment rates dropping, the demand for labour was high and wages tended to rise more rapidly than farm incomes. This was especially true for farmers with small holdings. The number of holdings with less than 20 hectares decreased while farms in other size classes increased for most of the post-war period (Table 8.3). Furthermore, in comparing Tables 8.2 and 8.3, it is apparent that the rate of decline in farms of less than 20 hectares rose in close correspondence to reductions in the rate of unemployment until the mid-1970s.

These developments were a matter of serious concern to the German Farmers Union (DBV). The DBV had become the chief representative of the farm sector in the post-war period, and had been more successful in maintaining unity within the farm sector than most of its European counterparts. Among its chief concerns was the maintenance of its constituency and thereby its influence *vis-à-vis* competing interests such as the growing export industry (Averyt, 1979; Kötter, 1983). However, the DBV realised that without some form of government intervention the changing structure of the German economy would undermine its position.

It is worth considering this structure in more detail. While both the overall economy and agriculture grew throughout the post-war

TABLE 8.3   *Annualised percentage in farm numbers by size of farm, Federal Republic of Germany, 1949–85*

| Years | Hectares | | | Total |
	1–19	20–49	50 +	
1949–60	−1.8	0.7	0.4	−1.5
1960–65	−2.5	2.0	0.9	−2.0
1965–70	−3.9	3.1	2.4	−2.9
1970–75	−5.1	2.2	6.1	−3.6
1975–80	−1.6	0.2	3.5	−2.5
1980–85	−2.7	0.9	3.5	−2.0

SOURCE: Table 8.1

period, agriculture's share of the gross national product declined steadily, from 10 percent in 1950 to just 2 percent in 1980. The declining relative position of agriculture in the national economy can be attributed to the fact that food consumption has not risen as rapidly as increases in income. Of course, this point is true not only of Germany, but of other nations with highly developed economies as well. Nevertheless, limits on growth in the demand for food have been rather firm in Germany, which has experienced limited population growth and saturated markets for agricultural commodities for more than three decades.

Rapid gains in per capita income were accompanied by unprecedented growth in farm productivity in post-war Germany. These gains in productivity can be attributed to tractorisation, expanded use of commercial fertiliser, and improvements in seed and breeding stocks (Henning, 1979). But technological advance merely steepened the decline in agriculture's economic position as productivity gains generally surpassed growth in demand, leading to production surpluses which exerted downward pressure on price levels (Schmitt, 1983). At the same time, German farmers competed with rapidly expanding industries for production inputs. As the demand for these goods rose, so did their prices. Yet, farmers could not forgo the purchase of these inputs, if they were to produce the quantity of farm commodities necessary to achieve income levels considered acceptable in society. Thus, they were trapped in a cost-price squeeze, that is, as productivity increased, the price of inputs rose and the price of farm commodities offered for sale declined.

This predicament for farmers became clear as Germany entered a period of rapid economic growth accompanied by a swift rise in incomes and consumption in the mid-1950s. While farm incomes rose absolutely, they tended to remain below those of comparable occupational groups. A sizeable gap between earnings in the farm sector and other sectors of the economy was developing in the 1950s (Planck, 1987).

Declines in farm numbers were attributed to this disadvantaged position of agriculture within the German economy and the DBV sought government intervention to reduce the structural transformation of agriculture. It based its appeals on a conservative ideology rooted in German romanticism. The loss of farms experienced in the 1950s was interpreted as a family farm crisis by the DBV. The family farm was presented as a bulwark of a democratic and capitalistic society. The DBV's argument in favor of the preservation of as many family farms as possible has been summarised as follows, 'The farmer on his own land is independent, a broad element of a true middle class, and a model for dispersed property ownership. Thereby the farm population constitutes a stable and solid counterweight against the uprooted, "red" urban proletariat' (Bergmann, 1975, 128). In the early 1950s, the governing administration was open to the appeals of the DBV, as it sought to stabilize the farm sector in an effort to establish a politically conservative element and a force opposed to the Social Democratic Party. Furthermore, calls for the preservation of existing family farms based on a conservative or fundamentalist ideology were particularly effective in the context of the Cold War (Kötter, 1983).

The DBV scored a major victory with the passage of the Agricultural Act (Landwirtschaftsgesetz) of 1955. Not only was the central importance of the family farm codified, but the parity principle that the farm sector should be given the opportunity to earn an income comparable to the industrial wage was established. By 1962, Germany's agricultural policy began to be integrated into that of the EEC. Nevertheless, income parity continued to be a clear and central element of agricultural policy. The agricultural policy objectives set forth in the Treaty of Rome included the maintenance of farm incomes 'to ensure a fair standard of living for the agricultural population, particularly by increasing the individual earnings of people engaged in agriculture' (Buckwell, et al., 1983, 10).

German agricultural policy during the 1950s and early 1960s, and later the Common Agricultural Policy of the EEC, both attempted to support farm incomes by means of a variety of price support mechanisms. Price support programmes were unable to stem the decline in farm numbers, which continued to be confined to farms of less than 20 hectares, and rates of decline in farms of this size increased until the mid-1970s (Table 8.3). However, farm programmes did play a part in successfully reducing disparities between farm and non-farm incomes.

Over time, price support subsidies made up an increasing proportion of farm income. It was estimated that by the late 1960s, the combination of direct and indirect subsidies accounted for approximately half of the income of all Germans employed in agriculture (Henning, 1979). These price supports, in conjunction with changes in farm structure, were largely successful in eliminating the income disparity between farm and non-farm incomes, as comparisons between the composite industrial wage and the earnings of family members on full-time farms indicate.[1] This disparity, which had been marked in the 1950s, virtually disappeared in the 1960s and the early 1970s (Brandkamp, 1982). Given the elimination of disparities between farm and non-farm incomes and continued growth of employment opportunities outside of agriculture, there was little concern with continued reductions in the number of small farms during the 1960s and early 1970s.

Recent trends in farm income have focused renewed attention on the farm income problem and the plight of small farms. Figure 8.1 displays recent trends in the earnings of fully employed family members on full-time farms and the industrial comparison wage. Aside from rather minor annual fluctuations, farm earnings remained very close to the industrial comparison wage through 1975. However, beginning in the mid-1970s these figures began to diverge substantially. By 1982, there was a difference of more than 6000 DM between farm earnings and the industrial comparison wage. This difference is now larger than at any time during the 1950s, whether in nominal or real terms (Brandkamp, 1982).

However, exclusive consideration of overall trends in farm income is somewhat misleading in that it obscures the persistent nature of the farm income problem. There is considerable variation in earnings within the farm sector. In fact, income disparities within the farm sector are more pronounced than the disparity between farm and industrial incomes (Planck, 1987). In other words, the gap between farm incomes and the industrial comparison wage is not experienced

FIGURE 8.1   *Net farm income for full-time farms and industrial comparison wage per year, Federal Republic of Germany, 1968–84*

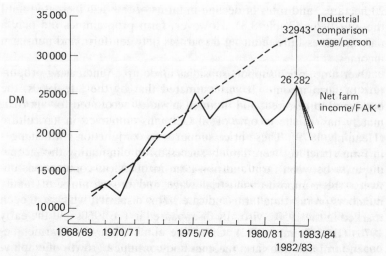

* FAK is the equivalent of a male family member fully employed on the farm.

SOURCE   Agrarbericht, 1984.

equally by all farmers. These disparities within the farm sector are illustrated in Figure 8.2. It is apparent that the earnings of small farms have consistently fallen below both those of medium-sized and large farms as well as the industrial comparison wage. This observation could be made even during the prosperous early 1970s. The significance of these disparities is underscored by the fact that only *full-time* farms (that is, farms earning less than 10 per cent of the combined income of farm operator and spouse off the farm) are being compared. Only after the mid-1970s did the earnings of medium-sized farms fall below the industrial comparison wage. Large farms displayed the most pronounced growth in earnings during the 1970s. Even as farm incomes dropped, the earnings of large farms remained comfortably above the industrial comparison wage.

Although these income disparities within the farm sector have persisted for decades, the farm income crisis of smaller farms was not as problematic prior to the onset of economic stagnation in the mid 1970s. Operators of small farms suffering economic hardship then

FIGURE 8.2 *Net farm income for full-time farms by size of farm * and industrial comparison wage, Federal Republic of Germany, 1968–85*

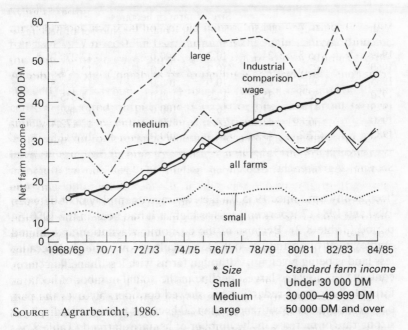

* Size	Standard farm income
Small	Under 30 000 DM
Medium	30 000–49 999 DM
Large	50 000 DM and over

SOURCE Agrarbericht, 1986.

could give up farming for employment in another sector of the growing economy, which resulted in a steady decline in farm numbers (Table 8.1). The land of those leaving agriculture was taken over by remaining farmers who were able to improve their incomes by expanding production (Brandkamp, 1982).

However, the economic stagnation of the past decade, together with saturated markets for major agricultural commodities, have limited the option of improving farm income by means of expanding production. The availability of land is steadily declining in Germany, as farm land is given up to alternative uses such as the construction of buildings and roads (Planck, 1987). Consequently, the possibility of a real expansion is limited, and takes place only by means of the reduction of land farmed by other operators. Prior to the 1980s, land shifted from farms of less than 20 hectares to those of 20 hectares or more. In the 1980s, only the largest farms as a group (that is, those with more than 50 hectares) captured an increasing share of the total number of hectares farmed (Table 8.4).

The unemployment rate in the early 1980s was higher than it had

TABLE 8.4   *Percentage distribution of land farmed by size of farm, Federal Republic of Germany, selected years*

| Year | Size of farm in hectares | | | | |
	1–19	20–50	50 +	Total	Number of hectares
1949	65.3	24.4	10.3	100.0	13 279.2
1960	62.6	27.1	10.3	100.0	12 934.8
1965	59.2	29.9	10.9	100.0	12 838.8
1970	52.2	35.5	12.3	100.0	12 645.5
1975	41.6	41.7	16.7	100.0	12 462.2
1980	36.0	43.9	20.1	100.0	12 172.4
1985	32.2	43.5	24.3	100.0	11 932.5

SOURCE: Agrarbericht, 1986.

been at any time since 1955. In fact, average unemployment between 1980 and 1984 (7.9 per cent) was as high as it had been in the 1950–54 period (Table 8.2). Because of the economic stagnation and limited employment opportunities outside agriculture over the past decade, less land is being given up. Although farms with less than 20 hectares continue to show the largest decline in the actual number of hectares farmed, the rate of reduction has slowed considerably over the past decade. Only farms with more than 50 hectares continue to display a strong rate of increase in the number of hectares farmed (Table 8.5).

The rate of decline in the number of small farms and the number of hectares they operate has slowed in the past decade. At the same time, the income-generating alternatives available to these farms are being narrowed. This statement is particularly true of livestock production, which has long been an important source of income for

TABLE 8.5   *Annualised percentage change in hectares farmed by size of farm, Federal Republic of Germany, 1949–80*

| Years | Hectares | | | |
	1–19	20–49	50 +	Total
1949–60	−0.6	0.7	−0.2	−0.2
1960–65	−1.3	1.8	0.9	−0.1
1965–70	−2.8	3.1	2.1	−0.3
1970–75	−4.8	2.9	5.8	−0.3
1975–80	−3.3	0.5	3.2	−0.5
1980–85	−2.6	−0.6	3.4	−0.4

SOURCE: Table 8.4

TABLE 8.6   *Concentration of selected types of animal production, Federal Republic of Germany, 1971 to 1983*

Type of animal	Size of holding	Percent of farms *		Percent of total animal holdings	
		1971	1983	1971	1983
Cattle	100 +	0.6	4.0	4.8	17.5
Milk cows	40 +	0.4	4.6	2.5	17.4
Breeder pigs	75 +	0.2	2.4	3.3	17.1
Feeder pigs	600 +	0.1	0.6	3.6	16.3
Laying hens	10 000 +	0.1	0.2	32.2	57.9
Feeding hens	25 000 +	0.6	0.3	48.3	79.4

* Per cent of farms with respective types of animal holdings.
SOURCE: Agrarbericht, 1986.

farms with limited assets in land. The German Ministry of Agriculture reports that one of the most important changes of the past decade has been the concentration of animal holdings. For example, between 1971 and 1983, the average number of milk cows and feeder pigs per farm increased by 80 per cent, while the number of hectares per farm grew by just 30 per cent.

Very high levels of concentration of animal holdings are observed only in poultry production. However, farms with larger inventories greatly increased their share of total animal holdings between 1971 and 1983 in the major livestock sectors (Table 8.6). This concentration of animal production is accompanied by greater specialisation of production (Agrarbericht, 1986), which typically requires increased investments in improved production facilities. Small farms, having only limited capital assets, are least able to make the investments necessary to remain competitive in livestock markets. Consequently, these developments in livestock production are likely to further limit income-enhancing alternatives available to small farms.

This farm income problem is not new, and over the years farm programmes have been implemented to address this issue. However, in recent years these programmes have failed to provide persons working on two-thirds of all farms in Germany with a parity wage. The farm income problem acquires an added dimension when one considers that small farms in Germany are geographically concentrated. This concentration, together with more general social and economic characteristics, poses special problems for particular regions. For this reason it is necessary to evaluate the regional dimensions of the current farm crisis.

TABLE 8.7   *Percentage distribution of full-time farms by size and region, Federal Republic of Germany, 1980*

Farm size *	Region		Total
	Agriculturally advantaged	Agriculturally disadvantaged	
Small	35.8	45.5	39.2
Medium	25.0	30.6	27.0
Large	39.2	23.9	33.8
Total	100.0	100.0	100.0

*	Size	Standard farm income
	Small	Under 30 000 DM
	Medium	30 000–49 999 DM
	Large	50 000 DM and over

SOURCE: Forschungsgesellschaft für Agrarpolitik und Agrarsoziologie.

REGIONAL DIMENSIONS OF FARM CRISIS

The farm income problem in Germany is most pronounced in agriculturally disadvantaged regions, which account for about one-third of all full-time farms.[2] Moreover, small- and medium-sized farms whose incomes have increasingly fallen below the industrial comparison wage since the mid-1970s make up more than three-fourths of all full-time farms in these regions (Table 8.7).

Farms in agriculturally disadvantaged areas are plagued by difficult operating conditions which constrain their ability to earn an income on a par with that of farms in more favorably endowed regions. About two-thirds of the West German landscape is made up of highlands and mountains, and a large proportion of this land mass is considered agriculturally disadvantaged (Planck, 1987). The characteristics of these agriculturally disadvantaged regions and their implications for agricultural production have been described as follows:

[These] regions [are] characterized by close alternations of sheltered valley and exposed uplands. These produce a highly differentiated geography of physically advantaged and disadvantaged farming areas, in which environmental differences are not just a matter of contrasts in temperature, insolation, and rainfall, but also include acute variations in terrain and soil quality. In the upland regions there are large tracts of steeply sloping land which, although they have been farmed quite intensively during past periods of population pressure, are hardly suitable for the application of present-day agricultural methods. The working of such ground by modern machinery is scarcely feasible: in many instances it is totally impossible.   (Thieme, 1983, 222).

These unfavourable natural conditions place rather severe limits on production alternatives. The majority of all land in agriculturally disadvantaged regions is devoted to pasture and not surprisingly, farms in such areas have higher than average stands of cattle and milk cows (Agrarbericht, 1984). It would seem that farms in these regions have a comparative advantage in various forms of livestock production. However, recent trends in the concentration of animal production are erasing any comparative advantage that farms in these regions might once have had.

As we have seen, livestock production is becoming more concentrated and specialised, and these trends also are accompanied by increasing geographical concentration in more fertile agricultural areas, particularly in locations close to processing plants and urban markets (Agrarbericht, 1986). These trends create a competitive handicap for farms in agriculturally disadvantaged regions. First of all, as a result of the tradition of partible inheritance, many of these farms are very small with highly parcellised holdings, inhibiting the development of larger, more specialised and competitive units. Secondly, farms in agriculturally disadvantaged areas have poor transportation links and market outlets, given their remoteness from large urban centres. These circumstances restrict the sale of farm produce to less lucrative markets.

The combination of farming with off-farm employment has been important in stabilising the populations of agriculturally disadvantaged regions. In these areas in 1980, about half of all farms were operated on a part-time basis (that is, more than 50 per cent of the combined income of farm operator and spouse are earned off the farm). An additional 25 per cent of all farms in these regions earned the majority of their income from farming, but relied on off-farm employment for more than 10 per cent of the combined income of farm operator and spouse (Forschungsgesellschaft für Agrarpolitik und Agrarsoziologie, 1980). However, economic stagnation since the mid-1970s has restricted this important option of combining farming with off-farm employment.

The combination of poor farming conditions and the absence of suitable alternative employment opportunities has aroused fears of depopulation, the abandonment of farm land, and the general social deterioration of such regions. A stable farm sector is thought to be instrumental in maintaining the population densities necessary for the provision of basic social and economic infrastructures and preserving the environment in such regions (Strauf, *et al.*, 1982). Environmental deterioration in agriculturally disadvantaged regions is a major concern. Because farms have often been operated on the steep inclines common to these regions, there is an ever-present danger of soil erosion. Farm abandonment poses the possibility of the deterioration of soils as well as the countryside's recreational value for the broader population (Thieme, 1983).

The economic well-being of the farm sector is generally considered as being crucial to the overall vitality of agriculturally disadvantaged regions. The special problems of such regions have long been recognised by agricultural experts and policy-makers, but existing agricultural policies have made little progress in solving the farm income problem in these areas.

Price support policies were at the heart of West German agricultural policy in the 1950s and 1960s. In 1968 the German price supports were superseded by those of the Common Agricultural Policy (CAP) of the EEC, but the operation of the EEC price supports is almost identical to those that had been in effect in Germany. The CAP includes some provisions for all major agricultural commodities produced in Germany.[3]

Price support policies are defective in ways that have especially important consequences for agriculturally disadvantaged regions. One basic defect of price supports is that they are tied to production. That is, benefits are realised per unit of the commodity marketed, with the result that larger farms receive more benefits. Income disparities between individual farms have consequently been exacerbated by price support policies. Furthermore, because the farm structure of agriculturally disadvantaged regions is characterised by the prevalence of small farms, price support policies have not only failed to alleviate regional disparities in farm income, but have actually broadened these differences.

Already in the late 1970s, recognition of the ineffectiveness of price support policies and, especially, the high costs of these policies led to calls for a fundamental reorientation of the CAP. Proposals for structural reform of the farm sector were made in response to mounting pressures within the EEC, brought about by overproduction and the high costs of disposing of agricultural commodity surpluses. These proposals emphasised structural reform of the farm sector and had pronounced implications for agriculturally disadvantaged regions. Farm numbers were to be reduced, farm size increased, marginal land taken out of production, and new jobs created. Obviously, such changes would result in a radical transformation of agriculturally disadvantaged regions where farming is the principal economic activity. The economic and social deterioration of these areas could only be avoided if structural reform of the farm sector were accompanied by adequate regional economic development.

Regional economic development is a key element of any plan for restructuring agriculture if it is to be both economically and socially effective. Of course, the West, and Germany in particular, experienced rapid economic growth through the mid-1970s. However, the ensuing recession and slower growth have prompted the reconsideration of agricultural policy (Haushofer, 1983). Economic recession has made calls for extensive reductions in the farm work force untenable in Germany, as alternative employment opportunities for people leaving agriculture are limited. The possibility of inducing rapid change in farm structure without guaranteeing requisite alternative employment opportunities is considered socially and politically unacceptable to German policy makers. This concern is especially pronounced with respect to agriculturally disadvantaged regions.

Falling farm incomes have a marked impact on these rural economies, where farming remains important and economic alternatives are limited. Given the economic constraints faced in agriculturally disadvantaged regions, some form of government intervention is needed to stabilise the remaining population and provide for its welfare. However, under current economic circumstances, neither price support policies nor structural policies are suited to this purpose. Economic stagnation has limited the possibilities for structural reform, and price support policies remain the centrepiece of EEC agricultural policy. Price support policies have been unable to stem the erosion of farm incomes relative to the industrial comparison wage over the past decade. In times of economic stagnation, when employment options are limited, farm families have few alternatives other than enduring reductions in their standard of living. Thus, the farm income problem takes on crisis proportions in agriculturally disadvantaged regions.

REGIONAL INTERESTS AND FUTURE POLICY
DEVELOPMENTS

Regional concerns are likely to weigh heavily in future policy considerations in Germany, because of growing regional disparities in farm income. Seventy five per cent of all larger, economically more successful farmers are concentrated in regions with natural conditions favourable for agricultural production, notably in the fertile plains of Northern Germany. Such producers benefit disproportionately from existing price support policies. The DBV has continued to lobby for price support subsidies for German farmers in recent years. But because the fiscal crisis of the EEC has all but eliminated the possibility of increased price support levels, the DBV has been forced to seek subsidies directly from the German government.

This partial 'renationalisation' of agricultural subsidies came about as a result of the introduction of marketing quotas for milk in 1984. In an effort to reduce rapidly expanding subsidies to milk producers, the EEC imposed a quota on the amount of milk that farmers could deliver and still receive a guaranteed price. The DBV sought compensation for income reductions resulting from the imposition of marketing quotas and the German government responded by offering tax reductions to 'qualified' farmers.[4] With the imposition of the EEC marketing quotas for grains, the same sort of compensation is now demanded for grain producers.

This renationalisation of agricultural subsidies is primarily a matter of political expediency, and provides no lasting solution to the farm crisis in West Germany. Tax breaks are a response to the increasing discontent of German farmers with the policy alternatives being offered by the DBV and the governing coalition. However, this rather shallow attempt to placate the farmers has merely exacerbated inequities within the farm sector. Tax reductions, like price supports, are tied to the volume of production. Consequently, small- and medium-sized farmers, hardest hit by the erosion of farm incomes, receive the least benefits from such policies. Furthermore, despite efforts to prevent large scale animal producers from benefitting from tax reductions, these restrictions have often been circumvented by various legal manoeuvers.

Thus, the German renationalisation of agricultural subsidies does not appear to offer an effective solution to the erosion of the incomes of most farmers or the economic crisis concentrated in agriculturally disadvantaged regions. This fact is apparent to many farmers, and these policies have fuelled rather than stifled farmer dissent. Farmers typically have been staunch backers of the Christian Democratic Party (CDU). However, the DBV has become increasingly ineffective in rallying support for the CDU, and in recent years farmers have been withdrawing, or threatening to withdraw, electoral support for the party.

Tax reductions for German farmers were instituted over the objections of the EEC, but other policy proposals emanating from the CDU's Minister of Agriculture are in line with the CAP and represent no significant departure from the existing price support regime. These proposals offer possible solutions to the problem of agricultural commodity surpluses, but assume a continuation of the existing price support system. For example, the Minister of Agriculture has proposed that imported soy-based feeds be substituted by EEC produced grains, as well as the production of alcohol from domestic grain and sugar beets as an alternative source of fuel. These proposals may open alternative markets for surplus EEC commodities, but again fail to address the roots of those surpluses and the inequities inherent in the existing price support framework.

Although market-orientated price support and structural reform policies have dominated agricultural policy discussions in the post-Second World War period, policies to preserve existing agrarian structures have been given greater consideration in recent years. Unlike market-orientated policies, substantive policies are most favorable to small- and medium-sized farmers. The growing interest in such policies also is related to environmental concerns. Environmental preservation is often seen as being opposed to market-orientated policies and the promotion of economic efficiency (Vogel, 1980). Some politicians go so far as to claim that the conflict between 'economy and ecology' will polarise future agricultural policy discussions (Deneke, 1980). The recent conflict between economic and environmental concerns in agricultural policy has been summed up as follows:

> In recent years there has been a strengthening awareness among the public that economic objectives in the sphere of food production have been pursued at substantial cost to the environment. In this awareness, consternation is coming from several quarters, ranging from doubt concerning the future of natural soil fertility to general dismay over the seemingly wanton destruction of the traditional image of the West German countryside. There is, therefore, a growing tide of feeling that too much latitude is being given to the needs of agricultural efficiency (Thieme, 1983, 242).

The Green Party offers an alternative view of agricultural efficiency. The Greens' agricultural policy platform proposes a departure from the production treadmill where economically hard-pressed farmers are forced to intensify production continuously in the effort to compensate for falling farm incomes. The Greens favor a reduction in the intensity of production through reduced petroleum-based inputs and less use of imported soy-based animal feeds. Implicit in this platform is the assumption that small scale, diversified farms would be best suited to engage in such production. However, the Greens offer no concrete proposals for promoting these changes.

The economic plight of small- and medium-sized farmers is most directly addressed in proposals for the replacement of the current system of price supports with direct subsidies to farm households that fall below some threshold of income. Such proposals have found favour in Social Democratic Party circles because they offer a means of reducing the subsidisation of agriculture while at the same time assuring that remaining subsidies are directed at those most in need. Policies offering subsidies directly to farmers have already been implemented in Germany. Regional policies implemented by the German government as part of the EEC Less Favoured Regions Directive, represent a concrete effort to address the problems of small- and medium-sized farmers in agriculturally disadvantaged regions. The main objectives of this directive are providing rural families with an acceptable income level, stabilising population levels, and preserving the countryside.

Under the auspices of the directive on less-favoured regions, the German Ministry of Agriculture in 1975 formulated a programme to provide subsidies to farms in agriculturally disadvantaged regions. These efforts are consistent with the regional policy objectives adopted by the EEC. Under the German programme, special investment subsidies are provided to farms in agriculturally disadvantaged regions in an effort to stabilise the social and economic structure of such areas. In 1986 these regions were expanded by 2 million hectares. With this addition, agriculturally disadvantaged regions account for more than 46 per cent of all West German farm land.

Extremely disadvantaged areas within regions considered unfavourable for agricultural production are also eligible for direct transfer payments (Ausgleichszulage). These subsidies are intended to raise farm incomes to an acceptable level, thereby stabilising the farm population. Inasmuch as these transfer payments prevent farm abandonment, they are also to play a role in preserving the traditional image of the countryside and its recreational value for the broader population (Peters, 1980). These extremely disadvantaged areas were expanded to encompass some 4 million hectares in 1985, thus accounting for more than 70 per cent of the farm land falling within the more broadly defined agriculturally disadvantaged regions, and about one-third of total farm land in Germany. The budget for direct transfer payments stood at 336 million DM in 1985. However, the importance of these payments should not be exaggerated. In 1984, average transfer payments per farm amounted to just 1473 DM per farm, which was less than 6 per cent of the average net income of farms in areas where such payments are available (Agrarbericht, 1986).

Agriculturally disadvantaged areas are concentrated in the southern states (Hessen, Rheinland-Pfalz, Baden-Württemburg, and Bayern), where small farms historically have predominated (Planck, 1987). Even within these states, agriculturally disadvantaged regions remain geographically concentrated, which is best illustrated by the geographic distribution of direct transfer payments. Almost three-fourths of these payments went to Baden-Württemburg and Bayern in 1984 (Agarbericht, 1986). Areas eligible for direct income transfers were concentrated in the Black Forest, the Alps, and sparsely populated areas along the border with the German Democratic Republic. The growth of direct income transfers and the expansion of areas eligible for special investment subsidies indicates the increasing awareness of policy makers that the farm crisis in Germany is geographically specific.

While regionally specific agricultural policy in Germany is in its infancy, it does suggest the outlines of possible future alternatives. Such alternatives would de-emphasise market solutions to the farm income problem, and instead promote policies focused upon substantive goals, such as the maintenance of existing agrarian structures and environmental preservation. New alternatives in agricultural policy are becoming imperative as commodity surpluses continue to place heavy strains on the EEC budget and economic stagnation limits the possibilities for structural reforms. Conflicts over the future direction of agricultural policy will be strongly influenced by regional interests based on differences in agrarian structures.

These conflicts pose a threat to the hegemony of the DBV since they bring to the fore inequities in the price support regime so forcefully promoted by the DBV. The DBV has enjoyed a virtual monopoly in farm interest representation in Germany since the

Second World War. It has justified this position on the grounds that all farmers share a common set of economic interests, and that these interests are best served through vigorous efforts to raise agricultural price support levels. The DBV has been very successful in pursuing this aim and prior to implementation of the Common Agricultural Policy (CAP), Germany had the highest prices for agricultural products in the EEC (Tangermann, 1979). The German delegation to Brussels, strongly influenced by the DBV, was effective in incorporating the same high price supports previously enjoyed by German farmers into the CAP (Henning, 1978).

The DBV now finds itself in a precarious situation. It must recognise the distinctive problems of agriculturally disadvantaged regions if it is to avoid giving up the initiative for dealing with these issues to state level affiliate organisations and government. This danger is very real in states like Bayern and Baden-Württemberg, where state governments and DBV affiliates are strenuously involved in efforts to assist small farms and agriculturally disadvantaged regions. Independent local initiatives threaten to undermine the DBV's claim of being the effective representative of all German farmers. This claim is a key legitimating factor of the DBV's role as a national political force.

On the other hand, greater recognition of the distinctive problems of small- and medium-sized farmers in agriculturally disadvantaged regions amounts to tacit admission of inequities in price support programmes on the part of the DBV. Any acknowledgment of this sort calls into question the DBV's longstanding position that, despite the tremendous costs involved, increases in price supports are the best means of improving the incomes of all German farmers. In short, the DBV is caught in a dilemma. Whatever stance it takes towards the economic problems of small- and medium-sized farmers in agriculturally disadvantaged areas, its position in the national political arena is diminished.

The growth of policies targeted at farmers in agriculturally disadvantaged regions represents a recognition on the part of policymakers of the failure of price support policies to address the needs of regions heavily dependent on agriculture. Official acknowledgment of differences in economic interests within the farm sector weakens the DBV claim to represent the interests of all German farmers, and poses the possibility of the erosion of DBV influence over the German delegation in Brussels. This change could result in a softening of the German position on price support levels, as well as in discussions of real alternatives to the existing price support regime. Obviously such changes can only be expected to take place over an extended period of time, but they are most likely if economic stagnation persists and the economic position of small- and medium-sized farmers continues to erode.

As the DBV's position in support of price support policies wanes, other pressures for changes in the CAP are on the rise within Germany. The CAP was long seen as the cornerstone of the EEC, but this perception is changing. Few Germans would dispute the importance of the European market for German industry. More than half of German exports go to other EEC countries. But there is increasing sentiment that more of the EEC budget should be spent on the development of European markets other than agriculture. Persistently high rates of unemployment are cited as evidence in support of this viewpoint. In this context, popular support for massive expenditures on agriculture is softening in West Germany.

Notes

1. On full-time farms, less than 10 per cent of the combined income of farm operator and spouse is earned off the farm.
2. Agriculturally disadvantaged regions encompass areas where the maintenance of minimum population levels are considered problematic and a minimum of farming activity is considered necessary for farmland preservation. These regions are officially designated by the German Ministry of Agriculture.
3. Price support policies attempt to raise farm incomes through government intervention in agricultural commodity markets by either purchasing domestic commodities or subsidising their export until market prices are raised to target levels, and by establishing levies on imports which fall below domestic prices, raising the prices of these imports to the target level.
4. That is, these tax reductions were only to go to farmers with less than the equivalent of 330 large animal units (Grossvieheinheiten), and operating a minimum of farmland. For example, farmers with 330 large animal units also had to operate at least 60 hectares. This rule was to limit benefits to traditional farms *with land*, and to prevent large farmers from benefitting from these programmes. However, these restrictions have been evaded in a number of ways.

Bibliography

Agrarbericht, Agrar- und ernährungspolitischer Berichte der Bundesregierung (Bonn: Bundesministerium für Ernährung, Landwirtschaft und Forsten, 1984, 1986).

Averyt, William (1977), *Agropolitics in the European Community: Interest Groups and the Common Agricultural Policy* (New York: Praeger).

Bergmann, Theodor (1975), 'Betrieb oder Scholle?' in Martin Greiffenhagen und Hermann Scheer (eds.), *Die Gegen Reform* (Hamburg: Rowohlt Taschenbuch Verlag 157–89.

Brandkamp, Franz (1982), 'Entwicklung der landwirtschaftlichen Einkommen', *Berichte über Landwirtschaft* 60, 494–510.

Buckwell, Allan, David Harvey, Kenneth Thompson and Keven Parton (1983), *The Costs of the Common Agricultural Policy* (London: Croom Helm).

Deneke, Diether (1980), 'Agrarpolitik in einem Industrieland: Konflikte zwischen Ökonomie und Ökologie', *Berichte über Landwirtschaft* 58, 20–5.

Forschungsgesellschaft für Agrarpolitik und Agrarsoziologie 'Arbeitseinasatz, sozialökonomische Lage und Probleme landwirtschaftender Familien in der Bundesrepublik Deutschaland', Bonn, 1980.

Hallett, Graham (1973), *The Social Economy of West Germany* (London: Macmillan).

Haushofer, Heinz (1983), 'Die Schlüsseljahre 1968/69 in der Agrarpolitik', *Bayerisches landwirtschaftliches Jahrbuch* 60, 5–21.

Henning, Friedrich-Wilhelm (1978), *Landwirtschaft und ländliche Gesellschaft in Deutschland, Band 2, 1750 bis 1976* (Paderborn: Schoningh).

Henning, Friedrich-Wilhelm (1979), *Das Industrialisterte Deutschland 1914 bis 1978* (Paderborn: Schöningh).

Kötter, Herbert (1983), 'Die Landwirtschaft', in Werner Conze und Rainer Lepsius (eds), *Soziolgeschichte der Bundesrepublik Deutschland* (Stuttgart: Verlag Gemeinschaft Ernst Klett).

Peters, Wilhelm (1980), 'Untersuchung zur Ausgleichszulage', *Berichte über Landwirtschaft* 58, 212–47.

Planck, Ulrich (1987), 'The Family Farm in the Federal Republic of Germany', in Boguslaw Galeski and Eugene Wilkening (eds), *Family Farming in Europe and America* (Boulder: Westview) 155–91.

Schmitt, Günther (1983), 'Die Strukturwandel der deutschen Landwirtschaft', in Hans-Georg Wehling (ed.), *Auf dem Lande leben* (Stuttgart: W. Kohlhammer 24–42.

Strauf, Hans-Georg, Jan Uhlmann and Gerald Westphalen (1982), 'Der Beitrag des Agrarsektors zur Bevölkerungsdichte im ländlichen Raum', *Berichte über Landwirtschaft* 60, 41–54.

Tangermann,Stefan (1979), 'Germany's Role Within the CAP: Domestic Problems in International Perspective', *Journal of Agricultural Economics* 30, 241–59.

Thieme, Günther (1983), 'Agricultural Change and Its Impact in Rural Areas', in Trevor Wild (ed.), *Urban and Rural Change in West Germany* (London: Croom Helm 220–47.

Vogel, Gisbert (1980), 'Konflikte zwischen Ökologie und Ökonomie: Begrenzungen durch Industrie und Verbrauchernähe, Konsequenzen für die Beratung', *Berichte über Landwirtschaft* 58, 329–42.

9 Mexican Agricultural Policy in the Shadow of the US Farm Crisis

Stephen E. Sanderson

Writing about the impact of the US farm crisis on Mexican agricultural policy[1] is a high-risk enterprise – for a political scientist doubly so. On the surface the US farm crisis is difficult to understand, thanks to the remarkable difference between scholarly treatments and popular renditions in the press and in the US Congress. Projecting the future relationship between the US farm system and Mexican agricultural policy is even more difficult, as both countries are wracked by major economic problems, policy reversals, poor policies that spawn more problems to be attacked by new policies, and so on. Most ominously, no one seems to have tried to relate the US farm crisis to the politics of Mexican agriculture, despite the topic's obvious attractiveness as a research and political issue. But, despite these cautions, there is a need to put a political perspective on phenomena that are generally considered economic. This paper offers a first encounter.

The landscape of agricultural policy is profoundly political, especially in view of the durable development crisis gripping Mexico in the 1980s and the deepening farm crisis in the United States. As one of the principal agricultural commodity buyers of the US, Mexico is especially important to export-led farm recovery. Mexico was projected to import over 6 million tons of grains and pulses in 1986–87, over 85 per cent of which would come from the US (USDA, 1986). As a leading farm product export market for Mexico, as well as the main provider of imported food and feedgrains, the US is an essential contributor to Mexican agricultural policy. The US takes 70 to 90 per cent of Mexican agricultural exports, which in recent years have approached US$ 2 billion, representing 15 per cent of Mexico's non-petroleum exports.

Accordingly, the relationship between the two countries' farm and development policies is complex. To begin to unwind the convoluted ties between the US farm crisis and Mexican agricultural policy, it is

205

helpful to trace the Mexican government's traditional agricultural policy strategies, to assess the role of US agriculture and its current farm crisis.

Before beginning, three limits must be imposed. First, the focus of this analysis will be the effects of Mexican agricultural sector policy-making on the poor. In Mexico, in contrast to the US, a pre-eminent link exists between agricultural development policy and the government's attention to the most deprived Mexicans. That does not mean, however, that agricultural policy, food policy, and rural development policy are synonymous. We will deal with the most production-orientated of these, agricultural policy, recognising the debate over favouring agricultural output instead of structural changes in rural property and other, more socially equitable possibilities for the Mexican system.

The second limit involves data. This paper will not offer a wide range of data in support of the arguments laid out. Again, in the interests of space and exposition, the reader is invited to repair to some recent publications that offer a broad range of data on Mexican agriculture.[2]

Finally, this paper makes no claim to a coherent treatment of the US farm crisis. It only seeks to use some commonly understood elements of the crisis to illustrate points of integration in the US – Mexican agricultural system. Even that limited mission will show that one of the continuing shortcomings of both US and Mexican agricultural policy analysis is an insufficient appreciation of the impact of the international system on domestic politics.

US AND MEXICAN AGRICULTURAL POLICIES: POINTS IN COMMON

Both Mexican and US agricultural policies have traditionally been made on the basis of domestic development goals, relegating the bilateral relationship to secondary status. While both nations have recognized that their agricultural systems are increasingly interactive with the world economy – vulnerable to market prices, highly dependent on world markets for some basic grains (in the US case, it is a determining factor in those markets) – the process and goals of the agricultural policy establishment have taken that reality into account only grudgingly. The result in the US has been that farm policy changes mainly respond to domestic concerns, with 'recapturing world markets' mainly invoked as a loosely-conceived policy goal, or a means of increasing farm income or balancing trade (McCalla, 1985). Only recently, and only in reference to the US, has agricultural policy included structural and equity issues more seriously in the political discourse surrounding farm legislation.

In Mexico, while equity concerns are a pillar of agricultural policy, the government has created an insular agricultural policy establishment that considers the US at worst to be a threat to domestic self-sufficiency and at best a residual provider of domestic production shortfalls. Traditionally, Mexican agricultural policy makers have perceived their system to be isolated from external (generally meaning US) 'shocks', and have managed a 'closed' agricultural policy. But such political insulation from the international environment has been torn loose by the debt and foreign exchange crisis under which Mexico has been labouring since mid-1981. Future vulnerability to food shortages, foreign exchange bottlenecks, and a real food crisis will depend to a growing extent on US agricultural policy.

The currency of US – Mexican economic relations in general is an intimate antagonism. Agricultural relations are no exception. But the antagonism is so institutionalised in the bilateral relationship that it has become a constant in the bilateral equation, more of a cliché than a threat. The tension is complicated further by the realisation that the two nations have a surprisingly similar set of agricultural problems and interests, which are often masked by conflicting political philosophies in rural development. In the case of agriculture, both the antagonism and the intimacy that dominate bilateral relations hinder resolution of the enduring Mexican food crisis. But what are the shared interests of the two systems, and what is the nature of the Mexican food crisis that is so compromised by the bilateral dynamic?

As to common interests, there are several. Both Mexico and the US have counted on agricultural trade for their successful export performance in the past. As overall external performance has deteriorated in the 1980s, both countries' agricultural trade has continued to perform relatively well, thereby becoming more important to long-term well-being. Both the US and Mexico have seen manufacturing exports remain weak despite some isolated glimmers of growth due to huge new investments and rapid currency devaluations. Even in those more positive moments, the exchange rate impact on imports in Mexico since 1982 and in the US since 1985 has tended to offset improved manufactured export performance. The result has been that agricultural trade in both countries has been an increasingly important producer of foreign exchange.

Second, both the US and Mexico have seen their agricultural trade mandate propelled even further by the debt crisis. Although the debt crisis is generally perceived by policy-makers and the public alike as a Latin American (or, at worst, a Third World) problem, the US is the largest debtor in the world. Mexico is the second largest Third World debtor, with indebtedness of more than US$100 billion. The traditional medicine for these debt problems is well known by now: fiscal austerity to reduce the public sector deficit, export growth to generate foreign exchange reserves, and what US Democrats would call 'competitiveness' – producing (preferably unsubsidised) goods that fare well in the international market.

Third, both countries are under severe fiscal constraints, the US because of unmanageable fiscal deficits, and Mexico because of a long-term programme of fiscal austerity that has come with its status as a model of Latin American external stabilisation programmes and sectoral adjustment in agriculture. While such constraints are a formidable limit to innovative agricultural policy, they have not managed to block subsidies to agriculture. The US lags behind Mexico in its desubsidising drive, spending in excess of US$25 billion in farm subsidies in 1986, despite a record fiscal deficit. Mexico, with a US$500 million World Bank sectoral adjustment loan for agriculture, and a four-year programme of economic stabilisation in place, will presumably continue to cut the most burdensome subsidies. Its first attempts, unfortunately, have focused on consumer price subsidies, a form of non-wage buffer against rampaging inflation.

Finally, the United States and Mexico have both suffered nearly a decade of low commodity prices, which coincide with high production levels in certain key crops. The result has been a series of policy initiatives totally at odds with the policy perspectives that held at the beginning of the 1980s. The US has embarked on a policy dialogue of reducing production and subsidies in a world 'awash in grain'. Mexico has been feeding wheat surpluses to livestock, even as it has reduced human consumption by raising bread and flour prices (USDA, 1986, 1986a). And neither has shown any particular acuity in predicting world food needs and prices, suggesting policies more circumspect than bold (Johnson, 1985, pp. 20–4).

The single most penetrating difference between the two agricultural systems is the close relationship between agricultural policy and rural poverty in Mexico, which, in effect, means a close relationship between a farm crisis and a food crisis. In contrast to the US, where poverty programmes are heavily urban-biased, and are less directly connected to the short-term performance of the economy, Mexican agricultural – food policy is the determinant of assistance programmes for the rural poor. The rural poor, despite their declining weight in the overall population, are primary claimants on the post-revolutionary Mexican system of entitlements and social programmes. To the extent that Mexican agricultural policy is vulnerable to the vicissitudes of US farm policy, the Mexican poor are directly affected.

To add to the burden of social policy, Mexico has been in a deepening food crisis for more than a decade. Mexico in many ways set a precocious example for the Third World by embracing an ambitious agrarian reform in the 1930s, by undertaking massive rural infrastructure development in the 1940s, and by hosting the Green Revolution in wheat in the 1950s and 1960s. The Mexican food system is still renowned for its technological modernity, its progressive technical assistance programmes, and its ambitious water resource management plan. And for much of the post-Second World War period, until the Echeverria years (1970–76), Mexican agriculture was well able to provide cheap food and rural employment for a growing population.

In the late 1960s, that system began to break down (CDIA, 1974) under the combined pressures of high population growth on an extremely limited resource base, the exhaustion of an agrarian reform built on usufruct, and the growing demands of urban consumers for sophisticated foodstuffs at low prices. The government, as the principal manager of a mixed agricultural economy, was forced to maintain high subsidies to production, protect large landholdings at the expense of agrarian reform, and guarantee cheap food to the urban populace, both as a political hedge against middle-class discontent and an anti-inflationary element in incomes policy. The result was a huge fiscal deficit, political polarisation over the agrarian reform, and growing inflation. The Echeverria presidency, seen in this light, became the battleground for resolving the future terms of agricultural production and imports. As Echeverria left office in 1976, it was clear that agrarian reform was dead, that agricultural investment was crippled, and that the system in fiscal and external payment crisis was unable to finance food imports for a damaged rural policy.

For a time the 'blessings' of Mexican oil papered over the food crisis by apparently resolving the fiscal crisis and providing huge budgets to maintain food and agricultural production subsidies. After suffering three embarrassing years of fiscal austerity and massive food imports, the Lopez Portillo government in 1980 inaugurated the Mexican Food System (*Sistema Alimentario Mexicano*), SAM).[3] The shock of Mexico becoming a food deficit nation after 30 years as the Third World's agricultural development model was softened artificially by expanding government disbursements of the tremendous cash windfalls of the oil boom. The US$15 billion SAM budget was a monument to the momentary conviction that the SAM could '*sembrar el petroleo*' (sow the oil). (Redclift, 1981, 1986) that is, turn oil revenues into food production through public investment in agriculture.

At the ignominious end of the Lopez Portillo government in 1982, with the oil crash destroying the myth of food self-sufficiency and exposing the dimensions of Mexican foreign debt, the food crisis was more real than ever. Food distribution has not improved, and production growth had been based on unsustainable levels of public subsidy to the rural poor. Enormous consumer subsidies – exceeding US$ 400 million for tortillas alone in one year of the SAM – fell long before inflation did, and both rural producer and urban consumer felt the impact of fiscal austerity on a state-dependent agricultural development model. Less obvious, but of equal importance, was the virtual abandonment of a food policy for the rural poor, based as it always had been on keeping poor farmers in production through public land and credit programmes.

Even after the agricultural policy ruin of the Lopez Portillo years, Mexico continued to strive for relative food self-sufficiency and to see US imports as adjustments to estimated production shortfalls. The articulation of that modest policy principle has changed according to import demand, fiscal solvency and good weather. But the Mexican self-portrait as a food deficit country represents a remarkable change in viewpoint from the 1960s. Before the breakdown of the post-war agricultural production 'miracle', Mexico had an explicit policy of export promotion in basic grains and surplus disposal problems similar to those of the US (Barkin and Esteva, 1981). Mexico's agricultural trade balance in the early 1970s was in surplus, and the food scarcities and high international commodity prices of the time benefitted its grain exports.

With the arrival of President de la Madrid in 1982, the food policy

equation again changed radically, due to the fiscal exhaustion of the
SAM, a poor record of private agricultural investment, and the
impoverishment of the Mexican government. Mexico is still a food
deficit nation (averaging a deficit of US $500 million currently), even
after two years of SAM and four years of its anaemic successor
PRONAL.[4] The government of Mexico has spent the last two years
dismantling many of the public sector enterprises through which
agricultural policy was managed (Sanderson, 1985). The Ministry of
Agriculture and Water Resources, once the repository of agricultural
policy development and a major contributor to general macroeconomic policy formation, has been marginalised and subordinated to
an inter-ministerial 'cabinet' (Goodman *et al.*, 1985). Mexico has
agreed to join the GATT and to liberalise imports, which will have a
serious impact on domestic agricultural policy (see below). And the
fiscal crisis of the Mexican government means that the budgetary and
administrative capacity to conduct traditional agricultural policy has
evaporated. The residual attempt to 'rationalise' agricultural policy
comes in the form of reducing 'market distortions' created by the
complex subsidy system, in favour of more traditional market mechanisms, such as credit and price policy. For the moment, these
policies escape the fiscal hatchet by the grace of the World Bank
sectoral adjustment loan in agriculture.

Over the past decade of growing import vulnerability, the US has
been the principal exporter of feedgrains and foodstuffs to Mexico.
The Mexican import bill from the US has varied year by year, but has
depended in some significant part on imports from the US since the
end of the Echeverria presidency. Because the public sector held a
virtual monopoly on foreign imports of basic grains, and because
Mexico took a highly visible position against import dependence, it
seems fair to infer that Mexican foodgrain imports are understated in
the data. Since 1985, when the government of Mexico began to open
grain tenders to the private sector,[5] a significant foreign exchange
constraint and continued government regulatory interventions persistently suppress effective Mexican demand (USDA, 1986, 1986a).

It is also reasonably clear that vulnerability to US exports is less a
function of public policy initiative, and more a function of weather.
Because of the structure of Mexican agriculture, maize, beans and
sorghum, and to a lesser degree, soya and wheat depend in different
ways on timely and adequate seasonal rainfall in Mexico. Although
weather in the 1980s has generally been kind to Mexican farmers, a
significant drought is the norm once in every three years (Roberts

and Mielke, 1986: 15). Devastating droughts and/or untimely rains sparked the worst import imbalances in the late 1970s. Mexican basic grain production is too close to its per capita limits to allow for even normal weather problems. And the Mexican policy plan is grossly unprotected from the effects of weather calamities that throw the basic grain supply – distribution system on the mercy of the US.

It is in this context of rapidly changing – and deteriorating – Mexican agricultural policy that the impact of the US farm crisis must be evaluated. In order to approach some rudimentary measure of that impact, we must turn to the aims of Mexican agricultural policy, the goals of US farm policy and crisis response, and some projection of the likely successes of both.

FISCAL CRISIS, THE FARM CRISIS, AND MEXICAN FOOD SELF-SUFFICIENCY

The US, as the stronger element in the bilateral equation and market leader in world agriculture, certainly has the upper hand in setting the bilateral agricultural policy agenda. Two clear political signs colour the discussion of that bilateral agenda, however. First, there is no indication whatsoever that the US agricultural policy agenda is concerned with its impact on Mexican agricultural policy. That is, US agricultural policy will be made without regard to Mexico, despite Mexico's proximity and its status as a leading agricultural trade partner. So, in the analysis that follows, we will consider US policy alternatives as the 'independent variable' in the bilateral equation, and Mexican policy alternatives as the 'dependent variable'.

Second, agricultural policy in the US is driven only partly by international and farm goals; to a great extent, overall US macroeconomic goals override sectoral policy. The proposition that US agricultural policy goals are vulnerable exclusively to farm-based or Mexico-based interventions is naive. Accordingly, this section begins with a brief analysis of exchange rate movements, which are certainly not governed by agriculture on either side of the border, but have enormous impact on the bilateral agricultural picture.

Bilateral Exchange Rate Policy

From the standpoint of Mexican agricultural policy, the relationship between the peso and the dollar is perhaps the worst of all possible exchange rate relationships. In essence, the decline of the dollar, accompanied by an ever greater decline of the peso, has meant an increased cost to Mexican agricultural imports. Both the commodity price impact of US devaluation and the relative devaluation of the peso against the dollar have hurt Mexico.

G. Edward Schuh has shown a number of economic principles at work in his pioneering studies on exchange rates and agricultural trade and development (Schuh. 1974, 1985). They all seem to have worked against Mexico for much of the 1980s. First, the peso has traditionally been tied to the dollar, which itself is unsurprising, given the uniquely bilateral nature of the Mexican external sector. Throughout the 1950s and 1960s, Mexico was able to maintain a stable exchange rate in a climate free of exchange rate controls, due to high growth, rapid foreign direct investment, a stable political system and low inflation. That began to break down in the early 1970s, made manifest in the devaluations of 1976 and 1982, and the secular, if bumpy, slide of the peso since.

During much of the time that the peso was pegged to the dollar, the Mexican currency was consciously overvalued as a part of development policy. Following the brief post-Echeverria stabilisation programme, the years of the oil boom (1978–81) also were characterised by an overvalued peso. Exchange rate policy allowed a transfer of resources from export activities to domestic development – consistent with import substitution strategies of the past – but artificially cheapened agricultural imports from the US and taxed domestic production. That same overvaluation created problems for trade with third countries, and dampened foreign direct investment.

When the dollar began to decline in 1985, the peso had already preceded it in freefall, and did not benefit from the cheapening of US commodities. In the past two years, the effects of a dollarised peso have been virtually all negative. The relative cost of US imports is still high, despite the low value of the dollar against major currencies. Partly because of previous exchange rate policies, trade connections with other countries have been occasional and weak. The decline of both peso and dollar have put further strain on the Mexican import bill.

It is clear that the impact of dollar devaluation on US commodity prices is to raise them. The rise in nominal prices has been estimated at 50 to 75 per cent of the decline of the value of the dollar (Johnson, 1985 p. 41; Longmire and Morey, 1982). The impact for Mexico is doubly devastating. Because of the fall of the peso, dollar devaluation has less impact on commodity import prices from the US. Because of the likely impact of devaluation on US commodity prices, nominal prices for those imports will increase, as well. The normal response in Mexico would be to encourage import-substituting production of agricultural commodities when they become expensive. Currently, Mexico is not able to count on that option, because of a general fiscal crisis limiting public stimuli to production, the commitment to sectoral adjustment and trade liberalization under GATT accession, World Bank loan and IMF stabilisation agreements, and the importance of some agricultural imports as agroindustrial inputs necessary for economic recovery.

US Agricultural Policy Goals

Like Mexico, the US makes its agricultural policy for domestic consumption. But the US debt and trade crises and their impacts on agricultural policy carry with them disruptive potential for the Mexican system. Because of the complexity of US farm and external sector problems and the focus of this paper on Mexico, I will discuss only selective aspects of the US farm situation.[6]

One of the primary concerns of US farm policy is the improvement of farm incomes, as a political response to the highly-publicised failure of so-called family farms in the US in the past few years. Various strategies have been employed to improve farm incomes, many of which have focused on improving commodity prices. Because of the importance of commodity prices to Mexican agricultural trade and food policy, these elements are also most revealing of the potential impact of US agricultural policy on Mexico.

The data on commodity prices in the 1980s show that the ambitions of the 1981 and 1985 US farm bills were not realised. Commodity prices in general continue to be low, as world food availabilities are good and the US system continues to overproduce. The role of the US in basic feed and foodgrains (especially maize, sorghum and wheat), and oilseeds (especially soya) is well known and in some cases still preponderant. But significant commodity price increases imply a series of contemporaneous changes, including increases in effective world demand, global crop shortfalls, steady and adequate economic growth in the principal consumer countries, and improved nutrition and distribution among the world's poor. Obviously, many of these factors fall outside the control of any single country.

Nevertheless, higher commodity prices are only one of a set of changes that might affect Mexican agricultural policy. And US agricultural policy includes a number of non-price interventions that might change Mexican agricultural and import policy, as well. A US strategy that addresses the farm crisis under current farm legislation involves stimulating agricultural exports.

The principal US agricultural exports to Mexico in recent years have been basic food- and feedgrains and oilseeds. Those exports have varied sharply according to Mexican national supply and distribution of the same commodities but Mexico remains a consistent importer of American agricultural commodities. Traditionally, Mexico was a cash customer for US agricultural exports, until the debt and foreign exchange crisis of 1982. Since the 1983 US 'bailout' of Mexico, which included agricultural export financing, Mexico has been incorporated into US Commodity Credit Corporation programmes, principally via credit guarantees (Sanderson, 1983). As a result Mexico has maintained its status as one of the top five agricultural trade partners of the US, despite its debt crisis, the strength of the dollar, the devaluation of the peso, and the deterioration of effective demand.

US agricultural policy is governed by target prices, loan rates and other mechanisms that are designed to bolster farm prices, improve farm incomes and manage commodity stocks in a policy environment that is anti-statist in ideology. Because the US is such a significant exporter of basic grains and oilseeds, subsidies for domestic production are equivalent to export subsidies. McCalla (1985, p. 183) makes the same observation about exchange rate devaluation as an *ad valorem* export subsidy.

The farm bills of 1981 and 1985 envisaged reductions in payments and changing the management of stocks, with an eye toward reducing the federal role in farming. The Payment-in-Kind (PIK) programme of 1983 had dramatic short-term effects (taking 70 million acres out of production), and early evidence on the 'Sodbusters' soil conservation provisions of the 1985 bill indicates great success in removing high-erosion areas from production. (USDA, 1985, 1985a) Likewise, the farmer-owned reserve has grown to replace some of the burden of government grain stocks. But target price calculations and loan rates have not reduced the overall cost of the American farm programme; nor have they improved farm incomes directly.

US farm legislation, the current international context, and the ongoing farm policy debate in the US Congress seem to ensure the future of several policy principles that can help frame our discussion of the bilateral agricultural policy scene. First, it appears clear that the increasing pressure of the US fiscal and trade deficits will provoke efforts to increase agricultural exports. Second, the continuing political debate over the US farm crisis will ensure that price policies and farm income are part of the export promotion programme, despite the uncertain connection between the two. Third, the declining dollar will exert some upward pressure on agricultural prices as exports increase (which in turn will influence the future debate about saving the US farmer by improving farm income). And, finally, the US will tie agricultural trade credit guarantees and other concessions to broad policy goals, including increased market access in importing countries, privatisation of agricultural imports from the US, and reduction in agricultural subsidies to competing foreign producers.

Mexican Agricultural Policy Goals

Mexican government agricultural policy goals include a wide range of productivity and social objectives, among which are land tenure reform, improvements in rural welfare and productivity, export promotion, technology development, rural social organisation, agro-industrial development, better nutrition, and control of environmental pollution. Those and other concerns can be collapsed into three areas: concern for accelerating the growth of agricultural production, promoting rural development, and satisfying the growing urban demand for food (Goodman, *et al.*, 1985).

Of these three areas, agricultural production has clearly led the political agenda in Mexico for several years. First, the food deficits of the late 1970s caused political embarrassment among Mexican leaders who had to justify exporting beef during a meat crisis in Mexico City and growing winter vegetables for the increasingly hostile US market, while basic grains displaced by those vegetables were in deficit (Sanderson, 1986). Second, the production-orientated strategy of the SAM and its successors displaced a discredited populist approach to the agrarian question, which focused on improving agricultural output and rural well-being through recourse to the 50-year-old land and resource distribution programme.

In the years since 1981, however, the debt crisis has provided the clearest motive for putting production at the head of agricultural policy. In 1982 and 1983, Mexico was unable to pay for food imports critical to domestic food supplies and agricultural inputs essential to agro industries. The centrepieces of the external payments crisis have been export promotion, peso devaluation (from 24 to 1200 pesos to the dollar in five years), fiscal austerity, and import reduction. In agriculture, because oilseed, food and feedgrain supplies were essential to domestic development policy, the only alternative to high-risk shortages was a combination of increased output in the domestic system, concessional imports from the US, and market-induced underconsumption. We shall examine the latter elements in more detail shortly.

Naturally, the emphasis on agricultural production does not preclude attention to rural development and a domestic cheap food policy. But there are limits to the compatibility of the three elements of Mexican agricultural policy. On the one hand, concessional credit, agricultural inputs and technical assistance are legitimate elements in rural development policy. As has been shown elsewhere, a certain stratum of the rural poor is served by a targeted small farmer rural credit policy, and improvements in output are also achieved. (Diskin, *et al.*, 1987) And a cheap food policy is most readily achieved by ensuring agricultural surpluses that permit retail price management of basic foods without the fear of black markets, hoarding, producer slowdowns and other horrors familiar not only to Mexicans but to Brazilians and Argentines, among others.

On the other hand, aside from well-placed critiques focusing on the too-exclusive dedication of public resources to rich farmers to meet production goals, improving agricultural production among smallholders in Mexico has been associated with conservative rural credit schemes, inattention to land reform, diversion of resources away from *ejidos* (public usufructs), and the depoliticisation of the agrarian question (Sanderson, 1981, 1986). Cheap food policy has also been doubly criticized for its extensive and multi-tiered subsidies to producers, processors and consumers, as well as its legendary incapacity to maintain adequate prices to stimulate production. Typically, production of basic grains and pulses that are the staple of poor diets in Mexico rest with very small producers (*microfundistas*) (Barkin and Suarez, 1982; Schejtman, 1981) whose own diets and economic opportunities are jeopardised by a cheap food policy.

In any event, with or without connivance by a politically conservative state management team, Mexico since 1982 has been forced into a production-orientated agricultural policy that gives short shrift to the grand tradition of rural populism and equity previously characteristic of the Mexican government. At the same time, the debt crisis has left Mexico more vulnerable to changes in US agricultural policy.

Mexican Agricultural Policy Alternatives

What are Mexico's alternatives, in a weak, interactive agricultural system on the border of the world's largest agricultural producer and almost exclusive agricultural trade partner? Crudely put, they are three: food self-sufficiency, market-oriented agricultural trade liberalisation, or export-promotion with growing imports. Thus far, it seems that the Mexican government has chosen a contradictory mix of the three. As we can see in the following sections, the role of the US farm system is to *clarify* Mexican agricultural policy alternatives and goals.

Food Self-sufficiency

Food self-sufficiency programmes in Mexico depend on the expansion of the agricultural frontier, the elaboration of subsidies and assistance programmes to include more farmers in preferential credit and rural development schemes, maintenance (and steady growth) of farm incomes, a progressive rural tax structure, and similar incentives.

Two principal constraints on food self-sufficiency in today's Mexico are the generalised fiscal crisis and the lack of material resources to achieve self-sufficiency in most basic grains. A third factor, of increasing importance to policy alternatives, is the US farm crisis itself, based as it is on deteriorating US farm income and aggregate exports.

The fiscal crisis in Mexico affects the central role that government played in keeping domestic producer prices above international prices in the 1970s. Combined with a policy that gave the official grain marketing agency, CONASUPO, complete control over basic food imports, the Mexican government imposed a somewhat artificial constraint on trade through layers of domestic subventions. Producer subsidies, a key element, were matched – albeit somewhat imperfectly – with consumer and miller subsidies in grains to achieve high production and cheap agro-industrial inputs and food. The purposes were to increase food production on land that had been diverted to crops outside the 'basic food basket', to bring marginal land into production by subsidising inputs and improving farm organisation, and to subsidize food production and delivery at several points to 'rationalise' the system according to domestic food policy goals. In large measure, the debt crisis and its fiscal constraints have ended the prospect of food self-sufficiency with growing consumption.

The fiscal crisis has meant the cutback of technical assistance and subsidised inputs in agriculture, and closer limits on subsidised credit and credit guarantee programmes managed through the central bank. It has also meant that large and small infrastructure projects alike have come to depend even more on World Bank and other external financing. Though it is too early to tell at this writing, it is reasonable to hypothesise that fiscal austerity will continue to emphasise 'economic efficiencies' as the premier value of agricultural development policy. While the arguments in favour of such efficiency orientation are familiar to all, less familiar are the impacts on the rural poor who depend on lamentably less efficient programmes of rural development. To show the complexity of the relationship between such straightforward variables as border and farmgate prices and agricultural policy goals, we can offer the following preliminary propositions. Of course, these propositions must be qualified by a multi-sectoral analysis of the economy, and are meant here for illustrative purposes:

(1) As US grain prices rise, international pressure on the Mexican producer subsidy system is lowered, as farmgate and border prices become more equal. The Mexican government subsidises domestic producer prices both as a farm income policy and as protection against competition from international sources. A shift upward in border prices without an equivalent shift in Mexican prices would reduce the subsidy required for protection and would focus attention on prices as an instrument to achieve higher farm income. Mexican price subsidies would become more strictly a domestic policy affair.

(2) As long as Mexican farmgate prices are higher than border grain prices, a double or triple subsidy system (producer, miller, consumer) is required in Mexico to achieve both production and income/nutrition goals. Because of high land and transport costs, and scarcity of key inputs, Mexico is unlikely to produce basic foodstuffs at 'reasonable' prices without consumer and processor subsidies. In recent years, the combination of producer, processor and consumer subsidies has been outrageous. But virtually no one argues that the goals of a cheap food policy – made more necessary by the protracted austerity programme now underway – can be met without massive public subsidies. In the context of reducing the fiscal deficit, those subsidies either have to come from tax reform in the sector, from capital transfers from other sectors, or from international development assistance (such as the World Bank in its new, broadened role as adjustment agent).

(3) When border grain prices exceed Mexican farmgate prices, the

overall grain subsidy cost to the Mexican government is a function of demand management and social welfare considerations connected to poor farmer production. If there is an inverse relationship between border prices and Mexican protection subsidy requirements, there is a direct relationship between domestic farmgate prices and demand management. In view of the low debt and input structure of poor Mexican farmers, there is a direct relationship between farmgate prices and farm income, as well, which implies that, assuming reduced input subsidies, farm prices become social welfare policies for producers.

(4) As long as border grain prices are above domestic farmgate prices, Mexican government options are freer to subsidise domestic production for import-substitution and social welfare reasons. Public expenditure stays at home, rather than leaving the country. There is a public windfall on high border prices, whether they are tariff- or market-induced. Such is not the case with 'voluntary' export restraints, where the price effect of restricted supplies often generates a rent to the importer or his domestic agent. This is a good reason to prefer tariffs and formal licensing to informal quantitative controls. If the international market forces border prices above domestic prices, the Mexican government benefits directly.

(5) As long as border grain prices are below domestic farmgate prices, a fiscally constrained Mexican government is better able to cushion food prices to the *urban* poor through imports. This is undoubtedly more efficient than subsidising import-substitution at high prices. Conversely, subsidising nutrition to the *rural* poor is better served by high US prices, because historically the cheap distribution of imported grains in the countryside has been almost a complete failure. Well-targeted producer subsidies have more redistributive effect in the countryside than a cheap food policy. To the extent that US farm programmes raise the border price of food grains, rural producers in Mexico are favoured. To the extent that US overproduction is not controlled, the Mexican urban poor are better off.

(6) Exchange rate management thus becomes a powerful tool for domestic food and agricultural production policy. The decline of the peso relative to the dollar – other things equal – increases border prices and reduces the protection subsidy required for domestic production. Such devaluation favours domestic production over imports and rural over urban welfare. Of course, with Mexico's continued dependence on agricultural inputs, this model must be specified at a

much more sophisticated level. Overvaluation, on the other hand, enhances import capacity in the short term, and could be used to benefit overall food supplies. The spread of such benefit is almost strictly urban, however.

Besides powerful fiscal constraints and the clumsiness of policy tools applied to the complex Mexican market, Mexico is governed by a resource 'constant': the lack of the natural resources necessary to create a self-sufficient food system. In fact, of course, self-sufficiency has for years been viewed as a relative term, and not as the autarky belaboured by critics of the SAM. But for some time agricultural specialists have proclaimed – and President de la Madrid endorsed – the closing of the Mexican agricultural frontier. Given Mexico's modest agricultural endowments and its regular resource shortages, it seems unlikely that the amount of land under production will expand by much in the near future. The implications of this argument for agricultural trade with the US are complex and politically delicate. Currently, Mexico is relatively self-sufficient in wheat production and, with good weather and improved rural development programmes, is potentially self-sufficient in beans and rice. Oilseeds and maize are another matter, as are such problematic agricultural commodities as milk and animal protein. Foodgrain and feedgrain import requirements in the future are the sum of the productivity of existing agriculture and Mexico's import capacity. In the current crisis, the US has become an ever larger factor in the latter term, because of its programmes of credit and credit guarantees, as well as its optimal position as Mexico's grain supplier.

Combined with the fiscal crisis, it seems clearer now than ever before that Mexico will be forced to accept at least part of the logic of comparative advantage, and concentrate on those products it is able to produce at competitive prices (again, relatively speaking) and import those in which the US is more efficient. That will mean continuing to import wheat as a function of domestic production, and oilseeds and oil, milk, maize and sorghum according to 'demand'.

The reason I have set 'demand' in quotes is that self-sufficiency can be approached from both the supply and the demand sides of the food system. With Mexico in crisis, a supply-orientated policy has been converted into a policy emphasising demand management. In the latter case, food and agricultural policy are turned on their heads: the principal value becomes the generation of domestic surpluses to reduce import requirements without incurring the costs of a SAM. Currently, the Mexican government artificially manipulates demand through purchase, storage, incomes and distribution policy. Demand in Mexico is not effective demand, unless one concedes a large role for government policy in the term. A clear example of such manipulated demand is the current combination of wage reductions and wheat surpluses. Except for a momentary blip in 1981, there has not been a real wage increase in Mexico since 1976. Current wages, in the wake of a decade of rampaging inflation and a moribund official labour movement, are very low. Moreover, rural wages always lag behind urban wages and often hover below the official minimum wage in the poorest areas.

The regressive incomes policy of the Mexican government has been an implicit element of recent agricultural and food policy, as concessional non-wage food distribution programmes do not exist, except, perhaps, in the subsidised stores of the urban labour élite. That incomes policy has combined since 1982 with consumer price increases in basic foods and generalized inflation in basic goods. The structure of food consumption in Mexico indicates that the poor are eating less because of high food prices, and devoting less of their household budget to food because they are chasing the unprotected prices of other goods as well. At the same time, in the crop year 1985–86 Mexico fed to animals one million tons of 'surplus' bread wheat – reclassified as feed wheat by CONASUPO to permit use by livestock producers (USDA, 1986). Those animals are most likely to end up on urban middle- and upper-class tables (poultry and hogs) or are exported (feeder calves and steers) to US consumers. Either way, the production of one set of foodstuffs under fiscal crisis implies a zero-sum game for the poor, and the forced reduction of demand by state fiat. (It should be recorded that tax and indirect subsidies to animal producers have not been threatened by government policies, in case it might be thought that the system's stress is equally shared).

Taking for the moment the two variables 'agricultural frontier' and 'demand management', the following propositions are offered about the relationship between the US farm crisis and Mexican agricultural policy. The objective is to show the policy consequences of market-based constraints which currently govern the bilateral food system. The central premise is that as population increases and wheat production stays relatively level, oilseed production continues to lag demand, and maize output fluctuates according to the weather, then foodstuff prices or supplies have to increase, or demand must decrease.

Domestic price increases imply pressure on incomes policy and inflation. With 120 per cent annual inflation, and a harsh economic stabilization scheme, Mexico must maintain some sort of price ceiling on basic foods. Incomes and inflation policy are already severe, and few Mexican politicians – or economists – would argue for freeing food prices.

Demand increases are a natural outgrowth of population increases, and are understated by a regressive incomes policy. In any event, even without real income improvement, demand is inching forward, putting pressure on supplies, which in turn implies more production, imports or underconsumption. Basically, only two alternatives permit prices to remain constant, if we assume that subsidies will be lowered for fiscal reasons: demand management or supply increases. Demand is currently managed aggressively. Supply increases are only possible via productivity changes, changes in cropping, and/or imports. Regarding the latter, if domestic prices increase relative to border prices, more pressure exists for imports.

If border feedgrain prices are low, and domestic food prices do not decline (as they probably cannot under current circumstances) there is a domestic food production dividend, especially on rainfed land, as food crops substitute for sorghum. This proposition, of course, assumes substitutability, responsiveness of poor farmers to market signals, and greater elasticities in food demand over feed demand. If border feedgrain prices are high, and imports are restricted, animal feed requirements put pressure on wheat and maize consumption, to the detriment of food consumption. Over the long term, however, it is possible that animal herds and flocks might be liquidated to compensate for such high feed prices. (These high prices are relative, of course, to livestock and dairy prices.) Past experience indicates that the first to suffer in herd liquidation are the poor backyard (*traspatio*) producers.

These observations suggest that a combined policy of agricultural imports and domestic rural development policy is necessary to reduce the 'demand management' (that is, underconsumption) aspect of Mexican food policy. Such a policy calls for maximising domestic output, but recognises that significant imports must be a part of any progressive future policy. In that regard, both the US farm crisis and US agricultural export policy play heavy roles. And the bromide of simple trade liberalisation is hardly cost free for Mexico.

Trade Liberalisation

This 'option' for Mexico to some degree has been a by-product of the debt crisis, as well. For years, the US has argued that Mexico should follow its comparative advantage and import grains and oilseeds while exporting more tropical and semi-tropical products such as coffee, winter vegetables, sugar, and certain fruits. In fact, the successes of the Mexican agricultural export economy in the last decade have come in precisely those products (minus sugar). But two-overriding concerns weaken the argument for agricultural liberalisation: the inevitable changes in domestic agricultural production and their consequences for Mexico's poor; and the ever-present external sector constraint.

As to the first, the complete liberalisation of Mexican agricultural imports – admittedly a rather far-fetched idea, these days – would clearly imply the destruction of much maize, wheat and soybean production, and probably the virtual disappearance of sorghum production. Likewise, dairy cattle, coffee, sugar and poultry would undoubtedly suffer great changes. On the export side, there are few clear winners, except for winter vegetables which themselves have shown a reluctance to grow past certain levels, in light of technological limits to cost-efficiency and the everlooming hostility of American producers.

Two problems haunt the liberalisation option: the lack of partners who will liberalise along with Mexico, and the social role of agriculture that would be destroyed with liberalisation. The first can be easily treated. While US farm policy analysts and trade specialists recommend the liberalisation of Mexican imports for the sake of food policy, there has been *no* equivalent movement on the US side. While the argument can be made that US markets are relatively open in traditional Mexican exports, the regional sugar and tobacco markets certainly operate under severe distortions because of US quotas. While the Mexican sugar industry is admittedly weak, relative to its Caribbean and Brazilian counterparts, the political symbolism of opening markets is a two-way street.

Much more serious than the call for one-sided agricultural trade liberalisation is the threat such liberalisation would pose to the social role of agriculture. What is Mexico to do with farmers displaced by maize, basic grain and pulse imports? To what extent would the marketplace substitute for the subsistence food system represented by the *minifundista* and *ejidatario* of the Mexican central plateau? To what extent would the cost efficiencies of importing according to comparative advantage be offset by the rising social welfare costs of labour force adjustment? None of these questions has an easy answer, and few of them have been addressed adequately. It is clear that agricultural trade liberalisation for Mexico means potentially explosive social changes in the countryside, in a country renowned for its rural jacqueries.

And, of course, a real concern for Mexico in a scenario of agricultural trade liberalisation is the lack of export alternatives. Mexico has been shown to be a vulnerable exporter, relying excessively on oil, tourism, labour and selected primary commodities. Manufactures have been notoriously inept in the international market, except when accompanied by competitive devaluations. Certainly, the long-term prospects of export promotion in manufactures do not look bright as long as the protectionist climate in the US continues to grow. And the accession to GATT over the long term almost certainly means a less favourable balance of trade for Mexico. Agricultural trade liberalisation would have to be accompanied by great confidence that the agricultural trade balance would favour Mexico, which it has not done since 1979, even with vigorous food import restrictions.

Export Promotion.

Given the impossibility of food self-sufficiency under current conditions and the political dangers of agricultural trade liberalisation, Mexican agricultural policy has taken a position that is the residual left after rejecting the first two 'options'. Mexico's current agricultural policy combines export-promotion with demand management. That means relative food trade balance achieved by underconsumption and growing exports. Unfortunately, relying on agricultural export promotion in a food deficit country is hard politics, made more difficult by fiscal austerity and the enduring uncertainties of the US market.

In order to examine the balance required in these policy matters, let us look briefly at some of the most interactive sectors of Mexican agriculture: beef, basic grains and winter vegetables (Sanderson, 1986).

US-Mexican Agricultural Policy and the Bilateral Beef Feeding System. In the 1970s Mexico began to capitalize on the integration of a bilateral beef production system that had deep historical roots. At its peak, the internationalised element of the Mexican beef cattle system was exporting 800 000 head or more of feeder steers to the US for finishing on US feedlots. Then the system broke down. In Mexico City in 1978 and 1979, beef shortages were common, reflecting problems in the domestic beef cattle system that were only very indirectly related to the frontier beef cattle industry serving the US market. Nevertheless, it became politically impossible for the Mexican government to sanction massive exports of live beef cattle to the US, while the residents of the capital (representing about one-third of the beef consumer market of the country) went without beef. And, with the stagnation in beef production for domestic consumption, development policy at the height of the oil boom dictated that future investments in beef cattle would be targeted toward the modern frontier industry 'turned inward'.

That scenario has already changed, once again revealing the volatility of the Mexican agricultural scene and the difficulty of making policy for the sector. First, the domestic market contracted severely in the crisis that began in 1982. That market contraction was matched by reduced investment in cattle-raising, partly because of reductions in public subsidies and concessional credit to the sector. At the same time, the US economy began to recover from the recession of the early 1980s, and beef demand grew. Cattle 'finishing' on feedlots, which had become expensive because of poor feed-meat price ratios, began to grow again, as feed grain prices remained low and meat prices recovered slightly. Of particular importance to Mexico, the US institutional beef industry – led by hospitals, frozen food producers and fast food outlets using the 'manufacture beef' produced by the Mexican feeder steers – began to perform well.

The implications for Mexican agricultural policy are unclear: in the context of external sector problems, an overall food deficit, and the contraction of demand for beef in the country, investment in beef cattle for export, and reinvestment in once-promising boxed beef and pork for third-country markets, seem possible once again. However, the performance of this cattle-raising sector depends on economic phenomena in the US, outside the control of Mexican cattlemen and policy-makers. And the cattle export industry is governed by short-term commercial contracts without any assurances of future demand or price. Mexican cattlemen, who operate on relatively long (and obviously inflexible) livestock reproduction cycles, are essentially thrown onto an international auction market with one bidder.

Given the high cost of developing feedlots in Mexico, the effective quarantine of the export market from domestic beef production, and the absolute inaccessibility of fed beef to the Mexican poor, two policy limits exist. They take into account not only Mexican government priorities, but the realities of the frontier beef cattle industry. First, feedlot development and beef cattle feeding in general cannot be encouraged in Mexico, irrespective of domestic input prices. Mexico's comparative advantage (and, not incidentally, culinary tradition) is built on range-fed beef. And feeding foodgrain 'surpluses' to livestock is already a scandal. Specialists have observed that technological and capital investments in this area would be better spent in ecologically sustainable, low-technology range management.

Second, live beef cattle exports can be stimulated only in limited ways through public policy, essentially by removing disincentives to export and by lobbying in favour of more secure frontier production contracts with US counterparts. Simpler licensing, removal of quotas, maintenance of realistic exchange rates, and technological improvements in stock and husbandry would all be welcome. But the Mexican government, under extreme fiscal duress, cannot afford to subsidise these exports, which are in effect subsidies to American consumers.

Likewise, it seems apparent that the US beef market is the main outlet for the frontier cattle industry, and no amount of cajoling can turn the beef industry inward for domestic consumption without effectively taxing the poor through agricultural subsidies to upscale markets. Export cattle can provide scarce foreign exchange, improve agricultural sector productivity, and integrate US and Mexican markets via a more Mexican-driven industry. Assuming normal variations in the long beef cycle, the frontier beef cattle industry will likely improve with lower feedgrain prices, perhaps finally institutionalising *maquila* beef (cattle raised in Mexico, fed in the US and returned for slaughter to Mexico) or a border boxed beef industry for export to third countries.

The Winter Vegetable Market. Since the early 1970s, Mexico has held a significant share of the US winter vegetable market, especially and most visibly the tomato market. Winter vegetables are significant to Mexican exports, generating US $200 million per year in recent years. But what relationship is there between this simple traded commodity and the Mexican and American farm crises?

Admittedly, the connection of winter vegetables to food policy is somewhat more subtle than is the case with feeder steers for export. Nevertheless, the relationship is real and problematic. The first aspect involves the comparative advantage of Mexican tomatoes (these arguments are generally true for other winter vegetables, as well). While devaluation has made Mexican tomatoes more competitive in US markets, their price was never the single reason for their entry; nor was it the constraint on their growth in the market. Mexican tomatoes entered the US market because it was growing and because Mexico had a regional and seasonal comparative advantage over US competitors. However, in the years immediately prior to the debt crisis, production of winter vegetables for export was declining because of exchange rate policy and deteriorating price competitiveness with US suppliers. Many producers shifted out of tomatoes in favour of other crops, especially in the heyday of the SAM.

Given the foreign exchange shortages of the Mexican government and the export mandate of the debt crisis, it is important for winter vegetables to continue to grow as an export crop, other things equal. That growth depends in part on continued devaluation of the peso, continued cheap labour in the fields to compete with productivity gains induced by technological advances in the US, and the continued substitution of winter vegetables for commodities with a domestic market – for example, wheat and safflower. All of these factors militate against an agricultural development policy that benefits the poor, whether through the price impact of further devaluation, the coercive suppression of the rural wage, or the state-managed cropping priorities of the irrigation districts where winter vegetables are grown.

The future of the winter vegetable market depends greatly on the tolerance of the US market and the relative prices and guarantees for competing crops in Mexico. It is unlikely that another SAM-like set of incentives and insurance will draw North–West Mexican producers away from tomatoes in favour of rice or other staples. However, increasing factor costs, especially in water and land values, might price Mexican winter vegetables out of the US market. On the US side, federal marketing orders and certain productivity improvements in recent years have dampened Mexican market prospects. In the expected absence of significant new capital investments in Mexican winter vegetables over the short term, producers will continue to hold a minority position in the US market, but are unlikely to displace land dedicated to food crops much further.

Food- and Feedgrains. Continuing debt crisis means suppressed demand for foodgrains in Mexico, with some negative impact on US exports. The cheap peso, lack of foreign exchange, and rising prices on commodity imports all constrain food imports into Mexico. These constraints have a clearly negative impact on US exports, though regular droughts and other production shortfalls in oilseeds and maize can be expected to keep Mexico close to its largest agricultural provider.

This scenario obviously has more negative aggregate effects for the US than for Mexico, hungry as the US is for increased agricultural exports. However, as US policy-makers showed in the Mexican 'bailout' of 1983, policy instruments do exist to stimulate US grain exports to Mexico, even in the current climate. For the moment, we will assume that there is some relationship between increased US food exports to Mexico and the availability of low-priced food to the Mexican population.

For years, policy makers have recalled regularly the 'special relationship' between the US and Mexico. Yet, as has been the case with US–Canadian relations, the concrete manifestations of that special relationship often give way to multilateral imperatives, US domestic policy constraints and other limits. Now that the US has embraced the possibility of a 'plurilateral' option in trade negotiations,[7] and has for years participated in a world sugar system governed by bilateral agreements and special deals, it is time that bilateral food aid and trade reforms be considered as part of a farm crisis policy.

The credit guarantee and concessional credit programmes of the Commodity Credit Corporation (CCC) offer a convenient starting point. In 1983, the US included Mexico in the CCC GSM–102 credit guarantee programme, at no cost to the US government (Sanderson, 1983). The programme allowed Mexico to borrow money to buy US agricultural products, with the co-signature of the US government. The credit guarantee programme is essentially governed by the Office of Management and Budget, in cooperation with the US Department of Agriculture. Providing credit guarantees based on expected agricultural import needs, and not fiscal year CCC programme ceilings, would permit a more flexible, unsubsidised facility for Mexican purchases.

Other CCC programmes are more problematic, but still offer possible avenues for increased exports to Mexico. The blended credit programme in effect provides an export subsidy by mixing concessional credits with commercial loans. Although Mexico is not eligible for such credits now, it seems reasonable to include Mexico as a special case, maybe along with other high-debt countries. The same is true for possible future concessional exports of grains that mix commercial sales with government-held stocks to reduce overall prices to the purchaser. On the Mexican side, these policies might offer a SIK option (subsidy in kind) with low prices to poor consumers and relatively high prices to producers, to be made possible by blending cheap imports with domestic purchases.

Such export promotion programmes create certain problems in Mexico. As mentioned above, free agricultural trade (or simply greater import levels) in Mexico may jeopardise subsistence agriculture, especially in maize. Food aid, which is already politically difficult to swallow in a country such as Mexico, is made more problematic when it threatens to throw small farmers off their land into the city by removing their protection.

Another prospect for the bilateral agenda comes from the 1983 bilateral agreement as well. At that time, the US advanced cash for future oil purchases so that Mexico could finance its imports. This seems little more than a glorified countertrade opption: oil for basic grains with a price trigger mechanism. Although the US in not in dire need of more oil imports, low prices and regional advantages may make short-term barter – a sort of progressive 'food for crude' – a reasonable policy instrument. Such barter has been undertaken several times with the government of Jamaica, trading CCC dairy stocks for bauxite (Grigsby and Jabara, 1985, p. 194).

CONCLUSION

Jack Burden, the protagonist in Robert Penn Warren's *All the King's Men*, proferred a 'web theory' of action, in which each individual's actions send ripples of effect to all others connected to the web. The US and Mexico are in a tightly woven web of agricultural policy, the effects of which are so important to the development of Mexico that one is tempted to advocate paralysing any movement on the US part for Mexico's sake. Since the agricultural sector in the US is itself suffering perturbations of macroeconomic policy, however, one can expect the bilateral ripples to grow stronger, not weaker, in coming years.

Both Mexico and the US have preferred to deal with the bilateral agricultural system on domestic terms, without significant appreciation for their partner's own crisis or a particularly acute vision of their own long-term development needs in the sector. Mexico has relativised its own food crisis according to a false standard: import levels. The result has been the forced underconsumption of food among the poor, for the sake of a false, import-obsessed idea of food self-sufficiency. The insularity of each country's policy reached absurd heights in April 1987, when the Mexican government apparently sought to promote the notoriously inadequate domestic dairy industry by forcing US milk products off the shelves for 'health reasons'. The United States, citing increases in Mexican live cattle imports in 1986 and 1987, threatened an investigation and possible 'action' against 'excessive' imports of Mexican cattle – demagogically ignoring the automatic quota trigger mechanism already in place in the Meat Import Act.

In order to break out of such insularity and bilateral pettiness, Mexico must make structural adjustments to its agricultural policy, to adapt to a truly integrated agricultural system – but on its own terms. The United States must show at least a modicum of appreciation for Mexico's development quandary, especially in light of the professed goals of new immigration laws, the Baker Plan, promised rewards for the Mexican GATT accession and myriad other contradictory foreign economic policies.

The trade climate in the US suggests that Mexico is on its own in devising new ways to make such adjustments. But, there are points of advantage where Mexico can exploit agricultural trade and growth as part of a coherent social policy. That possibility, sadly, seems most remote now, in the gloom of Mexico's endless stabilisation efforts. But the lines of the US farm policy crisis most relevant to Mexico are relatively clear. And, crisis or not, Mexican policy-makers would do well to study US farm legislation and research to find opportunities of its own. In view of the United States manifest lack of concern for the Mexican food crisis, agricultural policy for Mexico becomes a matter of how to avoid becoming hopelessly entangled in a web woven by others.

Notes

1. Agricultural policy is not synonymous with rural development policy or food policy. Agricultural policy is sectoral policy for agricultural supply and distribution, under which rural development, agricultural imports, agribusiness development and food policy considerations fall. The political basis of agricultural policy in Mexico is not at all identical with rural development advocates.
2. Data can be found in Goodman *et al.* (1985), Sanderson (1986), and Yates (1981).
3. The SAM (*Sistema Alimentario Mexicano*) was an interministerial oversight agency that presided over a two year (1980–82) food self-sufficiency

drive, fuelled by petrodollars. For relevant literature, see Redclift (1981), Luiselli (1985), Spalding (1984) and Austin and Esteva (1985).
4. PRONAL (*Programa Nacional de Alimentacion*) is the intellectual (but not the fiscal) heir of SAM. It had the impossible mission of continuing the SAM mission (now redefined as 'food security', not self-sufficiency) without a budget.
5. Before that time, CONASUPO held exclusive rights to grain tenders abroad, and dominated much of the domestic bean and maize market. CONASUPO continues to be a central factor in grain marketing, and continues to make difficult regulations about grading, licences, and so on.
6. For more serious treatments of US farm policy see Gardner (1985), Glaser (1986), Tweeten (1979) and USDA (1985b).
7. The 'plurilateral' option was devised as a means of offering an alternative to US bilateral and multilateral commitments. In arguing for a new GATT round, US trade policy-makers suggested that they would adopt a plurilateral approach as a last resort; that is, if the multilateral system did not agree to a new round, the US would negotiate agreements with 'anyone who would come to the table'.

Bibliography

Austin, James and Gustavo Esteva, (1985), 'SAM is dead—long live SAM,' *Food Policy*, 10:2.
Barkin, David and Gustavo Esteva, (1981), 'El papel del sector público en la comercialización y la fijación de precios de los productos agrícolas básicos en Mexico' (Mexico: UN Economic Commission on Latin America). Mimeo.
Barkin, David and Blanca Suarez, (1982), *El fin de autosuficiencia alimentaria* (Mexico: Editorial Nueva Imagen).
CDIA (Centro de Investigaciones Agrarias) (1974), *Estructura agraria y desarrollo agrícola en Mexico* (Mexico: Fondo de Cultura Económica).
Diskin, Martin, Steven E. Sanderson and William C. Thiesenhusen, (1987), *Business in Development: Betting on Winners in Rural Mexico* (Washington, D.C.: Inter-American Foundation).
Gardner, Bruce (ed.) (1985), *US Agricultural Policy: The 1985 Farm Legislation* (Washington, D.C.: American Enterprise Institute).
Glaser, Lewrene K. (1986), 'Provisions of the Food Security Act of 1985,' USDA Agriculture Information Bulletin 498.
Goodman, Louis W. *et al.* (1985), 'Mexican Agriculture: Rural Crisis and Policy Response,' Woodrow Wilson International Center for Scholars, Latin American Program Working Paper No. 168.
Grigsby, S. Elaine and Cathy L. Jabara, (1985), 'Agricultural Export Programs and US Agricultural Policy,' In USDA (1985b) 185–201.
Johnson, D. Gale (1985), 'World Commodity Market Situation and Outlook', in Bruce Gardner (ed.), *U.S. Agricultural Policy: The 1985 Farm Legislation* (Washington, D.C.: American Enterprise Institute) 19–50.
Longmire, Jim and Art Morey, (1982), *Exchange Rates, US Agricultural Export Prices, and US Farm Program Stocks* (Washington, D.C.: USDA).

Luiselli, Cassio (1985), *The Route to Food Self-Sufficiency in Mexico*, monograph 17 (La Jolla: UC San Diego Center for US-Mexican Studies).

Mccalla, Alex F. (1985), 'Assessment from Outside the Beltway', in Bruce Gardner (ed.) *U.S. Agricultural Policy: The 1985 Farm Legislation* (Washington, D.C.: American Enterprise Institute) 174–94.

Redclift, Michael R. (1981), 'The Mexican Food System (SAM) – Sowing Subsidies, Reaping Apathy', *Food Policy* 6:4 (November) 231–5.

— (1986), 'Agricultural Development in Latin America since 1960: The Unsustainable Options', *Bulletin of Latin American Research*.

Roberts, Donna H. and Miles J. Mielke, (1986), *Mexico: An Export Market Profile* (Washington, D.C.: Foreign Agricultural Economic Report 220. USDA).

Sanderson, Steven E. (1981), *Agrarian Populism and the Mexican State: The Struggle for Land in Sonora* (Berkeley and Los Angeles: University of California Press).

— (1983), 'The Complex No-Policy Option: US Agricultural Relations with Mexico,' *Working Paper* 134, Latin American Program, Woodrow Wilson International Center for Scholars. (Washington, D.C.: Smithsonian Institution).

— (1985), 'Trends in Mexican Investment Policy and the Forces that Shape Them'. Manuscript.

— (1986), *The Transformation of Mexican Agriculture: International Structure and the Politics of Rural Change* (Princeton, N.J.: Princeton University Press).

Schejtman, Alejandro (1981), 'Economía campesina y agricultura empresarial: tipología de productores del agro mexicano', mimeo (Mexico: UN Economic Commission on Latin America).

Schuh, G. Edward (1974), 'The Exchange Rate and US Agriculture', *American Journal of Agricultural Economics* 56, 1–13.

— (1985), 'International Agriculture and Trade Policies: Implications for the United States', in Bruce Gardner (ed.) *U.S. Agricultural Policy: The 1985 Farm Legislation* (Washington, D.C.: American Enterprise Institute) 56–78.

Spalding, Rose (1984), 'The Mexican Food Crisis: An Analysis of SAM', working paper (La Jolla: UC San Diego Center for US-Mexican Studies).

Tweeten, Luther (1979), *Foundations of Farm Policy*, 2nd ed. (Lincoln: University of Nebraska).

US Department of Agriculture (USDA) (1985), 'Analysis of Policies to Conserve Soil and Reduce Surplus Crop Production', USDA Agricultural Economic Report 534.

USDA (1985a), 'Sodbusting: Land Use Change and Farm Programs', USDA Agriculture Information Bulletin 536.

USDA (1985b), 'Agricultural-Food Policy Review: Commodity Program Perspectives', USDA Agricultural Economic Report 530.

USDA (1986), 'Grain and Feed Annual, 1986', USDA, Foreign Agricultural Service, US Embassy in Mexico, MX6024.

USDA (1986a) 'Mexico – Agricultural Situation Report', USDA, Foreign Agricultural Service, US Embassy in Mexico, MX6023.

Yates, Paul Lamartine (1981), *Mexico's Agricultural Dilemma* (Tucson: University of Arizona Press).

10 The Rural Crisis Downunder: Australia's Declining Fortunes in the Global Farm Economy

Geoffrey Lawrence

INTRODUCTION

The greater proportion of the income of most Australian farms is obtained from the sale of a combination of no more than two or three agricultural products. Wool, wheat and beef are three of the main commodities produced by the majority of Australia's 174 000 commercial farmers in extensive dryland systems. Dairy products, sugar and rice are produced by specialist farmers in higher rainfall coastal regions or inland irrigated areas. These commodities have dominated Australian agricultural production in past decades and can be considered the main products upon which Australia relies for the generation of overseas agricultural earnings.

The vast majority of Australian farms are properties owned and operated as family-farm concerns. Technologically sophisticated and economically efficient, these farms are, by international standards, quite large holdings. They are supported by a state infrastructure which includes railways, grain handling facilities, a Commonwealth Bank, a Federal Department of Primary Industry and Bureau of Agricultural Economics (BAE), State Departments of Agriculture, statutory marketing authorities and other bodies established to administer stabilisation schemes, rural reconstruction measures, differential pricing, quarantine, research, extension and overseas trade.

After a short period of hesitation and tight control federal government policies after the Second World War encouraged an expansion of agricultural output – including an expansion of sales abroad – and sought to foster capital accumulation in agriculture. Through a variety of export, output and input subsidies, tax breaks, concessional loans and other stimulatory measures Australian producers were encouraged to utilise the labour-saving, industrially-produced inputs to farming. They readily accepted the products of a growing agribusiness sector and were not reluctant to borrow heavily in an effort to capture the productivity gains from the latest agrichemicals, fertilisers and machinery.

As a result of domestic and international economic growth from the early 1950s to the mid-1970s (the so-called 'Long Boom' of capitalist development) Australian agriculture prospered. For a majority of those years the farmers' own party, the Country (now National) Party, was in government with its senior coalition partner, the Liberal Party. Although tensions existed over the latter's insistence upon retaining high tariff barriers as a means of fostering import-substitution industrialisation, the state, ever conscious of agriculture's crucial role in Australia's balance of trade, continued to underwrite agriculture.

After a period of structural adjustment, Australian producers were able to weather the stormy period following Britain's entry to the European Economic Community (EEC) by locating new markets in Japan and the Pacific Basin region. However, it was clear after successive wool, wheat and beef price collapses in the late 1960s and mid 1970s that conditions in international markets no longer favoured unfettered agricultural expansion. Following the crisis of the mid-1970s there was a re-examination of Australia's reliance upon farm products. Mineral extraction had proceeded in a spectacular fashion during the late 1960s and, within a decade, minerals all but matched agriculture as an earner of foreign exchange. Agriculture's relative contribution to Gross Domestic Product (GDP), to employment and to export earnings had deteriorated slowly, but steadily, throughout the post-war years.

There was no longer any perceived need for agriculture to be afforded the privileged status it had acquired during the Long Boom. Since the late 1970s federal governments of both political persuasions – the Liberal–National Party Coalition (parties supported by the farmers and graziers) and the Labor Party (which recruits most of its support from wage workers) – have implemented policies aimed, above all else, at removing the perceived barriers to increased efficiency in agriculture. The consequent restructuring of domestic agriculture has resulted in the further concentration and centralisation of capital in agriculture and the accelerated growth in output as farmers have responded to cost-price pressures by producing a greater volume for sale. The National Farmers' Federation (NFF) (a peak organisation established in 1979 in response to the declining power of the National Party and to the consequent implementation of tougher Federal policies for agriculture) has *not* argued for the continuation of state-subsidised benefits for farmers. It has adopted the consistent but economically 'dry' line that local and world wide subsidisation and the protectionist policies of competing countries disadvantage Australian producers.

The NFF argues that on the domestic front the solution lies in further deregulating financial and labour markets, lowering tariffs and reducing state expenditure. At the international level the crisis is seen to have been caused by restrictive trade practices, subsidies and other 'distortions' which prop up inefficient farming and prevent the guiding hand of free market forces from operating effectively. It argues for the removal of these distortions. Its only concession to domestic producers is its insistence that uneconomic farmers should be removed from the industry via the state-funded Rural Adjustment Scheme, thereby allowing those remaining to expand farm size in an effort to capture economies of scale.

There is no doubt that the expansion of existing farm units has encouraged capital accumulation through the resultant growth in the forces of production. Despite the efficiency-as-the-key-to-viability argument propounded by the NFF, Australian agriculture in the mid-1980's had become ensnared in a crisis of major proportions. It is a crisis resulting from the economic fragility of a world marketplace currently saturated through the subsidised dumping of rural commodities. And it is a crisis which has stemmed from the erosion of power and influence of family farmers in a domestic economy which has come progressively under the influence of both national and transnational corporate capital. The main features of the present crisis have been low returns to producers, steeply rising input costs, growing indebtedness, high interest repayments and falling land values. There is little likelihood of any immediate improvement. Current policies of the EEC together with the retaliatory action taken by the US against EEC encroachment upon world markets have been, and will continue to be, major factors in the deterioration of world commodity prices. Meanwhile, the farm crisis in Australia is having an important effect on the well-being of rural producers. In response to declining farm incomes, farmer militancy, which reached a high point in 1985 (when demonstrations were staged in most State capitals and where farmers staged the largest rally ever been held in the nation's capital) shows little sign of abating. In a matter of a year the NFF raised over A$15 million in a special 'fighting fund' aimed at dislodging Labor and other politicians who oppose further deregulation of the economy at the 1987 elections.

The farm crisis has spilled over into other areas. The deterioration of the environment has been one consequence of the strategy of many farmers to maximise production. The application of the products of agribusiness as well as overstocking, over-ploughing and over-irrigating have resulted in massive soil erosion, desertification, salination, eutrophication and chemical pollution of streams and waterways (Lawrence, 1987). These are particularly important problems for a continent with a very shallow, nutrient-deficient topsoil and a small and unreliable network of inland waterways.

The social costs have been no less important. In the absence of state intervention to bolster a flagging rural economy, the declining number of farms has had a significant impact on the viability of rural communities. Unemployment, underemployment and poverty rates are very much higher in rural than in urban areas. Rationalisation of private firms and public agencies throughout the countryside has led to reduced opportunities for employment, thereby compounding the effect of the crisis for farm families seeking alternative work options.

Unlike previous crises which have struck particular commodity groups for short periods, the present period of crisis appears to be consistent with a major international restructuring of capital. Australia is being required to undertake internal adjustment so as to cope with balance of trade difficulties. It is expected that Australia will emerge from the crisis ready to play a new role as a provider of cheap raw materials for an industrialising Pacific Basin region (Catley and McFarlane, 1981; Crough and Wheelwright, 1982).

The dominion capitalist (semi-peripheral) nature of the Australian economy means that it must continue to import increasingly expensive industrial items yet rely, for their payment, on the sale of increasingly cheaper primary products. This is part of the explanation for Australia's problems since it requires recognition of the dependent nature of internal economic development, as well as an appreciation of the importance of transnational capital in the determination of Australia's economic future. Another part of the explanation is that agriculture, as a competitive capitalist industry appears, in its articulation with monopoly capital, to be relatively disadvantaged and open to manipulation and exploitation.

In this chapter I will make three straightforward points: the crisis in
Australian agriculture is *real* and is having major on-farm effects as
well as causing significant problems beyond the farm gate; any
adequate assessment of the causes of the crisis requires discussion of
the 'dominion capitalist' role of Australia in the world system; and,
traditional responses to the crisis appear outmoded and would seem
to lead to 'adjustment' solutions which, while they may ultimately
enhance capital accumulation, will lead inexorably to the further
concentration and centralisation of capital in agriculture, to increasing economic pressures on those family farmers remaining, and to the
demise of Australian rural communities.

IMPACT OF THE CRISIS

On-Farm Dimensions

The rural crisis of the mid-1980s has occurred neither accidentally nor
spontaneously. Signs of deterioration in the agricultural economy
were clearly evident during the boom – bust decade of the 1970s.
Following a price slump on world markets, Australian wheat producers suffered in the late 1960s and early years of the 1970s. As a
consequence the unusual step was taken of introducing delivery
quotas for wheat. Prices recovered in the mid 1970s but fell again in
the early 1980s. The price of wheat on international markets fell by
some 13 per cent in 1986–87 and the average Australian wheat farm
received an income, after deduction of costs, of some A$2200. About
half the wheat farmers in New South Wales faced the prospect of loan
default during 1987. The BAE has estimated that land values in
Australia's prime sheep-wheat zone have decreased by 40 per cent
over the past two years (*National Farmer*, 4 February 1987,12). The
current US export enhancement programme and the 1985 Farm Bill,
which have been implemented in response to the contradictions of
US farm policy have had a direct bearing on Australian wheat sales
and on world price levels. When the 1981 US Farm Bill was enacted
market prospects appeared good. Price support (loan levels) for
grains as well as government stock release prices were set at relatively
high levels compared with prevailing world prices. With the appreciation of the US dollar in the early 1980s there was a consequent
reduction in the US share of world grain markets and a significant
increase in government held stocks. Throughout the US farmers were

facing increasing financial pressure as interest rate levels began to
climb. Implementation of the 1985 Farm Bill was in response to the
need to deplete stocks (through subsidised exports) and was aimed at
providing assistance (through increased deficiency payments) to an
increasingly vocal farm sector (Curran *et al.*, 1987). As US economist
Gale Johnson told Australian farmers at the beginning of 1987:

> The farm bill was designed to once again make the US farm
> products competitive on world markets, regardless of what these
> costs were either in terms of governmental expenditures or nega-
> tive impacts upon producers in countries that do not protect their
> producers to a significant degree . . . . Unfortunately for us all –
> US farmers and taxpayers and Australian farmers – US grown
> stocks at the end of the 1986-87 crop year are predicted to be . . .
> 25 per cent larger than a year earlier. (*National Farmer*, 4 February
> 1987:17).

Since 1980–81 world wheat stocks have risen by 70 per cent at the
same time as prices have fallen by 45 per cent (Miller, 1987:12). The
current US Farm Bill, which is now in place until the 1990s, is costing
the Australian wheat industry between A\$250 million and A\$500
million annually and dislocating world trade patterns.

Australian wool producers are faring somewhat better in the mid-
1980s than they did in the years of price collapse a decade earlier.
However, despite buoyant prices, approximately 25 per cent of sheep
producers received negative incomes in 1985–86. The current industry recovery is therefore not one which has reached all producers.
Indeed, while prices are currently climbing (at a time when the
Australian dollar hovers at historically low levels) it is expected that
competition from synthetics and from cotton will compete away
profits in the medium to long term. Prospects of a strengthening
Australian dollar, the continuation of low prices for world oil and the
likelihood of the subsidised dumping of US cotton stocks on international markets are unhealthy prospects for an industry which is
reliant upon the sale of over 90 per cent of its product on a volatile
world market.

The beef industry provides perhaps the best example of the roller-
coaster ride experienced by Australian farmers in recent years. After
the boom years of the late 1960s – a time when industry leaders were
telling farmers that the demand for Australian lean beef was 'limit-
less' – the sudden imposition of barriers to the Japanese and US

markets left Australian producers with an unsaleable commodity. Farmers shot and buried their animals. (Calves, for example, were costing more to take to the auctions than the price received for their sale.) Farmers who had attempted to move into beef production with the onset of the deterioration in wool and dairy product prices (many of of whom had often borrowed heavily to convert their farms into beef properties) were trapped. Bankruptcies and poverty level incomes were a feature of this sector until the price recovery of the late 1970s. By mid-1984, following the exposure of a racket which substituted horse and kangaroo meat for beef destined for the US, the industry was in crisis. Again, in August 1987, Australia's entire A\$750 million beef export industry was threatened when pesticide-contaminated meat was discovered in a shipment of beef to the US. Although US authorities did not immediately retaliate, one month later all Australian meat exports to the US were banned with the imposition of the protectionist US Meat Import Law. During the middle years of the 1980s Australia's three main customers the US, Japan and South Korea had been setting quotas, buying cheaper meat from subsidised competitors or, in the case of the US, simply producing more of its own product for domestic consumption.

The EEC is currently seeking means of penetrating new markets. It has been discounting its beef by up to A\$1500 per tonne in an effort to attract buyers in some of Australia's new markets in the Middle East, Africa and the USSR. It is feared much of the EEC surplus is destined ultimately for the Pacific Basin region. Yet Australian producers continue to rebuild herds in the face of the weakening consumer demand for beef, despite the cheapening of its main substitutes, chicken and pork, and without any plan to counter continued EEC subsidisation and the breakdown of voluntary restraint agreements in world trade (BAE, 1986). Overproduction in the industry is again predicted for early years of 1990s (BAE, 1987a:8).

Australian dairy producers have struggled to find markets since Britain joined the EEC in 1974. The world market for dairy products is chronically oversupplied and high levels of undisposed stocks remain in competing countries. It is believed that major exporters may fail to observe minimum prices set by GATT, placing Australian producers in an ever tightening cost-price squeeze (BAE, 1987a:36). The BAE has predicted little improvement over the next five years as the excess production of the EEC is dumped on international markets. The number of dairy farmers, which stood at 62 000 in 1964, had contracted to 18 000 some 20 years later. While the exit rate is expected to be lower than that of the 1970s, average farm size and productivity per cow are expected to increase over the next decade. The high incidence of poverty amongst dairy farmers which was a feature of the mid-1970s is still apparent in some regions. In the 1985–86 financial year over 25 per cent of dairy farmers were recording negative farm incomes.

In recent years Australia's sugar, dried fruit and rice producers have also become victims of depressed world prices. In 1985–86 over 75 per cent of Australia's cane producers registered a negative farm cash operating surplus, with the sugar industry in a state of virtual chaos and prices, in real terms, at their lowest level in 200 years. Australian growers' costs have been in the order of A\$240 per tonne at a time when world prices had dropped to A\$90 per tonne. Restrictions on sugar imports to the US and state support for US domestic producers is estimated to be costing Australian cane growers up to A\$310 milllion per annum and has resulted in lower and more variable world sugar prices (Borrel, Sturgiss and Wong, 1987). It has been calculated that about 40 per cent of Australia's 7000 cane producers will be removed from the industry if conditions do not improve immediately. The drive for self-sufficiency in many sugar-importing nations and the harnessing of new biotechnologies in the manufacture of sugar substitutes would seem to counter the optimism of those predicting increased international demand in the medium to long term (see BAE, 1987a:53).

In the dried fruit industry one in three producers is currently experiencing a loss, and for rice farmers the average income this year is expected to be negative A\$3200 (*National Farmer*, 4 February 1987:13). Approximately one third of Australia's rice farmers are currently unable to meet basic monthly fuel repayments. Competition in the world market and reduced requirements by Australia's rice customers has eroded world prices by some 13 per cent in the past year. The current debt per rice farm stands at about A\$100 000, and, with 25 per cent of growers having less than 60 per cent equity in their properties, exit rates from the industry are predicted to increase. One problem for those seeking to move is that property values in the main rice growing regions have declined by as much as 35 per cent in the past year. Close to one-third of Australia's rice farmers are considered close to bankruptcy and may be forced from the industry if prices do not improve (*Daily Advertiser*, 7 February 1987:1–2).

Aggregate figures also provide an indication of the extent of current difficulties in Australian agriculture. During the last financial year the average commercial farmer (by Australian definition one who sold in excess of A$10 000 worth of agricultural commodities per year) received a net farm income of A$6700. This is about one-third of the average yearly income of Australian wage workers. The net real value of rural production – an indicator of the economic performance of the agricultural sector – decreased by 24 per cent during the same period and stands today at less than 50 per cent of its value in the late 1970s in real terms. Real farm incomes have declined by half since 1983–84 (Miller, 1987:2). In 1986–87 the return to capital in agriculture is expected to remain negative, averaging minus 6.9 per cent. Over 43 per cent of Australian farmers are expected to sustain cash losses from agriculture – although about one-third of all farms will receive off-farm income in the vicinity of A$6000 to supplement farm income (*National Farmer*, 4 February 1987:10). Figures from the BAE indicate that over the past 15 years 19 000 farmers and their families have left agriculture, the farm work force has decreased by about 32 000 and the total rural workforce by 100 000; farm costs have increased by 375 per cent, about twice the rate of farm returns; and that although Australia now produces in volume 27 per cent more agricultural goods than it did 15 years ago, gross value has risen by as little as 4 per cent (Cribb, 1985:10).

While highlighting general trends these aggregate figures do tend to hide internal divisions. Not all producers have fared equally during the crisis. There has been an economic polarisation amongst commercial farmers with the larger, more financially secure producers receiving a disproportionate share of the total value of agricultural production. There is also evidence that small, non-commercial producers – especiallly those with permanent off-farm work – have had some measure of protection from the current problems of agriculture (Lawrence, 1987). In contrast, the normally efficient family farmers – those involved in the operation of 'traditional, dependent enterprises' to use a more sociologically exact categorisation (Whatmore *et al.*, 1987:33) — appear to the ones who have suffered most in the recent period of commodity price decline (Curran *et al.*, 1987: 96). These farmers have relied heavily upon agriculture for the generation of income and have borrowed substantially in the past years to fund farm expansion and machinery purchase.

It is these producers who have marched the streets calling, among other things, for government action to reduce prime interest rates; rates averaged 18.9 per cent through 1986 but have been in excess of

20 per cent at particular times over the past two years(BAE, 1987:11). Rural indebtedness to major lending institution rose to A$8000 million in 1986, an 11 per cent increase over the previous year. Farm debt is expected to increase at the (reduced) rate of 3 per cent during 1987 (BAE, 1987:84). The index of prices paid by farmers is expected to increase in 1986–87 and again in the following year (BAE 1987:83).

The depreciation of the Australian dollar initially helped to increase sales abroad. But it also resulted in increased prices for imported goods. While fertilizer costs are likely to be static in 1987–88, fuel costs are expected to increase by about 10 per cent, and farm machinery costs by about 8 per cent during the year. In real terms the prices-received index is expected to slowly decline and then fall sharply at the beginning of the 1990s as a result of an anticipated reduction in beef and wool prices on international markets (BAE, 1978a:9; Curran, *et al.*, 1987:98).

The prospects for Australian rural producers are bleak. Rural exports are expected to stagnate and farm incomes are not expected to recover to the levels obtained in the more buoyant years of the late 1970s. The Common Agricultural Policy of the EEC has depressed world prices for beef, wheat, coarse grains and sugar by between 9 and 17 per cent and for butter by 28 per cent. Price decline and market encroachment is costing Australian farmers A$1000 million per annum (Stoeckel, 1986:157). Australian agriculture is expected to remain in its depressed state for the foreseeable future (BAE, 1987a:9–10).

Social Dimensions

Economic difficulties associated with farming have led to increasing social stress in rural Australia. The displacement of hired male labour as a cost-cutting measure has been associated with increased labour force participation by farm women. While this reflects a rational attempt by the farm family to utilise more effectively its labour resources in the face of rising costs, it also highlights the added burden being placed upon farm women during the present crisis. Research has confirmed that pressures on family farm members to work harder – both off and on the farm – has led to the breakdown of voluntary community networks amongst farm families, has decreased the opportunity for social interaction between family members, has increased problems of health and has led to an upsurge in domestic violence (*National Farmer*, 4 February 1987:18). One survey has revealed that rural people have 25 per cent more accidents, 10 per cent more illness, and a 28 per cent higher incidence of hypertension and psychiatric disorder than urban populations (*Australian*, 14–15 February 1987:2).

In one rice-growing region of New South Wales treatment of stress-related illnesses such as heart attacks, hypertension, asthma, ulcers, insomnia and alcoholism is known to have more than doubled over the past few years. Suicide is becoming an increasingly acceptable option among those who feel unable to survive economically (Wright, 1985:27; Australian Government, 1986:79). The rate of suicide among farmers has risen by some 70 per cent during the past three years (*Australian*, 4 March 1987:3).

It is not only the farming community which has suffered in recent times. Reductions in the number of farmers and farm workers have important implications for the provision of government services, the overall level of economic activity of service towns, and ultimately, of the life chances of the non-farm rural population. Population losses from agriculture set other wheels in motion which undermine the viability of small country towns and lead to increasing levels of poverty and unemployment. In many rural districts unemployment has reached Depression levels of around 30 per cent of the workforce (*Australian*, 14–15 February 1987:2).

It is estimated that for each person leaving agriculture one further job is lost from the towns which have grown to service the district farms (Harris *et al.*, 1974). The Australian rural labour market is characteristically more brittle than its urban counterpart; specialisation in activities related to natural resources increases a rural town's vulnerability to weather conditions and international markets; strong linkages to other industries means fluctuations in agriculture have a direct impact on country towns; there is little 'depth' in particular occupations; and, because of the diversity of country towns, it is difficult (in a planning sense) to formulate any blanket strategies for employment growth (Powell, 1986:19–20).

Approximately one-third of Australia's country towns (those with 200 residents or more) are considered to be in irreversible decline (Rural Development Centre, 1985:14). The isolation of people living in smaller towns, the poor access to public services and amenities and the concentration of both public and private investment exacerbates social welfare problems (McKenzie, 1986; Rural Development Centre, 1986). Rural poverty, which appears to be running at about twice the rate of poverty in the large cities, is most severe in small country towns with population levels below 10 000 (*National Farmer*, 18 October 1984). Research has revealed that between 15 per cent and 20 per cent of NSW farmers have been living below the poverty line during the last ten years, their limited expenditure having had direct and profound consequences for country town survival. Where the quality of life in rural towns is eroded, many of the more able, better trained, younger and more upwardly mobile citizens are encouraged to leave (Lawrence, 1987).

Recent rationalisations in the meat processing industry have added to the economic difficulties of smaller country towns. Between 1978 and 1981 about 20 domestic abbatoirs were closed and another eight forfeited their export licenses. Direct job losses from the closures have been put at between 10 000 and 25 000 (Lawrence, 1987). The seven country abattoirs which closed in NSW were virtually the only sources of secondary industry employment in the towns in which they were located. The Bureau of Industry Economics in its study of the impact of abbatoir closure in one northern NSW town found that the people displaced represented a high proportion of the region's total workforce. Most workers had few transferable skills and there were few alternative work options available. Unemployment in the town remained high, with only 40 per cent of workers who chose to remain finding jobs after 12 months. Local business suffered as the salaries of the meatworkers was lost to the town (Bureau of Industry Economics, 1983). Other research has indicated that workers over 40 years of age find moving from a country town to be both a difficult and daunting experience. Country towns lack a proper basis for retraining, educational opportunities are limited and facilities are scattered (Australian Rural Adjustment Unit, 1983). Furthermore, there is little scope for geographical mobility. In the context of a depressed regional economy, houses cannot be sold for prices necessary to allow the unemployed to settle elsewhere. Many residents remain for long periods on welfare and, in the process, become candidates for rural poverty.

The declining economic and social base of inland towns and farming communities supports what is known in the US as the Goldschmidt thesis (Buttel, 1981a). The thesis proposes that the development of capitalist agriculture leads to the *underdevelopment* of rural communities. With the increasing size and reduction in number of farms, and with increased technology and corporate rationalisation in rural areas, the socio-economic basis of small rural towns tends to decline. With the displacement of farm and farm workers from agricultrure a downward multiplier is set in motion undermining town viability. As people move from the town the tax base is lowered and the community becomes poorly serviced (Goldschmidt, 1978; Buttel, 1981a).

The Australian government appears to have been unable or reluctant to alter the forces threatening family-farm agriculture and the economies of small inland towns. There is now general agreement that most of the previous decentralisation initiatives have failed to bring about desired results (Lonsdale, 1971; Jarrad, 1981; O'Connor, 1986). The approach of 'scattered decentralisation' or provision of small amounts of assistance to many country towns as occurred in the 1950s and 1960s did little to increase work opportunities, and failed to halt population outflow. It now remains largely discredited (O'Connor, 1986). There is little evidence today of any real concern of the major political parties over issues of industrial decentralisation, although some State and federal governments have recognized the economic advantages of regional administrative decentralisation.

Private firms have found that it is the large cities of Australia which provide the best basis for surplus generation and cost savings (Mullins, 1977). As Stilwell (1974) has pointed out, direct intervention in population and manufacturing industry location to promote social equity must, of necessity, oppose free market forces. Yet government intervention in the Australian economy only seems to gain support when it actively enhances the profit-making opportunities for private firms, rather than opposes them. Within this framework Stillwell notes 'the forces of centralization have clearly outweighed those of decentralisation' in Australia (1974:153).

Limited growth is occurring in some of the larger inland regional centres. Advantaged by regionalised government departments, these centres have generated their own (albeit small) multipliers pulling population and economic activity to them – not from the coastal cities – but from surrounding towns, hamlets and farms. It is in such centres where educational, training, and more general social welfare services are located, and it is to those centres where the surplus rural population is tending to drift. As the Green Paper on rural policy noted, this leaves those remaining in less populated rural areas with restricted access to health, welfare, housing, education and other community facilities and services (Harris, *et al.*, 1974).

Unlike the United States (and to some extent Britain) Australia has not experienced any significant 'population turnaround' with disaffected urban dwellers looking to agricultural regions for a quieter, more satisfying, lifestyle. Those moving from Australian cities prefer *coastal*, rather than *agricultural*, areas for retirement or retreat. So while there has been some closer settlement of rural regions surrounding larger coastal towns such developments cannot be construed as the revival of family farming or as confirming a desire to engage in agriculture.

The forces of capital accumulation have led to structural polarisation in the Australian economy and to the social malaise accompanying the economic demise of rural regions. Without alteration to the conditions governing production and exchange within agriculture, it is unlikely that the flow-on effects of the crisis in agriculture will be successfully addressed.

EXPLAINING THE CRISIS

Australia in the World Economic Order

Following a century of pastoral development Australia emerged from its white settler colonial days as a major trader in staple commodities. Pastoral and small-scale farming which had expanded after the 'unlocking of the lands' in the 1860s produced ideal conditions for the accumulation of capital in agriculture. Surplus value created in agriculture was not consumed by a landlord class but was reinvested, enriching not only farmers, but bankers, merchants and other fractions of urban capital (Bedgood, 1978). Capital accumulation resulted in three important developments on the local and world stage. First, capital reinvestment allowed for the continued expansion of family-farm agriculture. Second, agriculture provided the basis for increased urban expansion in Australia. Small urban manufacturers, aided by state expenditure on infrastructure, were able to prosper as a result of the increased domestic demand brought about by population increase. Third, the provision of cheaper food and fibre to Britain (something facilitated by developments in transportation and refrigeration) lowered the cost of labour power in Britain and so contributed to preserving the competitive edge which British manufacturing industry had established in the world arena (Bedgood, 1978). Justified on the basis of comparative advantage, the relationship between Britain and its Southern Hemisphere colonies was one in which raw materials were sent from Australia and New Zealand and manufactured goods were returned. The surplus capital generated from British industry found its way back to the colonies. Australia was therefore not left in an underdeveloped state, but was provided with sufficient funds to undertake nascent, local industrialisation.

The outcome of this type of economic development was that Australia, along with Canada and New Zealand, came to occupy the 'middle ground' in the world economic order (Ehrensaft and Armstrong, 1978). Neither a fully industrialised centre nation nor part of the economically underdeveloped periphery, Australia grew to become a nominally independent country bound inextricably to a world of transnational corporate capital.

Philip Ehrensaft and Warwick Armstrong (1978:352) have sought to highlight the unique features of semi-peripheral – or what they term dominion capitalist – countries like Australia:
– they have been established in temperate or semi-temperate regions only sparsely inhabited by indigenous populations;
– the indigenous populations have been either assimilated or eliminated during the period of white colonisation;
– their levels of urbanisation, birth rates and life expectancy, are similar to those of modern Western nations;
– the contribution to GDP by the primary, secondary, and tertiary sectors are similar to those of other Western nations;
– labour-power is sold on the marketplace. Wage levels are comparable with those in other advanced capitalist societies;
– exports are primary products generated by technologies and capital/labour ratios typical of industrial societies;
– industrialisation is usually limited to first stage processing, import substitution with tariff barriers being a local means of stimulating domestic industrial growth;
– transnational corporations – often those originating in the North Atlantic economies or Japan – occupy an important position in both manufacturing and mineral production.
The authors developed these points as part of a first statement on dominion capitalism. Unfortunately it has remained the *only* statement. While it is a useful ideal – typical description of Australia, it does not explain how Australia's position in the world order places limits on both industrialisation *and* agricultural expansion. Nor does it expose the economic vulnerability of dominion capitalist economies during periods of recession.

Marx argued in Volume Three of *Capital* that it is useful to distinguish between capital involved in production and that specialising in circulation and, further, that the spatial location of each form will have different consequences for social structure (Marx, 1967). Where, as in Britain, there was a predominance of production capital over circulation capital, industrialisation could occur in a revolutionary manner, altering fundamentally the structure of social relations and destroying older, pre-capitalist forms of production. Where circulation capital predominated, however, it was typical for the capitalist mode to accommodate pre-capitalist production, thereby preventing a thoroughgoing transformation of society. Such truncated industrialisation (Ehrensaft and Armstrong, 1978; Clement, 1978; Stilwell, 1986a) has been a feature of the dominion capitalist economies,countries which have developed a reliance upon agricultural and mineral exports to support domestic economic growth. It is in this sense that the dominion economies can be considered *developed* as well as *dependent* (Stilwell, 1986a). In times of crisis this ambiguous status (or contradictory location) in the world economic order poses specific problems for a country like Australia which leans heavily on export agriculture and upon branch transnationals in manufacturing industry, yet supports a wage structure more typical of advanced centre countries. In the face of declining overseas revenue, enormous pressures are placed on the state to restructure the conditions of surplus generation throughout industry. This includes subsidising infrastructural expenditure and facilitating wage reductions as a means of appeasing transnationals. Governments fear that the corporate sector may stage a capital 'strike' by withholding investment or (more seriously), might move its activities to the Free Trade Zones and other low cost labour regions of South East Asia (Stilwell, 1986a).

Another condition for extended reproduction is the removal of tariffs and other restrictive forms of domestic industry protection. Even before the federation of the Australian States in 1901 it was apparent to domestic capital and labour alike that local industry and jobs would need to be protected through the state imposition of tariffs and trade restrictions. Barriers were set in place and local capital received other forms of state support. The farm lobby initially complained bitterly about the subsequent higher prices of imported manufactured goods (and those of their local substitutes) but these protests were quickly dissipated with the state's generous underwriting of agriculture and the restrictions placed upon the importation of farm products from abroad. That tariffs are again in the political spotlight is a consequence of the hegemony of monetarism within the NFF and underlines the increased power of transnational capital in the Australian economy.

Monopoly capital arrived in its transnational form after the end of the Second World War when the US and Britain (and later West Germany and Japan) encouraged firms to invest abroad. Incentives were provided by these countries to enable firms to export capital and to establish subsidiaries and branch plants in under-capitalised countries (Crough *et al.*, 1980; Crough and Wheelwright, 1982). Transnational coporations are typified by one or few firms in the market, large scale capital investment, technological sophistication, and high income generating potential. They are able, as a result of their level of market control, to manipulate prices and markets and to negotiate investment deals on favourable terms with host governments (Hymer, 1982; Scott, 1979).

Through mergers and takeovers foreign ownership in Australia increased rapidly in the post-war period, doubling in the 20 years to the mid-1960s (Crough and Wheelwright, 1982). It has now reached major proportions with Australia second only to Canada in regard to the level of foreign ownership amongst developed countries (Stilwell, 1986a:119). Levels of foreign control in some representative sections include: motor vehicles 100 per cent; oil refining 90 per cent; basic chemicals 78 per cent; brown coal and petroleum 84 per cent; black coal 59 per cent and iron ore 47 per cent (Crough and Wheelwright, 1982:1).

Transnational agribusiness has also grown in importance in the post-war years. Three large transnationals – Kelloggs, Sanitarium and Nabisco – control approximately 90 per cent of the breakfast cereal market; Steggles (UK) and George Western (UK) have merged with Inghams (Australia) to dominate Australia's poultry industry; in the wine industry Adsteam controls 13 per cent of sales and Philip Morris (US) 15 per cent; in oilseeds, Unilever (UK) and Allied Mills hold about 80 per cent of the market. Foreign interests control over 20 per cent of meat and milk products, over 70 per cent of vegetable products, approximately 70 per cent for confectionary and cocoa and over 50 per cent for soft drinks and for canned fish (Crough and Wheelwright, 1982:21). In farm chemicals transnationals again dominate. ICI, for example, with sales of at least A$70 million a year, commands one-third of the animal health market and a quarter of crop production sales (*National Farmer*, 8 March 1984:

24). The supermarket chains, Cole's and Woolworth's, now account for about 45 per cent of total grocery sales, representing the biggest concentration of food retailing in any country in the world (*Australian Business*, 5 October, 1985:45).

Figures from the Australian Bureau of Statistics indicate that, as a measure of corporate concentration, the top four companies in pesticides and agrochemicals control 43 per cent of the Australian market. For agricultural machinery the corporate concentration level is 44 per cent and for malt processing 80 per cent; biscuit making 95 per cent; margarine, oils and fats 67 per cent; vegetable products 58 per cent; poultry meat 49 per cent and starch gluten 80 per cent (Sargent, 1986:24). This level of concentration has occurred in tandem with industry rationalisation associated with the slower growth of export markets in the 1970s and 1980s and the entry of Britain into the EEC.

As a result of the high levels of foreign ownership and control in Australia it is conservatively estimated that in excess of one-third of after-tax profits accrues to foreign investors (Crough and Wheelwright, 1982:2). Many transnationals repatriate their profits, so that while corporate profits have risen over the past five years, corporations have withheld or exported their capital rather than reinvesting it in Australia (Stilwell, 1986a:47).

In this context it is useful to discuss Australia's changing role in the world order. According to Robert Catley and Bruce McFarlane, the Australian economy is becoming integrated into a corporate-initiated Pacific Rim Strategy which

> involves reorganizing the international economy of the Pacific on four tiers – the US and Japan acting . . . as providers of capital, technology and planning; Canada, Australia and New Zealand delivering foodstuffs, raw materials and energy and deindustrializing; . . . the former colonial areas of [the region] maintaining their role as neo-colonial providers of raw commodities and cheap labour, supplemented by new infusions of industrial capital; [and] the socialist countries of east Asia . . . . being invited or cajoled to join the system. (Catley and McFarlane, 1979:10).

What is posited here is a changing role for dominion capital – one which is premised upon deindustrialisation and the return to a pre-Federation staple-producing economy (with all that means for organised labour). The problem, however, is that in the face of overseas levels of agricultural protection and subsidisation, Australian agriculture has diminished ability to compete internationally. Consequently, the barriers set up to protect a growing secondary industry in Australia are now considered to be both economically costly and inappropriate in the competitive world of international trade. Since protectionist barriers in Australia have advantaged domestic manufacturing industry *and* labour, their removal is seen to clear the way for cost savings in the purchase of agricultural inputs and a lowering of the costs of labour (through increased unemployment and a challenge to the bargaining practices of trade unions). With the removal of the structures promoting industrial inefficiency, it is anticipated that Australia will be capable of securing a competitive advantage in international trade. While this is fervent hope of the proponents of free market agriculture, the production of commodities for exchange value in a stagnant world economy will ultimately limit the scope of any 'rural-led' recovery.

Production for exchange value relies upon the operation of a national and international market for agricultural goods. Farmers produce food and fibre not for farm consumption but for sale for money in the marketplace. While the prices of some farm goods sold on the domestic market can be manipulated in favour of the farmers by quasi-governmental instrumentalities (such as statutory marketing boards which have monopoly powers) the condition of the home market – where most people are already well fed – is of steady, rather than of accelerated, demand (Campbell, 1980). Any extra expenditure by consumers tends to go not on more food, but on the substitution of more expensive foods for the cheaper items. This results in an increased proportion of the consumer's dollar going to food processors and food preparers (restaurateurs) rather than into the farmer's pocket (Campbell, 1980).

While domestic sales are virtually static, home prices can be manipulated to some extent through government intervention. In contrast, prices on the international market are much less able to be controlled. Australian farmers supply a high proportion of their output to an international market which is vulnerable to violent price movements, which is regularly flooded with dumped goods from foreign competitors, and which is typified by falling (or at best slowly rising) prices (Harris, 1982). As is so regularly stressed by agricultural commentators, farmers are price takers, not price makers. The booms and busts of international trade prove to be economically damaging to agricultural producers hoping rationally to plan production. Unpredictable returns will negate attempts to offset the increasingly high costs of inputs. Indeed, Australian farmers, responding to price uncertainties, have tended to produce a *greater* volume for sale on the market with aggregate farm output having increased at a rate of about 3 per cent each year over the past 30 years (Vincent, *et al.*, 1982). Ironically, Australian farmers have actively contributed to conditions of over-supply on the world market thereby jeopardising their own futures in agriculture.

While in past decades farmers have lobbied for price support, the bipartisan approach to agriculture by the two competing political groupings has required farmers to respond to market forces. Agricultural producers are being exposed to the very conditions which have led to the development of monopoly capitalism in the wider economy. The problem for the farmers is that the market forces to which they are being forced to react are fuelled by (and are the products of) the actions of national and transnational agribusiness. Those farmers able to succeed in this economic environment are required to operate according to the dictates of agribusiness. Those utilising the latest inputs, or producing for the corporations, may have an edge on their rivals forcing them out of business and taking a greater portion of the available market. This 'cannibalism' as it has been called (Cochrane, 1979; Buttel, 1981b) is an outcome of economic competition, another significant feature of Australian farming.

Unlike monopoly capitalists who have high levels of market control and can set prices through manipulative (although often improper and illegal) means, farmers remain within the framework of competitive capitalism. Those who innovate and can lower the costs of production will be more able than non-innovators to survive any downturns in product prices or capture gains from price improvements. Utilising new innovations is a rational step for all farmers so long as sales from increased output from the use of new technology offset the costs of that technology. A difficulty for most farmers, however, is that the new technology is costly. The only way the farmer will be able to repay loans for new techology is to specialise and to extend production – which often means using the new technology over a greater area (or for a longer period). Where land on the farm is already used to full capacity the farmer must look to purchase adjacent lands if the new technology is to be most efficiently utilised. In this way the larger, more credit-worthy, farmers are able to improve their economic position by borrowing money for new innovations and by purchasing the land of their less viable neighbours.

The trend is towards bigger farms. The median size of Australian farms, which grew by about 20 per cent in the 30 years to 1971, continues to grow (BAE, 1983). This process of farm amalgamation is actively supported by State and federal governments through the Rural Adjustment Scheme. Given the existing conditions of economic competition within agriculture, the only way some can survive is through continual acquisition of the land of others – something which orthodox economists consider desirable and necessary, but which, as Marx recognised in the 1860s, was a manifestation of the concentration and centralisation of capital under conditions of cutthroat competition (see Dowd, 1977).

The conditions which allow some producers to become bigger and others, in relative terms, to become smaller, help to transform agriculture from an industry dominated by family farms to one dominated by what has been called 'larger-than-family-farms' (Buttel, 1981b). These farms may continue to be family-based (the agribusiness corporations have little reason to purchase farmlands so long as they can extract surplus from farmers through conventional mechanisms; Davis, 1980) but will begin to take a greater proportion of returns to agriculture. As the BAE has acknowledged:

Productive resources are allocated such that . . . some 70 percent of a particular product is produced by less than 35 percent of producers. This is evident in the income distribution pattern where well over half the producers earn net incomes below the average value. (BAE, 1983:46)

Calculations from Australian Bureau of Statistics data show that the polarisation in farming is greater than the BAE suggests. For most commodities produced in Australia the top 10 per cent of producers receive well over 30 per cent (often close to 40 per cent) of the entire income received by the industry, while the bottom 10 per cent usually receive less than 1 per cent (Lawrence, 1984). The polarisation of Australian agriculture is a direct result of the processes of capital accumulation under conditions of unknown market prices and intense competition. It is likely to increase with any moves towards the deregulation of Australian agriculture.

Household Production in an Era of Monopoly Capital

While it is necessary to consider features of the macroeconomy it is also important to recognise that family farming, as a sector of competitive capitalism, has direct links with urban industry (Goodman and Redclift, 1985; Whatmore, *et al.*, 1986; Whatmore, *et al.*, 1987). The outcome of the articulation of these two sectors provides yet another reason to doubt the efficacy of free market agriculture in curing the ills of Australian capitalism.

Farmers, as independent commodity producers operating within the sector of competitive capitalism, are structurally unlike most of the firms upon which they are dependent. First, they do not have vast economic resources at their disposal and find it difficult to integrate horizontally (and especially vertically) their activities (Barkley, 1976). Second, farmers as individual producers have very little market power, something which places them in a position of comparative disadvantage in relation to firms in the monopoly capital sector (Martinson and Campbell, 1980). Third, while farmers in the past have traditionally owned and controlled the means of production, they have not employed vast amounts of non-family labour. Farming tends to be family based – much more on the scale of a cottage industry rather than of a large industrial factory (Barkley, 1976; Goss, *et al.*, 1980). Harriet Friedmann has made a useful distinction between a household *form* of production in modern agriculture, and the capitalist *mode* into which it is embedded (Friedmann, 1980; Green and Fairweather, 1984, but see for discussion of difficulties in employing the concept Goodman and Redclift, 1985 and Whatmore *et al.*, 1986). Household production is based upon the family (and kinship networks) as the basic labour unit, while capitalist production (including large corporate farming) is based upon an owner/employee structure (Friedmann, 1980). Both types have in common a dependency upon commodity exchange and the mobility of factors of production.

Friedmann argues that in the white settler colonies where factors of production have been relatively mobile, household production has been able to coexist with capitalism. Time delays in the production process in farming, the requirement that machinery be moved to materials (rather than vice versa), and the capacity of the family labour unit to harness economies of new technologies has militated against the transformation of household production into capitalist production. This is not to say, however, that household production can function independently: household production remains both subservient to, and dependent upon, the wider economic structure of capitalism (Friedmann, 1981:8). Competition between firms in the agricultural sector will lead to the eventual disappearance of some farms and to a growth in the size and output of those remaining. But the reproduction of the household form within capitalism allows for foodstuffs to be produced (relatively) cheaply and in a stable manner (Barkley, 1976) and for surplus to be extracted from the rural sector (Goss, *et al.*, 1980; Lianos and Paris, 1972).

The relationship between household production and monopoly capitalism in agriculture is one providing the basis for unequal exchange and for exploitation (see Denis, 1982; Davis, 1980). Farmers produce foodstuffs and other perishable products which must be sold quickly if quality (and hence price) is not to deteriorate. Farmers are thereby in a weak bargaining position. This problem remains whether or not the state intervenes (via statutory marketing boards and in other ways) to control sales. Where, because of rationalisations, few firms remain in an industry, the farmer has little choice to whom to sell produce. To the extent that few firms comprise the processing and other downstream industries, bidding for farm produce might not be expected to reach the level which might occur in a more competitive market (Martinson and Campbell, 1980). In other cases the farmer may have a limited choice of agents from whom to purchase inputs. Research in the US has confirmed that economic concentration in the farm machinery industry has allowed manufacturers to overcharge farmers and has led to practices, amongst franchised farm implement dealers, such as 'kickbacks' and overbilling for repairs (Martinson and Campbell, 1980, p. 230). In Australia during the late 1970s, for example, a number of transnational firms sought to expand their share of the 'new machinery' market by understocking and overpricing component parts for older vehicles (Lawrence, 1985a). With markets for both farm inputs and food products having remained somewhat static over the past years of rural decline, new product *brands* have proliferated as agribusiness firms have sought to expand sales. New products contribute to the overall price increases in farming with product differentiation and advertising allowing for a movement away from competition and towards the manipulation of price levels. Australian farmers, like their counterparts abroad, have carried the economic burden of unnecessary product proliferation (Sargent, 1986:24).

As Martinson and Campbell (1980) have argued, the relationship between the farmer and the industrial economy has become one of asymmetric interdependency:

> To the extent the [farmers are] subordinate to the institutions and actions in the marketplace, [they are] open to exploitation. And to the extent that farmers are exploited, the rural economy based on a healthy farm sector suffers as well. (1980:234)

The operations of agribusiness are based upon maximum extraction of surplus from agriculture and maximum returns to corporate shareholders. Since agribusiness is guilty of, among other things, 'administered' rather than competitive pricing it is thereby adding considerably to the costs of agricultural production and to the erosion of returns to producers. Realistically, however, it is highly unlikely that Australian farmers could compete on international markets without employing the products and services of agribusiness. Farmers are trapped by the structural relations of a declining competitive capitalist sector embedded within the wider world of corporate capitalism.

One important effect of the necessity for Australian farmers to utilise new technology and of the particular conditions of the markets which those farmers supply is the intensification of what has become known as the cost/price squeeze (Wessel, 1983). In simple terms, the prices received by farmers from the sale of their products are growing at a slower rate than are the prices paid by farmers for the inputs to agriculture. In Australia in the last 20 years the index of prices received for farm products has declined by some 40 per cent relative to the index of prices paid for farm inputs and the situation has deteriorated in recent years (BAE, 1983; BAE, 1987a). Government statistics indicate that the cost of farm inputs is currently rising at four times the rate of farm returns. Since 1980 the cost of inputs has increased 55 per cent while the price of farm commodities has risen by 14 per cent (*National Farmer*, 23 January 1986:16). The farmer has little choice but to adopt the more productive technology. This *technological imperative* (Wessel, 1983; Whatmore, *et al.*, 1987) means that it becomes mandatory for farmers to adopt more productive technology if they are to remain in business. Yet in increasing their reliance upon new technology, farmers are pushed further into dependent relations with agribusiness – relations which require use by farmers of larger and more expensive machinery and equipment,

chemical fertilisation and pest control, and the introduction of mono-
cultural practices and other techniques which threaten the environment (Merrill, 1976; Humphrey and Buttel, 1982).

The cost/price squeeze appears unable to be solved within the
existing system of capitalist agriculture and corporate agribusiness. It
can be ameliorated through government actions to prop up family
farming but this requires increasing levels of regulation, price support
and market controls – which are anathema to large property owners
(particularly the graziers), to agribusiness and to the leadership of the
NFF. The present leader of the NFF believes that government
intervention has 'retarded adjustment' preventing farmers from
being exposed to the 'efficiencies of the market' (McLachlan, 1985).
As if to push the cause of agribusiness, the NFF has called for
increasing government deregulation of the financial sector, of the
labour market, and of the wider state regulatory apparatus (*National
Farmer*, 30 October 1985 and 8 April 1985; McLachlan, 1986).

RESPONSES TO THE CRISIS

On-Farm Responses

Farmers have attempted to cope with the present rural crisis through
a combination of altering their production mix, borrowing money for
the acquisition of new land and equipment, displacing hired labour,
reducing farm household expenditure, engaging in off-farm work, or,
where circumstances permit, becoming pluriactive. Where some or
all of these measures fail to alleviate the problem one final step is to
engage in social protest. These responses will be described briefly
below.

Alteration of the existing production mix is a rational response to
falling prices of farm commodities. Such on-farm adjustment – the
altered combination of particular commodities – has always been a
feature of Australian agriculture (Davidson, 1982). When wool
prices have fallen, extra wheat or other grain crops have been
produced; when wheat prices have been low, cropping land has been
turned to pasture and sheep or cattle number increased. While such
decisions have been a requirement of commercial family-farm production, the degree to which this option remains possible in today's
crisis must be questioned. When the prices of nearly all suitable
substitutes are depressed there is little advantage in moving away

from existing production. Even where an alternative commodity might be bringing higher prices it may not prove economically sensible to begin producing it. Should all producers read the same price signal, over-production may follow (Mauldon and Schappper, 1974), a symptom of the 'anarchy' of commodity production under capitalism.

At present, for example, Australian producers have been looking for alternatives to wheat. The area sown is projected to fall as world stocks remain high (BAE 1987a:41). As a consequence sheep and cattle numbers have been growing, with farmers hoping to take advantage of the strengthening market. However, by the time the wool is baled and the cattle turned off:

> there is a strong possibility of deteriorating market prospects for beef as a result of a triggering of the US beef import quotas . . . the medium term consequence of the increase in wool production is downward pressure on wool prices. This effect will be greatest . . . when production increases are most significant. (BAE 1987a:21)

There appears little scope for producers in the wheat-sheep-beef farming sector to escape from the cycle of commodity overproduction and price decline. In fact for some farmers – such as those producing grain crops in established dryland areas – crop production is now a highly specialised operation. The costs of turning to other forms of production – even if climate and soil types were suitable – are prohibitive. For all producers with large specialised operations (including those in dairying, rice, sugar and poultry production) it is simply not feasible to abandon existing production, to write off existing machinery, and to start again. Apart from the obvious financial limitations, nearly all specialist farming operations require specialist skills. Australian farmers may not have the training, nor wish to be trained, for the production of alternative commodities. While the market signals may clearly show that it is better to produce angora goats or pecan nuts than sheep or wheat the opportunities for major product change are, in reality, very limited. The average age of the Australian (male) farmer currently stands at 57 years (Campbell, 1980). It is unrealistic to expect that people in this category would have the money, the motivation or energy to embark willingly upon major structural change.

It is structural change, however, which is being *forced* upon agriculture. For those who recognise that continuation in agriculture will only come through increased productivity and/or new products, financial borrowing becomes a major consideration. While farmers who borrow expect to repay their loans through the sale of new high-priced products or through the sale of a greater volume of traditional products, conditions in the marketplace tend to militate against this (Wessel, 1983). Nevertheless, the level of borrowing has increased greatly in the recent period of crisis especially for the financing of production expansion (Curran, *et al.*, 1987:95).

The level of farm debt has been rising at about 11 per cent per year since the mid-1980s (Shearer, 1985:20; BAE, 1987a) with interest repayments constituting about 12 per cent of total farm costs (BAE, 1987a:88). Some farmers, especially wheat producers, have found their debt levels increasing because of the problem of low returns in an economy experiencing high interest rates. With some 15 per cent of wheat producers close to bankruptcy the financial institutions have been rescheduling debts rather than foreclosing. There is virtuallly no demand at present for second-hand machinery (*Sydney Morning Herald*, 29 September 1986:31) and an unacceptably low demand for real estate (*Australian*, 14–15 February 1987:4). It is anticipated that about 9000 farmers will eventually be forced from farming because of their inability to repay loans (*National Farmer*, 14 November 1985:29). Most of these will be otherwise efficient family farmers who borrowed heavily in an attempt to expand production (Curran, *et al*, 1987:96).

Another course for the increasingly marginalised farmer is to dispense with existing hired labour. The purchase of new machinery facilitates this. However, where labour is shed in an effort to save on input costs and where new machinery is foregone, farmers and their families will be required to work harder to maintian farm viability. With men and women working harder on Australian farms, limits are placed on social interaction, altering the basis of rural community involvement and curtailing civic obligation. Children's education is also known to suffer as their labour becomes increasingly important in the reproduction of the farm. Increased on-farm work duties may reduce involvement in, and commitment to, education thereby producing lower educational standards in future generations of farmers (Bell and Nalson, 1974; Schapper, 1982).

While the phenomenon of 'belt tightening' (reducing farm and household expenditure) is another option for farmers in their attempts to remain competitive, it is a short-term measure at best. Farmers may reduce their fuel purchases, utilise fewer chemical inputs, delay applications of fertilisers or begin to consume more of the produce of the farm rather than purchasing off-farm food items. This 'peasant response' as it has been termed (Campbell, 1980) may assist in cost reductions but it may also act to marginalise the farmer further. Reductions in inputs to farming will often result in lower yields, declining productivity and reduced earnings. For some farmers it will herald the economic decline from periodic to long term poverty (University of New England, 1974). 'Belt tightening' will also restrict opportunities for recreational and social activities, further eroding the structural basis of rural communities (Kingma, 1985).

Off-farm work – another option – is regularly undertaken by between 20 and 30 per cent of Australian farm-family members (BAE, 1983). In cases where labour is underemployed on the farm it may be beneficial to the individual and to the farm unit to supplement farm income with that obtained from work undertaken on neighbouring farms or in the non-agricultural sector. Off-farm work is desirable so long as the farm is not run down through neglect and so long as family members do not overburden themselves with excessive workloads. The problem for many would-be off-farm workers is the spatial isolation of many farms. Large population centres do not exist in close proximity to many of the regions where farmers are in crisis. In cases where farmers do decide to travel the long distances the farm may become something of a halfway house, placing an extra burden on remaining family-farm adults to work the property (Jensen, 1977).

While seriously limiting opportunities for a diverse range of off-farm employment, the great distance of farming regions from large urban centres has another consequence: it greatly limits opportunities for pluriactivity. Many European farmers have found it possible to avoid some of the vagaries of markets and prices by adopting a more-or-less permanent combination of agricultural and non-agricultural activities as a survival strategy (Newby, 1986). Agricultural work is supplemented by part-time work in the manufacturing and/or the growing service sectors. In some regions, farmers open their doors to weekend visitors anxious to purchase regional agricultural produce. While value-added activities and the direct sale of agricultural products to the public may provide a ready source of available cash for farmers in Europe, it is not an option for those in Australia who produce specialised bulk products for the export market. Pluriactivity may be an important option for small-scale hobby farmers but it is not an option for commercial farmers – those requiring assistance in the present crisis.

Farmer protest has been a final response to the declining fortunes of Australian agriculture over the last few years. Some 10 000 farmers joined in protest marches through the streets of the state capitals during 1984. The major concerns of farmers were steeply rising input prices, increased government charges, new taxes and the threatened introduction of a capital gains tax (*National Farmer*, 1 November 1984). In 1985, as farm fortunes declined, the level of protest increased. An estimated 110 000 farmers and their supporters marched on state and federal parliaments demanding action on farm costs (*National Farmer*, 2 January 1986:12). A primary focus was the economic policies of the federal Labor Government, but farm costs and stagnant world prices were also highlighted. Farmers sought a change in government policy in relation to agriculture. During 1986 the demonstrations continued. Wheat and manure was dumped on city streets, farmers raised money for a fighting fund to challenge the Labor Government at future elections,and threats were made by the NFF to implement measures aimed at destabilising the Australian dollar (*Sydney Morning Herald*, 17 January 1986:3; *Australian*, 23 January 1986:3; *National Farmer*, 2 January). The aim of the latter was to drive the dollar down to a level at which Australian export prospects would improve.

Today, while some farmers remain uncertain about the causes of their problems, farm leaders have identified the Labor Government's tariff policy and the wage awards granted to the unions through arbitration (the wage Accord) as two of the main factors. The NFF has vowed to challenge the unions over industrial matters in agriculture (*National Farmer*, 25 July 1985, and 2 January 1986). Unfortunately for the farmers, it has been shown that input prices will continue to rise despite any wage agreements, tariff reductions or fuel rebates (*Financial Review*,) 8 November 1985:14). It has also been shown that the wage Accord has kept increases in farm labour costs below the levels of increase of other inputs to agriculture and, significantly, below the prevailing rate of inflation (BAE, 1987a:83; *Financial Review*, 16 January 1986:2). The general cost of labour in Australia is at its lowest level in a quarter of a century (Stilwell, 1986a:53). Despite this some farmers have spoken of the prospect of bloodshed in the streets (*National Farmer*, 3 October 1985:11) and of the guerilla tactics which might be employed should the crisis worsen:

The farmers could probably muster 120 000 armed combatants counting women and teenagers, 40 000 all-terrain vehicles, 60 to 100 spotting planes, unlimited heavy equipment for blocking or destroying roads and unlimited bagged nitrogen for the production of explosives. (*Sydney Morning Herald*, 22 January 1986:2)

Whether or not it would be the union leaders and the working class who would constitute the enemy in such a battle was not disclosed. What *is* revealed is the extent of farmer anger during the period of crisis and the degree of farmer frustration with existing state policies.

Political Responses

The so-called economic rationalists within the present Labor Government (who, unlike the pro-interventionist Left, hold the reigns of power) have tried to ensure that Australia's economy conforms to its 'client' status in a changing world order (Crough and Wheelwright, 1982). The easing of restrictions on foreign ownership of Australian resources, the floating exchange rate policy, financial deregulation, tighter fiscal measures, and containment of wages under the Accord were moves designed to stimulate economic growth by providing local and overseas capital with increased profits and hence an incentive to reinvest (Stilwell, 1986a). In reality, the very conditions which the free-market proponents considered would pave the way for enhanced capital accumulation, have contributed, instead, to a deepening crisis. Deregulation did not stimulate competition between lending institutions and so lead to a reduction in interest rates; the currency float did nothing to stem the balance of payments problems; the greater returns to capital did not materialise in the form of new factories but were used in speculative manoeuvres on the stock exchange; and the wages Accord was rejected by many groups such as small business and farmers who claimed they did not have the capacity to pay workers cost-of-living increases (Stilwell, 1986a; Stilwell, 1986b; *Australian*, 26 November 1986:3).

The main response to the failure of Labor's moves has not been a re-evaluation of the policies and assumptions of the economic rationalists. Rather, it has taken the form of a hardening of the commitment to deregulation and to attacks on the living standards of wage workers. The emerging political discourse – that of the anti-labour forces – has come to prominence with the strengthening of the New Right in Australian politics.

As a loose affiliation of the representatives of foreign and local big business, the 'moral right' (opposing feminism, abortion, homosexuality and state support for the unemployed and socially disadvantaged), and the farming fraternity, this group has successfully moved the political debate from one of the need for job creation and state protection of a diversified industrial sector to a questioning of the supposed excesses of government expenditure, the distorting effects of current wage policies and social security measures, and the need to free the economy from the shackles of government regulation (*Bulletin*, 23 December 1986; Coleman, 1986; Stilwell, 1986a).

The leader of the NFF, a millionaire grazier who sits on the board of Australia's largest agribusiness, is considered to be the spearhead of the New Right (*Bulletin*, 23 December 1986:28). He has been instrumental in orchestrating several successful measures against organised labour (including taking the NFF out of the federal arbitration system) and has been the main force behind the 'fighting' fund to be used in anti-labour campaigns. He opposes subsidisation of agriculture, putting forward instead plans for cuts in government expenditure, a 12-(preferable 24) month wage freeze for workers, the scrapping of new taxes introduced by Labor, and an end to the Reserve Bank's support of the Australian dollar in international trading (*Australian*, 26 November, 1986:3).

The family-farm sector – once unswervingly behind the National Party and its pro-interventionist stance for agriculture – has followed the NFF leadership to the Right. The farmers have had, to some extent, little choice. The National Party has been out of office for five years and its leadership has been derided as complacent and ineffectual (*Australian*, 8 October 1986:3; *National Farmer*, 13 November 1986:33). Moreover, it was clear to the farmers as early as the mid-1970s that continued state support for agriculture could not be justified on economic grounds. After years of constant dialogue and disputation with the Industries Assistance Commission regarding the levels and forms of state support, farmer representatives finally recognised that their arguments were being ignored by Treasury. So although the political excesses of previous National Party governments (which provided farmers with precisely the sorts of subsidization and price support currently afforded US and EEC farmers) acted to protect and enhance family farming throughout the 'Long Boom', it is no longer considered to be appropriate as a form of assistance during recession. Subsidisation is viewed as impeding 'adjustment' to market forces. This argument has been developed and refined by the NFF which, as a logical extension of its free market philosophy, insists that since Australian farmers are no longer heavily protected – the average effective rate of assistance to agriculture dropped from 28 per cent in the early 1970s to less than 8 per cent in the early 1980s

(*Land*, 5 May 1982:5) – it is the distorting effects of *overseas* protectionism that is to blame for the demise of Australian farming. In
accepting this analysis farmers have become victims of their own free
enterprise rhetoric unable, on the one hand, to achieve price support
at home and incapable, on the other, of bringing about changes to the
levels of protection and price support for farming in competing
nations (Lawrence, 1985b).

As in the past, the National Party might have been expected to be a
vocal proponent of moves to compensate Australian producers for
the economic effects of such distortions. Today, in the presence of a
coalition partner and an NFF endorsing fiscal austerity, it has
adopted the stance of the economic rationalists in decrying international protectionism and demanding that GATT move to dismantle
trade barriers.

Several neo-populist figures have emerged in the vanguard of the
New Right. One, the Queensland Premier, is a champion of small
government. He wishes, as well, to contain unionism and to impose a
flat rate tax. Another spokesperson is demanding a better deal for the
small business sector and has called for the formation of an Enterprise Party. She has had her policies cryptically described as 'abolish
the dole, stomp the [union] militants, kill the compromisers, save the
family' (*Rydges*, September 1985). This peculiar modern-day variant
of populism is significantly different from that which arose in the late
1800s in the Canadian and the US wheat belt. There the populists
were concerned with the exploitative practices of the railroads,
banks, grain elevators and other private monopolies (Lipset, 1968;
Graham, 1966). A solution was sought through governmental intervention to reduce excessive private profit and to improve the
bargaining position of rural producers in a free enterprise economy
(Graham, 1966). In Australia most of those supporting the New
Right are opposed to any form of 'agrarian socialism'. The movement
is pro-big business and is anti-interventionist. With its calls for the
dismantling of bureaucracy, reduced taxation, a return to the virtues
of hard work and independence and small government, the movement has to date successfully diverted attention from the activities of
the mining companies, the foreign banks and the agribusiness corporations.

It is therefore inaccurate to consider that the groundswell of
support is part of a general populist sentiment emerging in a time of
economic uncertainty. The ideology of the New Right, while *popular*
in some sections of the community, is not *populist*. To consider it as

such is to disguise one crucial fact – what is being promoted are the conditions necessary for the further penetration of the Australian economy by big business.

Despite attempts by the Australian press to give the new ideology legitimacy by identifying it as the voice of the people, the narrow sectional interests being pursued by the New Right require its ideology to be more accurately labelled radical conservatism (Lawrence, 1987). Yet, the free market stance of Australia's farm leaders and the representatives of corporate capital is crucial to the realignment of the Australian economy from its older dominion capitalist role to its new position in the Pacific Rim strategy. As Greg Crough and Ted Wheelwright (1982:86) have convincingly argued:

> With the increasing transnationalisation of production, distribution, and finance it was to be expected that a new ideology would be created to justify the export-oriented, world market strategies. Increasingly the import-substitution policies followed by many countries in the post-war period [have run] counter to interests of the transnationals. Trade barriers and the restrictions on the movements of capital obviously interfere with global integration of the transnationals' operations, and must be dismantled if their interests are to be served. . . . it is now strongly argued that Australia should adjust its economic structure to the world economy [and] that efficiency and international competitiveness should [replace protectionism as an industrial strategy].

The policy stance advocated by the BAE and followed by the Government is to allow the farm sector to adjust to the realities of international markets and to argue at GATT meetings for reform of farm programmes in competing nations (Stoeckel, 1986; Miller, 1987; Curran et al., 1987:97). The first 'solution' will result in the inevitable decline in the number of farm families (with a consequent contraction and/or economic marginalisation of the non-farm rural population). The second provides the opportunity for the Government to grandstand on the protection issue and to argue the virtues of free trade to an international audience which finds it politically uncomfortable to heed the advice. For example, while the OECD in its Venice Economic Summit of June 1987 endorsed the reform proposals agreed to at an earlier meeting in Paris, most experts readily acknowledge that agricultural policy reform is restricted by other considerations in surplus-producing countries (BAE, 1987b). Negotiations have been, and are likely to continue to be, protracted and difficult.

Despite President Reagan's stated intention of phasing out subsidies and removing import barriers to agricultural products over the next ten years, such action would not be taken unilaterally. Yet for the EEC, which is being blamed for encroaching on US markets, expenditure on agricultural support has been running at a level of almost four times the rate of increase in agricultural output (BAE 1987b:266) reflecting the intransigence of member nations of the EEC. In 1987–88 CAP support prices remained at levels well above prevailing world prices and were responsible for the creation of further surplus production. In fact, since the benefits of continued protectionism have been capitalised into land values in competing countries, any withdrawal of concessions will lead to substantial welfare problems and political protest abroad. As President Reagan revealed in his endorsement of the 1985 Farm Bill, economic considerations are conveniently overlooked when the wrath of farmers threatens the withdrawal of their political support. Despite the verbal commitments at Punta del Este to the reversal of protectionism and removal of distortions in agricultural trade, there will continue to be the political problems of putting such sentiments into practice. Importantly, Department of Agriculture economists have begun to warn that with new technologies being adopted in competing nations, the removal of subsidies abroad may not provide any dramatic improvement in the position of Australian farmers (*Daily Advertiser*, 14 February 1987:15). GATT would not seem to be the key to any short-term success for Australian agriculture.

THE FUTURE

Continuation of existing policies will result in Australia's incorporation in the New World Economic Order, an economic and political structure characterised by the centralisation of production, marketing, technology and finance in key areas of the economy. The growth of corporate agribusiness will be one outcome of the adoption of *laissez-faire* policies for agriculture. The increasing vulnerability of the economy to international price movements and the possibility of Australia's deterioration to Third World status in the event of worsening terms of trade are other possible outcomes. To summarise the argument, because Australian producers grow food for an unplanned volatile international market there is no guarantee that what is produced will be sold, or that if it is sold it will return a price sufficient to cover costs of production. As trading patterns remain distorted and as stockpiled commodities are dumped on international markets, Australian farmers face bankruptcy, rural service centres contract and social welfare problems increase.

Yet economic competition, a major feature of household production within advanced agriculture, tends to impose upon farmers a technological imperative: purchase the modern, more productive, innovations or lose ground in the race for profits. While in the present crisis a number of more ambitious family farmers have been disadvantaged by having had the misfortune of expanding in times of recession, it nevertheless holds that those who can increase farm size and take advantage of new technology will achieve considerable benefit from the application of new techniques and production methods. In very general terms, the larger, more innovative farmers increase the scale of their activities becoming in the process 'larger-than-family farm' operations defined by employer/employee relations. The era of corporate franchise farming will complement such developments (Summons, 1984). It is expected, in line with the American example, that large food corporations will enter medium-term (perhaps ten-year) contracts with farmers who agree to supply particular products at given times for negotiated prices. The model of the poultry industry, where Australian growers operate under the control of two large agribusiness corporations, is the model considered most likely to evolve. It is predicted that as a result of the reorganisation of agriculture the number of commercially viable farms will decrease from the present level of 174 000 to about 70 000 within the next 25 years (Summons, 1984). These farms, more capital-intensive, demanding the skills of specialised operators and utilising the latest technologies, such as genetic engineering, will be those supplying the Pacific Basin with its agricultural products. This transformation will be one premised upon agricultural polarisation. The bigger farmers will prosper while the smaller family-farm operators try various means of remaining in agriculture. Some will alter production levels and types, or borrow money to improve productivity levels. Others may work themselves or their families harder or reduce household expenditure so as to maintain investment levels in agriculture. Those closer to large towns may become pluriactive or engage in permanent off-farm work, seeking to gain through wage

–labour more than may be lost through lower labour input and hence decreased production on the farm. If prices continue to trend downward, increased rural militancy is a definite likelihood. Importantly, the more dependent the agricultural economy becomes on free-market forces, the more likely it is that inequities between rural and urban regions will increase.

Although a detailed examination of options is beyond the scope of this chapter, it is worth considering how *increased* state intervention may help to alleviate hardship while allowing for improvement in agricultural efficiency. Rather than providing emergency relief to beleaguered sugar or wheat producers, the state might purchase what is an otherwise embarrassing food surplus for conversion to fuel ethanol. This would lead to reduced dependence upon imported energy. The state might seek to limit agribusiness profiteering by strengthening marketing boards and producer cooperatives. In an effort to address the problem of growing inequities between rural and urban regions the state might embark upon a major programme of decentralization (Lawrence, 1978 and 1987). Should people begin to move back to rural areas to take advantage of cheaper housing and improved living conditions, new service industries would be encouraged to expand. Local markets might become increasingly viable, possibly challenging the reason for agribusiness expansion (the delivery of processed and packaged foods for a growing urban population). Public participation and devolution of power at the regional level might help to resolve issues of conservation, country town development and social welfare problems. This might be facilitated by public planning and co-ordination of rural production, preferably at the regional level (Lawrence 1978; Stilwell, 1986a).

There are a number of other options for the state in its attempts to find alternative solutions to the rural crisis. Farm syndication is perhaps the most obvious. Financial incentives could be provided to those farmers who engage cooperatively in sharing land and equipment. Costs of production might in this way be lowered, borrowings reduced and any concessional state initiatives directed to the new syndicates rather than, as happened in the past, to the larger, more wealthy farmers. The sharing of machinery and the implementation of regional management plans might allow farmers to reduce their reliance upon the products and services of agribusiness. Research in Australia has confirmed that syndication reduces plant capital costs, limits yield fluctuation and reduces work pressure – allowing risks to be shared and more rational on-farm planning to be introduced

(Kennedy, 1977; Bartholomaeus and Hardaker, 1981). State governments might redirect their extension/advisory services to provide special encouragement and assistance for those choosing to join farmer co-operatives. The government may, in this way, support and legitimise what is a potentially more socially beneficial form of family-farm agriculture.

For smaller and/or poorer farmers, especially those too old to embark upon syndication or economically unable to contribute to syndicate viability, the state might offer assistance under a farm pension scheme. This might not only help to relieve rural poverty but become the basis for rational land use planning in agricultural regions. A central funding agency could be created to purchase marginal farms and to pay a pension or annuity to the owners. The farm would remain under full control of the farmers until death, at which time the property would revert to government control.

A land bank is yet another option. When land is held in trust by the state it can be conserved in times of poor prices and released, in times of higher prices, to syndicated farmers. This might stem the trend towards farmers exploiting as much land as possible in the mistaken belief that higher incomes will automatically ensue from the sale of an increased volume. A land bank scheme – perhaps similar to that existing in Canada – might be the only realistic alternative to that of increasing the level of foreign ownership of Australian farmlands.

These suggested interventions may be criticised on the grounds that they would be difficult and costly to implement, would be acting against the existing forces of capital accumulation and that their 'state socialist' character does not sit well with the spirit of free enterprise and individual hard work enshrined in rural fundamentalism. The point, however, is that for those in the family-farm sector who wish to continue farming, there may be little choice but to endorse the evolution of a more interventionist – even state planned – agriculture.

Bibliography

Armstrong, W., 1978, 'New Zealand: Imperialism, Class and Uneven Development', *Australian and New Zealand Journal of Sociology* 14, 3 (Part Two).
Australian: 27 February 1985; 23 January 1986; 8 October 1986; 26 November 1986; 14 February 1987; 4 March 1987.
Australian Business, 5 October 1983.
Australian Government (1986), *Economic and Rural Policy* (Canberra: Australian Government Publishing Service).

Australian Rural Adjustment Unit (1983), *The Current and Prospective Conditions of Rural Industries and Communities* (Armidale: University of New England).

Barkley, P. (1976), 'A Contemporary Political Economy of Family Farming', *American Journal of Agricultural Economics*, 58, 5.

Barr, N., G. Ronan and A. Volum (1979), *Farmers in a Changing Agriculture* (Melbourne: Victorian Department of Agriculture).

Bartholomaeus, M. and J. Hardaker (1981), 'Farm Syndication and Risk Sharing: A Case Study', *Australian Journal of Agricultural Economics*, 25, 3.

Bedgood, D. (1978), 'New Zealand's Semi-Colonial Development: A Marxist View.' *Australian and New Zealand Journal of Sociology*, 14, 3 (Part Two).

Bell, J. and J. Nalson (1974), *Occupational and Residential Mobility of Ex-Dairy Farmers on the North Coast of New South Wales* (Armidale: Department of Sociology, University of New England).

Borell, B., R. Sturgiss and G. Wong (1987), 'Global Effects of the US Sugar Policy', *Quarterly Review of the Rural Economy*, 9, 3.

Bulletin, 23 December 1986.

Bureau of Agricultural Economics (BAE) (1983), *Rural Industry in Australia* (Canberra: Australian Government Publishing Service).

BAE 1986, *Quarterly Review of the Rural Economy*, 8, 1.

BAE 1987a, *Quarterly Review of the Rural Economy*, 9, 1.

BAE 1987b, *Quarterly Review of the Rural Economy*, 9, 3.

Bureau of Industry Economics (1983), *Job Losses in Small Country Towns* (Canberra: Australian Government Publishing Service).

Buttel, F. (1981a), 'Farm Structure and Rural Development', *Cornell Rural Sociology Bulletin Series*, No. 118 (New York: Cornell University).

Buttel, F. (1981b), 'W(h)ither the Family Farm?', *Cornell Journal of Social Relations* (New York: Cornell University).

Campbell, K. (1980), *Australian Agriculture* (Melbourne: Longman Cheshire).

Catley, B. and B. McFarlane (1979), 'An Australian Perspective on the New International Economic Order', *Australian Left Review*, 71.

Catley, B. and B. McFarlane (1981) *Australian Capitalism in Boom and Depression* (Chippendale: Alternative Publishing Cooperative).

Clement, W. (1978), 'Uneven Development: Canada and the World System', *Australian and New Zealand Journal of Sociology*, 14, 3 (Part Two).

Cochrane, W. (1979), *The Development of American Agriculture*. (Minneapolis: University of Minnesota Press).

Coleman, K. (1986), 'The "Moral" Meets the "New": Alliances on the Radical Right', *Australian Left Review*, 98.

Cribb, J. (1985), 'Buying Back the Farm', *Inside Australia*, 1, 3.

Crough, G., T. Wheelwright and T. Wilshire (eds) (1980), *Australia and World Capitalism* (Ringwood: Penguin).

Crough, G. and T. Wheelwright (1982), *Australia: A Client State* (Ringwood: Penguin).

Curran, B., P. Minnis and J. Bakalor (1987), 'Australian Agriculture in the International Community', *Quarterly Review of the Rural Economy*, 9, 1.

Daily Advertiser 7 February 1987; 14 February 1987.

272   *The International Farm Crisis*

Davidson, B. (1982), 'The Economic Structure of Australian Farms', in D. Williams (ed), *Agriculture in the Australian Economy*, 2nd ed. (Sydney: Sydney University Press).

Davis, J. (1980), 'Capitalist Agricultural Development and the Exploitation of the Propertied Labourer' in F. Buttel and H. Newby (eds), *The Rural Sociology of the Advanced Societies* (Montclair: Allanheld).

Denis, W. (1982), 'Capital and Agriculture: A. Review of Marxist Problematics', *Studies in Political Economy*, 7.

Dowd, D. (1977), *The Twisted Dream*, 2nd ed. (Massachusetts: Winthrop).

Ehrensaft, P. and W. Armstrong (1978), 'Dominion Capitalism: A First Statement', *Australian and New Zealand Journal of Sociology*, 14, 3 (Part Two).

Financial Review, 8 November 1985; 16 January 1986.

Friedmann, H. (1980), 'Household Production and the National Economy: Concepts for the Analysis of Agrarian Formations', *Journal of Peasant Studies*, 7. 2.

Friedmann, H. (1981), 'The Family Farm in Advanced Capitalism: Outline of a Theory of Simple Commodity Production in Agriculture', Paper presented to the Thematic Panel 'Rethinking Domestic Agriculture', American Sociological Association. Toronto, August.

Goldschmidt, W. (1978), *As you Sow* (Montclair: Allanheld).

Goodman, D. and M. Redclift (1985), 'Capitalism Petty Commodity Production and the Farm Enterprise', *Sociologia Ruralis*, 25, 3/4.

Goss, K., R. Rodefeld and F. Buttel (1980), 'The Political Economy of Class Structure in US Agriculture: A Theoretical Outline' in F. Buttel and H. Newby (eds), *The Rural Sociology of the Advanced Societies* (Montclair: Allanheld).

Graham, B. (1966), *The Formation of the Australian Country Parties* (Canberra: Australian National University Press).

Green, G. and J. Fairweather (1984), 'Agricultural Production and Capitalism. . . . .' *Sociologia Ruralis*, 24, 2.

Harris, S. (1982), 'Agricultural Trade and Its International Trade Policy Context' in D. Williams (ed.), *Agriculture in the Australian Economy*, 2nd ed. (Sydney: Sydney University Press).

Harris, S., J. Crawford, F. Gruen and H. Honan (1974), *The Principles of Rural Policy in Australia – A Discussion Paper* (Canberra: Australian Government Publishing Service).

Humphrey, C. and F. Buttel (1982), *Environment, Energy and Society* (Belmont: Wadsworth).

Hymer, S. (1982), 'The Multinational Corporation and the Law of Uneven Development' in H. Alavi and T. Shanin (eds), *Introduction to the Sociology of 'Developing Societies'* (London: Macmillan).

Jarrad, J. (1981), 'Success or Failure? A Study of Victorian Decentralisation Policies', *Regional Journal of Social Issues*, 7.

Jensen, R. (1977), 'Small Towns in Rural Areas: Problems and Structural Change', *Kellogg Rural Adjustment Unit Contributed Paper No. 2* (Armidale: University of New England).

Kennedy, G. (1977), 'Some Social and Economic Aspects of Farm Syndication', *Melbourne Notes On Agricultural Extension No. 14* (Victoria: University of Melbourne).

Kingma, O. (1985), 'Agribusiness, Productivity Growth, and Economic Development in Australian Agriculture', Transnational Corporations Research Project. *Research Monograph No. 22* (Sydney: Faculty of Economics, University of Sydney).

Land, 5 May 1983.

Lawrence, G. (1978), 'Regionalism as Internal Imperialism', Unpublished Masters Dissertation, University of Wisconsin-Madison.

Lawrence, G. (1984), 'The "Poor Old Farmer" Revisited' in D. Cottle (ed.), *Capital Essays* (Sydney: University of New South Wales).

Lawrence, G. (1985a), 'Progress and Poverty: The Farmer's Plight', *Arena*, 72.

Lawrence, G. (1985b), 'The Answer Doesn't Lie in the Soil', *Australian Society*, 4, 8.

Lawrence, G. (1987), *Capitalism and the Countryside* (Sydney: Pluto).

Lianos, T. and Q. Paris (1972), 'American Agriculture and the Prophecy of Increasing Misery', *American Journal of Agricultural Economics*, 54.

Lipset, S. (1968), *Agrarian Socialism* (New York: Anchor).

Lonsdale R. (1971), 'Decentralization: The American Experience and its Relevance for Australia', *Australian Journal of Social Issues*, 6, 7.

Martinson, O. and G. Campbell (1980), 'Betwixt and Between: Farmers and the Marketing of Agricultural Inputs and Outputs' in F. Buttel and H. Newby (eds), *The Rural Sociology of the Advanced Societies* (Montclair: Allanheld).

Marx, K. 1967. *Capital*, vol. 3 (New York: International).

Mauldon, R. and H. Schapper (1974), *Australian Farmers Under Stress in Prosperity and Recession* (Nedlands: University of Western Australia Press).

Merrill, R. (1976), *Radical Agriculture* (New York: Harper Colophon).

Miller, G. (1987), *The Political Economy of International Agricultural Policy Reform* (Canberra: Australian Government Publishing Service).

McKenzie, B. (1986), 'Axe Grinding on Rural Poverty', *Inside Australia*, 2, 1.

McLachlan, I. (1985), 'Turning the Tide of Regulation', *Inside Australia*, 1, 2.

McLachlan, I. (1986), '1986 A Challenge for the Farm Sector' in *National Farmer*, 2 January.

Mullins, P. (1977), 'Urban Problems and the Renaissance of Urban Sociology', *Social Alternatives*, Summer.

National Farmer, 8 March 1984; 1 November 1984; 8 April 1985; 25 July 1985; 3 October 1985; 14 November 1985; 2 January 1986; 23 January 1986; 13 November 1986; 4 February 1987.

Newby, H. (1986), 'Survival Strategies in Rural Society — Continuity and Change', Chairman's Address to the 13th European Congress of Rural Sociology, Portugal, April.

O'Connor, K. (1986), 'Why Towns Change', *Inside Australia*, 2, 1.

Powell, R. (1986), 'Forgotten Workers', *Inside Australia*, 2, 1.

Rural Development Centre (1985), 'The New Rush for the Land', *Inside Australia*, 1, 2.

Rural Development Centre 1986 *Inside Australia*, 2, 1.

Rydges, September 1985.

Sargent, S. (1986), 'Living with Agribusiness', *Inside Australia*, 2, 1.

Schapper, H. (1982), 'The Farm Workforce' in D. Williams (ed.), *Agriculture in the Australian Economy*, 2nd ed. (Sydney: Sydney University Press).

Scott, J. (1979), *Corporations, Classes and Capitalism* (London: Hutchinson).

Shearer, C. (1985), 'The Outlook for Rural Credit', *Quarterly Review of the Rural Economy*, 7, 1.

Stilwell, F. (1974), *Australian Urban and Regional Development* (Sydney: ANZ).

Stilwell, F. (1986a), *The Accord . . . And Beyond* (Sydney: Pluto).

Stilwell, F. (1986b), 'After the Accord: Looking for an Alternative Economic Strategy', *Australian Left Review*, 98.

Stoeckel, A. (1986), 'Australian Agriculture: What is the Future?', *Quarterly Review of the Rural Economy*, 8, 2.

Summons, M. (1984), 'The Big Battalions will Dominate' in Rural Review, *Australian*, 6 February.

Sydney Morning Herald, 1 January 1986; 17 January 1986; 22 January 1986; 29 September 1986.

University of New England (1974), *Rural Poverty in Northern New South Wales* (Canberra: Australian Government Publishing Service).

Vincent, D., A. Powell and P. Dixon (1982), 'Changes in the Supply of Agricultural Products', in D. Williams (ed.), *Agriculture in the Australian Economy*, 2nd. ed. (Sydney: Sydney University Press).

Wessel, J. (1983), *Trading the Future* (San Francisco: Institute for Food and Policy Development).

Whatmore, S., R. Munton, J. Little and T. Marsden (1986), 'Internal and External Relations in the Transformation of the Farm Family', *Sociologia Ruralis*, 26, 3/4

Whatmore, S., R. Mutton, J. Little and T. Marsden (1987), 'Towards a Typology of Farm Business in Contemporary British Agriculture', *Sociologia Ruralis*, 27, 1.

Wright, L. (1985), 'The Crisis of Selling Out', *Time*, 4 November.

11 Aims and Constraints of the Brazilian Agro-Industrial Strategy: The Case of Soya

Vincent Leclercq

Until the end of the 1960s, Brazilian agricultural exports were essentially confined to traditional tropical commodities (coffee, sugar, and cocoa). However, major changes occurred from the early 1970s as Brazil rapidly expanded and diversified its exports. Thus it is now among the leading world exporters of soybean oil and soybean meal, chicken, beef, and orange juice. An important supplier to the EEC (mainly soybean meal and coffee), Brazil is today, with the United States, one of the EEC's principal competitors in certain world agricultural markets.

However, this undoubted commercial success should not disguise the crisis which has enveloped this strategy since the late 1970s. In this new period, economic conditions have been far less favourable to the Brazilian agricultural sector. On the one hand, the worsening financial position forced Brazil to resort to the International Monetary Fund (IMF) in November 1982, which led to a marked decline in the level of direct and indirect subsidies to the agricultural sector. On the other, world commodity markets have been less favourable for Brazilian exports in the 1980s due to the weaker growth of demand and falling prices. Here we will focus on the case of soya, the main recipient of state credit for both production and marketing and the flagship of Brazilian agricultural exports (Figure 11.1). A better understanding of the crisis gripping the soybean sector requires an analysis of the historical background to its development in the 1970s.

FIGURE 11.1   *World exports of soybean meal, 1970–85 (million tonnes)*

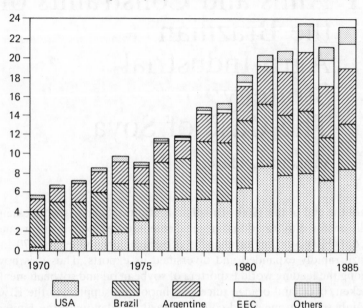

SOURCE   Oil World, ISTA, Hamburg.

A NEW ROLE FOR AGRICULTURE IN THE MODEL OF ACCUMULATION

Between 1929 and the early 1960s, Brazil pursued a protectionist policy of industrial import substitution. Within a framework of economic policy which gave clear priority to industrial development, agriculture was assigned a triple role: to provide a reserve army of labour for industry, supply urban food requirements at stable prices to restrict the rise of urban real wages, and to generate export earnings in order to finance imports of industrial capital goods and raw materials. In this period, it is impossible to speak of an explicit policy of agricultural development. Even though successive governments introduced rural credit schemes and minimum price programmes, the taxation of export commodities continued to be unfavourable. Furthermore, the question of urban food supply did not present major problems in this period, with the output of foodstuffs continuing to grow principally by extending the area under

FIGURE 11.2 *Soybean production of Brazil (million tons)*

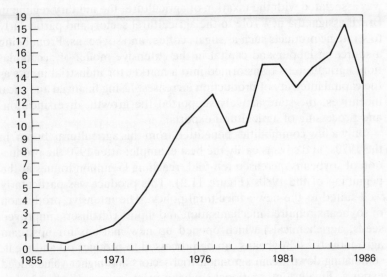

SOURCE IBGE.

cultivation. While the staple food sector successfully executed its role in the process of industrial development, the performance of the export sectors on the other hand was very much more uneven, and was determined largely by the fluctuations of the international coffee market and the overvaluation of the *cruzeiro*.

The military coup of 1964 marks a decisive break in the history of Brazilian agriculture. The so-called 'economic miracle' from 1967 until the first oil shock in 1974 was based on the strong stimulus given to industrial exports and increasing recourse to external financing. Within this framework, the state encouraged the rapid modernisation of selected agricultural sectors via the discriminatory expansion of rural credit at highly subsidised rates of interest. Without raising the issue of land ownership, this modernisation policy stimulated the input industries and processing sectors of the agro-industrial complex and encouraged the diversification of Brazilian agricultural exports. The modernisation strategy which took shape in Brazil in the late 1960s recalls similar processes which occurred in United States' and European agriculture after the Second World War. The model of agricultural growth disseminated by the advanced industrial countries places the agricultural sector at the heart of the accumulation process. Breaking away from the period of import substitution, which was associated with the taxation of agriculture, the military regime in Brazil assigned a new role to the agricultural sector, and particularly to strategic products such as sugar, coffee, and soybeans. From being a source of labour and capital in the extensive model of accumulation, agriculture is transformed into a market for industrial inputs as the capital intensity of production increases. Using financial and fiscal incentives, the state actively supported the growth, diversification, and processing of agricultural exports.

Only a few commodities benefitted from this agricultural 'boom' in the 1970s, and soya is easily the best example: after 1970 the production of soybeans increased ten-fold, reaching l5 million tonnes at the beginning of the 1980s (Figure 11.2). This product was particularly well-suited to the new agricultural policy. The intensive production of soybeans required mechanisation and inputs (fertilisers, improved seeds, agrichemicals) which opened up new markets for upstream agro-industries. Soybeans can be processed to produce oil and meal, stimulating downstream agro-industrial sectors and higher value added exports. Finally, international soybean prices increased sharply following the United States embargo of 1973, which brought to an end the period of relative price stability after the Second World War. Prices fluctuated around US$100 per tonne between 1950 and the early 1970s, before climbing to US$138 in 1972 and US$290 in 1973 (Bertrand *et al*, 1983.)

What are the social and technological foundations of the expansion of soybeans? Geographically, production in the 1970s was concentrated in the southern states of Rio Grande do Sul and Parana, which have favourable climatic conditions. Above all, however, these two states have similar agrarian histories, which have given rise to the juxtaposition of large *latifundio* properties and the small holdings established by European settlers. In the 1960s, both these forms of production were in crisis and seeking alternatives. In Rio Grande do Sul, the large cattle ranches which had partially shifted to mechanised wheat production in the 1950s had encountered serious technical problems. Similarly, the European settlers who practiced extensive cultivation based on the clearance of the forest were now facing the end of the agricultural frontier. Further north, in Parana, coffee production, hitherto the main source of the state's prosperity, was declining as the result of the federal coffee tree eradication programme introduced in the mid-1960s within the framework of the first International Coffee Agreement. In Rio Grande do Sul, the intro-

FIGURE 11.3 *Total rural credit, production credit (custeio) and investment credit in real terms, 1969–85*

(1969 Cruzeiros billions)

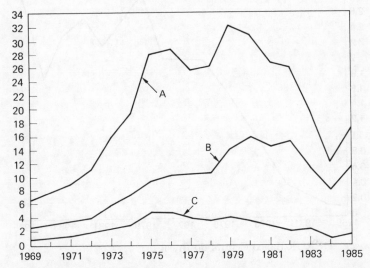

NOTES   A: Total Rural Credit; B: Production Credit; C: Investment Credit.

SOURCE   DERUR/Banco Central do Brasil.

duction of soybeans as a summer crop to follow winter wheat increased the utilisation of machinery and harvesting equipment already acquired for wheat production. In Parana, coffee producers were induced by official financial incentives to make soybeans the central focus of crop diversification. The strategy to overcome the crises in coffee and wheat production involves more than simply exploiting the fertility of the soil: it is based explicitly on achieving higher yields by greater use of modern inputs. The concomitant implementation of fiscal and trade policies to encourage the development of domestic agro-industries ensured that this strategy did not result in the rapid growth of imported inputs. However, the rising international price and the need for crop diversification do not explain the soybean 'boom'. In the late 1960s, the technical backwardness of Brazilian agriculture and the under-capitalisation of small and medium-sized producers were the main obstacles to the

FIGURE 11.4 *Credit for soybean production in real terms, 1969–85*

(1969 Cruzeiros billions)

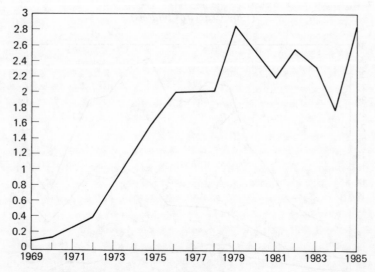

SOURCE DERUR/Banco Central do Brasil.

technological innovation implied by soybean production. In contrast to previous agro-export cycles, the state promoted the capitalisation of farmers and co-operatives by making increasing financial transfers to agriculture through the National System of Rural Credit (SNCR), the key instrument of agricultural policy in the 1970s. As the main vector of technological diffusion in agriculture, resource transfers through the SNCR enjoyed budget priority: the state via the Bank of Brazil accounted for more than two-thirds of rural credit, while the share of private commercial banks declined steadily. The supply of rural credit increased five-fold in real terms in the years 1969–78, and soybeans attracted the lion's share: this sector absorbed 3 per cent of production loans (*custeio*) in 1969, 14 per cent in 1973 and 21 per cent in 1979, displacing coffee from its traditional first place (Figures 11.3 and 11.4). The financial transfers were effected through the interest rate mechanism. This rate remained stable at around 15 per cent per year, whereas inflation, already much higher, continued to rise, increasing from 30 per cent to 77 per cent between 1974 and 1977. Soybean producers were in a position to benefit most from these official programmes, which subsidised agricultural inputs (interest free loans for purchases of seeds, lime, and machinery) and significantly reduced costs of production.

PRIORITY FOR THE SOYBEAN PROCESSING AGRO-INDUSTRY

The soybean crushing industry was the great beneficiary of this period of rapid economic and commercial expansion since it secured both financial transfers and protection. Within the framework of the new economic policy introduced after the first oil shock, the state provided financial and fiscal support to exports of processed, higher value added agricultural products but restricted exports of unprocessed commodities in order to guarantee supplies for national agro-industries and domestic markets. Until the early 1970s, Brazil was a net importer of soybean oil and essentially exported unprocessed soybeans (Bast, 1981). However, with state support for the development of a national crushing industry after 1974–75, exports of unprocessed soybeans reached 2.8 million tonnes in 1976 but fell continuously thereafter. Concomitantly, exports of soybean meal rose from 1.5 to 6.5 million tons between 1973 and 1980 as Brazil became the world's leading exporter. Soybean oil was used to meet domestic needs and won 90 per cent of the market thanks to price controls imposed as part of anti-inflationary policy.

What are the forms of state protection for the national soybean crushing industry? The Brazilian agro-industrial strategy rests on state control of competition in the soybean sector, which was inspired initially by the experience acquired over the years with coffee. The creation of the Brazilian Soybean Institute is especially evocative: it would guarantee a minimum price to producers, stockpile temporary surpluses, and centralise exports. This model can work for coffee, cocoa and sugar, where Brazil has a dominant position in the world market. However, its inadequacy in the case of soybeans was quickly revealed as Brazil does not have the means to influence trends in international prices. Despite several unfortunate experiences, the State has emphasised that a guaranteed supply of soybeans for the national crushing industry remains the first priority of its commercial policy in this sector. Thus the three soybean products cannot be exported freely in Brazil. Exports of unprocessed soybeans (*em grao*) are only authorised after satisfying the needs of the national crushing industry, whose processing capacity increased from 7 to 20 million

FIGURE 11.5   *Monthly soybean prices in Rotterdam and Porto Alegre, January 1973—December 1979*[1]

(Current dollars per tonne[2])

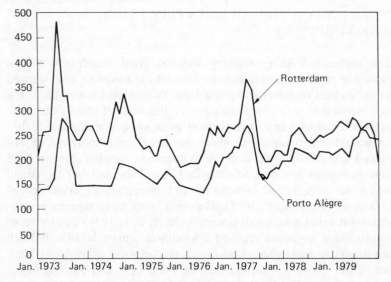

NOTES   (1) The price series for Porto Alegre is incomplete.
        (2) The cruzeiro/dollar exchange rate used is the monthly average.

SOURCE   CFP/Associacao Commercial de Porto Alegre and Oil World/ISTA, Hamburg.

tonnes between 1974 and 1979. Exports of soybean meal are often conditional on agreements by the processing industry to provide the domestic market with a certain volume of supply at controlled prices in order to encourage the development of modern poultry and pig industries. The most sensitive question concerns exports of soybean oil given its decisive weight in Brazilian food consumption. In this case, exports again depend on agreements made by the crushing industry to supply the domestic market at prices fixed by the government. This can provoke domestic shortages if international prices rise above domestic price levels. Without going into further detail (Leclercq, 1987), this interventionist strategy did not always work effectively given changing world market conditions, but the state at that time had sufficient financial capacity to offer compensating fiscal exemptions, export credits or direct subsidies to the different actors in the industry.

The decision to confer a high level of protection on the agro-industrial sector presupposes State financial transfers to soybean producers. Contrary to their American counterparts, the price received by Brazilian soybean producers is well below the international market price due to the high tax burden (the 15 per cent value added tax – *Imposto Sobre a Circulacao de Mercadorias* – does not exist in the US) and the strict controls on exports of unprocessed soybeans (Figure 11.5). Often, the co-operatives have been unable to exploit the competition between European importers and the national crushing industry due to the strict restrictions on soybean exports and have had to be satisfied with a price to the producer which is considerably below the international price. In addition, this selective protection of the processing industry has created a divergence of interest between the state, the co-operatives, and the agro-industrial sector. This has impeded the emergence of a 'soybean complex' along the lines of that in the United States, and means that there is only a conjunctural convergence of interest between the aims of state economic policy and those of the various agents in the soybean system or *filière*. The co-operatives, the great losers in this industrialisation strategy, have seen their access to international markets progressively diminish due to the rapid growth of national crushing capacity.

In more general terms, participation in the growth process in Brazil is much less complete than in the advanced countries. Even though the rapid economic growth in Brazil in the 1970s facilitated the emergence of a middle-class, almost half the population is marginalised, reducing the weight of the internal market. Moreover, the intensification of agricultural production only affected a limited number of crops, regions, and producers. Thus the soybean 'boom' was accompanied after 1977 by the stagnation of staple food production, although population growth continued. While the expansion of soybeans has occurred partially on lands previously used for staples, this stagnation of food production cannot be attributed entirely to this change in land use. Certainly the concentration of rural credit on selected 'industrial' crops, the lack of agricultural research on food crops, and strong state price control have depressed the profitability of staple foodstuffs. But the true underlying problem is the wages policy imposed by the model of economic development. The extremely limited purchasing power of half of the population is undoubtedly the principal barrier to any significant increase in the price of staple foods. This problem arises in similar terms for soybeans, since the indirect domestic consumption of soybeans via meat, milk and eggs is also restricted by low average purchasing power.

QUESTIONING THE FOUNDATIONS OF THE SOYBEAN 'BOOM'

Following the second oil shock in 1979 which brought a sharp decline in Brazil's trade balance, soybean producers began to question the durability of state financial and commercial intervention and of rising world demand for soybeans. While these conditions have ensured the extremely rapid development of production and exports in Brazil, they equally define the limits of this process. Indeed, few developing countries have become successfully integrated into world agricultural trade on the basis of an internalised process of capital accumulation. In the 1980s, the soybean sector finds itself facing financing difficulties due to the debt crisis, and renewed competition in the international market.

The debt crisis forced the state to greatly reduce the level of financial transfers. The analysis of the International Monetary Fund which underlies the structural adjustment policy imposed on Brazil is inspired by an orthodox monetarist vision which focuses on the balance of payments deficit. According to the IMF, this arises from internal excess demand. The economic measures implemented in 1983 thus envisaged a reduction in domestic demand and higher exports in order to re-establish equilibrium and lower inflation (Bacha, 1983). This led to strict controls and limitations on the volume of credit, which were felt immediately by the soybean sector, the principal 'consumer' of subsidised rural credit. In fact, the most controversial aspect of the new economic policy introduced in 1983 concerns rural credit, the cornerstone of modernisation in the 1970s. Successive policy changes after 1980 resulted in a 55 per cent fall in the real value of rural credit between 1979 and 1984. In addition, the real rate of interest paid by the producer rose above the official rate (inflation + 3 per cent) since the state now would finance only part of the costs of production, forcing producers to seek the remaining financing at commercial market rates (inflation + 30–35 per cent). This led to an extremely rapid increase in the share of financial charges in total production costs (Figure 11.6). In Rio Grande do Sul, this share rose from 7 per cent to 47 per cent between 1980 and 1985 (Trevissan, 1985; Leclercq, 1986).

The immediate logical counterpart to the elimination of rural credit subsidies would be an increase in minimum guaranteed prices. This is precisely what the Minister of Agriculture decided to do for the 1984–85 crop year. The Guaranteed Minimum Price Programme was established in 1951 and constitutes *par excellence* a short-term

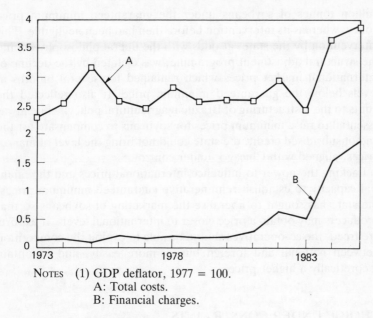

NOTES (1) GDP deflator, 1977 = 100.
A: Total costs.
B: Financial charges.

SOURCE FECOTRIGO

FIGURE 11.6 *Trends in financial costs and total costs of production of soybeans per hectare, 1973–85 (1977 Cruzeiros thousands[1])*

instrument of agricultural policy to effect production adjustments. As regards soybeans, the minimum price had very little impact before 1984 since it was systematically maintained at levels well below the market price set by reference to the Chicago futures market.

Although it may seem paradoxical, the 1984–85 harvest broke all records: soybean output reached 18 million tonnes while the production of traditional staple foodstuffs increased slightly. This agricultural 'boom' at the height of the financial crisis must be qualified by the most favourable weather conditions experienced in Brazil since 1977. This new record level of soybean production certainly did not represent, as in 1974, the response to an increase in international market prices. On the contrary, soybean prices declined from late 1983. It is above all the higher minimum price for soybeans and relative prices *vis-à-vis* staple foodstuffs which explain this performance.[1]

Despite its avowed intention to restrict its credit policy, the state was forced to intervene on a massive scale in stockpiling when the 1984/85 harvest came on to the market. Thus in 1985 it acquired 2.5

million tonnes of soybeans under the guaranteed minimum price policy, whereas its intervention before then had been negligible. This intervention by the state, at odds with the liberal philosophy behind the structural adjustment programme, was dictated by the decline of international market prices which remained for several months at levels below the guaranteed minimum price. It also reflected the limits to the restructuring of Brazilian agricultural policy: while it was essential to raise minimum prices for soybeans to compensate for the end of subsidised credit, the state could not bring the level of market prices, aligned with Chicago, under control.

Lacking the power to influence international prices and the financial capacity to establish remunerative guaranteed minimum prices, the state has sought to liberalise the marketing of soybeans so that producers may obtain a price closer to international levels. If exports are freed, the co-operatives should be able to exploit the competition between national and foreign buyers more easily, and so obtain theoretically a higher price.

CHOICE UNDER CONSTRAINTS

The modernised fraction of the crushing industry favours this liberalisation but on condition that it is no longer subject to the constraint of having to supply the domestic market with soybean oil and meal at prices fixed by the government and often below international prices. This reduction in protection in exchange for the freeing of domestic prices equally reflects growing pressures exerted by the EEC and United States, which are threatening commercial retaliation if Brazil does not reduce the level of protection enjoyed by its agro-industry.

Theoretically, the adjustment of the Brazilian soybean sector to the new financial and commercial conditions therefore is based on less credit for producers and lower protection for its processing branch. But the trend in international prices is the decisive element in this adjustment. An increase in world prices will allow the less productive producers to withstand the rise in financial charges but this will also lead to higher domestic prices of soybean by-products. Lower world prices will facilitate the liberalisation of marketing but tend to marginalise less efficient farmers (Figure 11.7).

The 1980s have turned out to be very much less favourable to Brazilian exporters, notably from the supply side. Although Brazil has successfully won certain traditional American export markets

Figure 11.7 *Soybean meal prices in Dollars and ECUs, January 1980-September 1986*[1]

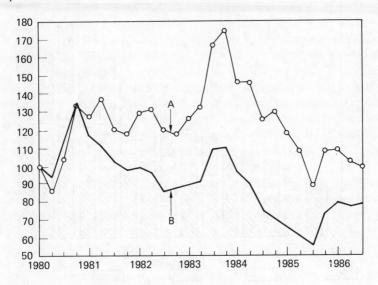

Notes (1) First quarter, 1980 = 100.
A: ECU prices; B: dollar prices.

Source IMF International Financial Yearbook.

thanks to an aggressive trade policy backed financially by the state, today it is suffering from the competition of American export subsidies for soybean oil, and its own export credits are under dual pressure from the financial crisis and the GATT. This situation is aggravated by the growing supply of soybeans from Argentina and Paraguay since the early 1980s, which makes it easier to offset the effects of output fluctuations in Brazil and the United States. At the same time, the irregular but indisputable expansion of palm oil production in Malaysia offers a new alternative to traditional buyers of soybean oil. In the medium term, Asian production of palm oil, less dependent on the animal feed market, is likely to take a growing share of the international market.

On the demand side, the concentration of Brazilian soybean exports on the EEC (65 per cent of its soybean meal exports and 85 per cent of unprocessed soybeans) is arousing protectionist sentiments among European oilseed millers (Figure 11.8). Between 1974 and

FIGURE 11.8   *World imports of soybean meal, 1970–85 (millions of tonnes)*

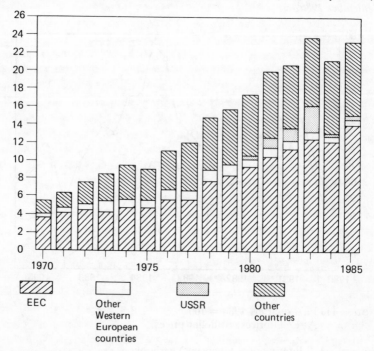

SOURCE   Oil World/ISTA, Hamburg.

1985, Brazilian exports of soybean meal to the EEC rose from 0.6 to 6.5 million tonnes, whereas the production of European crushing mills has stagnated in the last few years. European soybean millers argue that Brazil has succeeded in increasing its share of the EEC market thanks to higher indirect subsidies and price discounts: representations about these practices were made to the EC authorities in Brussels. Although the disputes of 1977 and 1984 were resolved by the Brazilian concessions, these conflicts could quickly re-emerge in the current period of CAP restructuring and the revival of European oilseed crops (Marloie, 1987).

Although during the past 25 years world demand for soybean meal has grown more rapidly than that of soybean oil, this trend may well be reversed in the future (ISTA Mielke, 1983). In relation to its main competitor, the United States, Brazil has two handicaps. First, the concentration of its exports in a restricted number of markets makes it more vulnerable to a revival of competition. Second, the size limitations of its domestic market and the agro-industrial strategy it has chosen to follow oblige Brazil to export two-thirds of its production of soybean meal, whereas the United States possesses a significant internal market and is rather more specialised in exporting unprocessed soybeans.

The financial and commercial elements of the crisis are reinforced by the 'social crisis', which can be defined as the negative social consequences arising from the expansion of soybean production in Brazil. These effects have led to the emergence or strengthening of social movements opposed to the agricultural development model that soybean production implies. The political 'opening' (*abertura*) of the military regime in 1979 reinforced these movements and today, as the re-democratisation of political life continues, they are seeking to influence the reformulation of agricultural policy.

The intensive agricultural development model of soybean production supported by the state accelerated the rural exodus and provoked an increasing concentration of land ownership. In the absence of any social policy to attenuate the effects of modernisation, the exodus of rural population has aggravated urban unemployment and under-employment. Furthermore, even if the different types of producers within the co-operatives had been able to reach a 'social pact' to mitigate the consequences of agricultural modernisation, this pact would have been undermined by the present financial and commercial conditions. The small and medium-size farmers who have failed to achieve high productivity levels will have difficulty in continuing to produce soybeans. Financing costs now represent the principal category in total production costs and high productivity (1900–2000 kgs per hectare) is required to make the crop profitable. This is likely in the long term to provoke a redistribution of soybean production between both producers and regions. Small farmers unable to attain the required productivity levels perhaps will revert to staple food crops, with soybean production becoming increasingly concentrated on the most modernised farms. Concomitantly, production regions where soybean productivity is lower, notably Rio Grande do Sul, will also diversify into staple foodstuffs after having been the original birthplace of soybeans in Brazil. The new financial conditions therefore are likely to accelerate the regional redistribution of soybean production toward the Central-West.

The growth of Brazilian agriculture has been achieved more by extending the area under cultivation than by raising yields. The 1970s were characterised by the substitution of traditional food staples by crops with higher value added potential (soybeans, oranges, sugar-cane for ethanol). Now, with the increasing national deficit in staple foodstuffs, the small and medium-size farmers have thrown their political support behind the diversification of production systems and the revival of food crops at the expense of soybeans. In this period of financial restrictions, will the Sarney government be able, as it claims, to reconcile the revival of staple food production with the maintenance of Brazil's agro-export potential?

If one argues from the Brazilian case, it is clear that the debt crisis has called into question the agro-industrial development strategy based on the growth of the domestic market and the intensification of agricultural production. Effectively, domestic consumption of soy-bean oil is stagnating, and soybean meal is not widely used as animal feed. Since the internal market no longer represents a vector of expansion, one can easily predict the reorientation of the soybean economy toward the world market. This is the strategy preferred by industry as the way out of the crisis. But this step, theoretically seductive, conflicts with the constraints now imposed on the model which had functioned so well in the 1970s. As we have seen, Brazil is not in the classic situation of an agricultural-exporting country, and soybeans via processed by-products have gained a significant part of the domestic market for foodstuffs. As a condition for a greater export effort, and also to compensate for the stagnation of the internal market, the industrial processors are demanding domestic prices equal to those on the international market. This is unaccept-able to consumers, except when world prices are falling, as has been the case since the end of 1984. On the other hand, this demand would mean sacrificing those producers whose productivity is insufficient to absorb the decline in world prices. It is at this level that such an undertaking is unacceptable to the State.

Are we facing simply a crisis of competitiveness which, in the United States as well as Brazil, must lead to an adjustment of agricultural production in accordance with the norms of stronger competition? In our view, the crisis is more widespread. Indeed, the questioning of the role of the state and the level of public expenditure on agriculture is neither specific to the soybean sector nor character-istically Brazilian. This question is presented in similar terms in most of the great agricultural exporting countries of the North. Brazil in fact applied to selected agricultural sectors the same growth model used in the North, at least its central principles: protection and state financial transfers. In this period, American and European producers, strongly supported by the state, constituted an important market for the capital goods industries. Exports, subsidised by various mechanisms, permitted the capitalisation and intensification of agricultural production to continue.

The regulation of the world market is based on this capacity of the advanced countries to finance agricultural sectors with structural surpluses. Yet, this model of production and trade can be established only in a period of strong economic expansion and increasing effective demand for food products. Today, the weak growth of the world economy and the changing orientation of economic policy cast doubt on the appropriateness and the cost of this method of regulating farm incomes and world prices. While one cannot foresee the strategies that will be followed to resolve the crisis in the United States and Europe, one can anticipate that the greater social flexibility and financial adaptability will facilitate a faster adjustment in Brazil than in the United States.

Notes

1. For the 1984–85 crop year, the minimum prices of 19 basic products were increased, but this general policy measure concealed some significant disparities. Thus, the minimum price for soybeans rose by 361 per cent, whereas the average increase for five products directed to the domestic market (rice, black beans, corn, cassava and sorghum) was 248 per cent.

Bibliography

Bacha, E. (1983), 'Prologo para uma terceira carta', Revista de Economia Politica, vol. 3 (4), October-December.
Bast, J. C. (1981), 'Analise retrospectiva da soja no Brasil', in ITAL, A Soja no Brasil (Sao Paulo).
Bertrand, J. P., C. Laurent and V. Leclercq (1983), Le monde du soja (Paris: La Découverte).
ISTA Mielke (1983), The past 25 years and the prospects for the next 25 in the market for oilseeds, oils, fats and meals (Hamburg: ISTA Mielke).
Leclercq, V. (1986), 'Conditions et limites de l'insertion du Brésil dans les échanges mondiaux de soja', Economie Rurale, No. 174, July-August.
Leclercq, V. (1987), Conditions et limites de l'insertion du Brésil dans les échanges mondiaux de soja, thèse de doctorat de III ème Cycle (Paris: Université de Paris I, Panthéon-Sorbonne).
Marloie, M. (1987), Les échanges de céréales, d'oleo-protéagineux et de produits de substitution aux céréales France/CEE/Bassin méditerranéen 1985, série Notes et Documents, no. 77 (Montpellier: GEI/ESR/INRA)
Trevissan, P. (1985), Consideraçoes solve a rentabilidade da lavoura da soja no Rio Grande do Sul (Porto Alegre: FECOTRIGO).

Index

IMF (International Monetary
 Fund) 34, 57, 92, 284
income distribution
 France 95
 Germany (FDR) 184, 188–91,
  198
 UK 116
indebtedness *see under* farm debt
 and farm sector debt
inflation 67, 164–5
interest rates 46, 67
international agreements
 bilateral 23, 230
 'compensatory' 34
 multilateral 30, 33
international division of
 labour 15, 68, 76, 93
international farm crisis 1–2, 71,
 176
 Australia 236
 Germany 185
 Mexico 212
international regulation 9–12
International Wheat Council 30

labour *see under* farm labour force
labour displacement 49, 165
'Long Boom' (Australia) 235
land diversion schemes 38, 100,
 151
 extensification 150
 set-aside 17, 78, 131
 targetting 151
land values
 Australia 238
 UK 119–20
 US 54–5, 77
LDCs 23

market regulation 9–12
Mexico
 bilateral beef feeding
  system 225–27
 CONASUPO 218
 exchange rate
  management 218–23
 food systems 210, 211
 see under individual subjects
Milk Marketing Board

 (UK) 125–6
milk quotas
 disparities 102–3, 124, 198
 France 93, 101–4
 Germany (FDR) 198
 outgoers scheme 124
 Spain 179
 UK 122–8
models
 agricultural technology/policy
  model 6–9
 organisational model of world
  trade 28
 theories of long waves of
  expansion and
  construction 64
Monetary Compensation Amounts
 (MCAs) 88–9
monopoly capitalism 256
multiple jobholding 80 *see also*
 farm adjustment

nationalisation of agricultural
 land 77–8
neo-liberal policies 14
Net Farm Income, NFI (UK) 118
new entrants 74, 96–7, 126
'New Right' 129, 263–6
New World Economic Order 267

off-farm employment 60, 195, 261
 see also farm and adjustment
off-farm income 73, 242 *see also*
 farm adjustment
OECD 2
Office of Technology Assessment
 (OTA) 73
overproduction 2, 84–5, 120–1

part-time farming 107, 144, 195,
 261 *see also* farm adjustment
pluriactivité see part-time farming
policy developments
 Australia 267
 Germany (FDR) 198–9
 Mexico 208, 216–17, 223
 UK 152–3
production control mechanisms *see*
 under land diversion schemes